Idiots

Studies in the
Postmodern Theory of Education

Joe L. Kincheloe and Shirley R. Steinberg
General Editors

Vol. 154

PETER LANG
New York • Washington, D.C./Baltimore • Bern
Frankfurt am Main • Berlin • Brussels • Vienna • Oxford

R. Daniel Linneman

Idiots

Stories about Mindedness and Mental Retardation

PETER LANG
New York • Washington, D.C./Baltimore • Bern
Frankfurt am Main • Berlin • Brussels • Vienna • Oxford

Library of Congress Cataloging-in-Publication Data

Linneman, R. Daniel.
Idiots: stories about mindedness and mental retardation / R. Daniel Linneman.
p. cm. — (Counterpoints: studies in the postmodern theory of education; vol. 154)
Includes bibliographical references.
1. Mentally handicapped children—Case studies. 2. Mental retardation—
Social aspects. 3. Mentally handicapped children—
Education—Case studies. I. Title. II. Series.
HV891 .L56   362.3'082—dc21   00-062958
ISBN 0-8204-5017-0
ISSN 1058-1634

Die Deutsche Bibliothek-CIP-Einheitsaufnahme

Linneman, R. Daniel:
Idiots: stories about mindedness and mental retardation / R. Daniel Linneman.
_New York; Washington, D.C./Baltimore; Bern;
Frankfurt am Main; Berlin; Brussels; Vienna; Oxford: Lang.
(Counterpoints; Vol. 154)
ISBN 0-8204-5017-0

Cover design by Dutton and Sherman Design

The paper in this book meets the guidelines for permanence and durability
of the Committee on Production Guidelines for Book Longevity
of the Council of Library Resources.

© 2001 Peter Lang Publishing, Inc., New York

Printed in the United States of America

This book is dedicated to Clinton, Abby, Rachel and Bobby:
Children who understand.

Table of Contents

Acknowledgments

This book began as a dissertation, one that I completed at the University of Illinois at Urbana-Champaign. I would like to thank the members of my dissertation committee for their support during that prolonged affair: Tess Bennett, Michael Bérubé, Norman Denzin, and Margery Osborne.

Tess Bennett taught a course about families who have exceptional children, and required that each of her students meet and come to know such a family. It was here that I began to experience the truth beyond textbook truisms.

Michael Bérubé wrote a book about his family and son that—although frustrating in that I wish I had written such a book—offered some confirmation that I was walking down a less traveled but fruitful path.

Norman Denzin allowed me to breathe life into *L'Enfant Sauvage de l'Aveyron* and forced me to tell him "in twenty-five words or less" just what the hell I was writing about in this book. Norm provided concrete advise on turning the "what I *had* to say" into "what I *wanted* to say."

Margery Osborne read the meandering initial drafts of this book and urged me to be "explicit, explicite, expliciiit." The advice she offered was invaluable, both in terms of the book's content and construction, as well as the implicit but powerful support she offered.

Robert Stake, patiently, and then not so patiently demanded that I use the word 'book' to describe what I was writing, and not some vaporous term like 'manuscript.' He also gently and then not so gently explained to me that the purpose of a book is something other than a platform from which one has authority to rant and rave. His reading and incisive commentary forced me to write beyond my capabilities.

Janis Chadsey deserves special recognition as my teacher, doctoral advisor, dissertation advisor, and finally colleague. There would have been no dissertation without her courage and support of a project that something other than business as usual if not downright dangerous. She was my coach in a game in which neither of us knew the rules. She has the knack of making apparently offhand comments that keep me thinking for days.

My family and friends provided food and shelter and love while all of this was going on—an impossible and inexplicable task, considering. My mother, Annabelle Linneman was especially helpful—reading and providing gentle "suggestions" with respect to drafts which "only a mother could love."

Melynda Bahrmasel gave to me more than she knows. She was there and she helped me by keeping me focused on the children, who they are, and who they could become.

There is always music. My students and I reveled in it. Wonderland Music Company was kind enough to grant me permission to use a very cool song from Disney's movie, *The Jungle Book*. Thanks for:

Finally, I would like to thank the families who let me write about them. They became my friends and gave generously of themselves for reasons unclear to me.

Chapter One
Introduction

...Why has our inner life become so impoverished and empty, and why has our outer life become so exorbitant, and in its subjective satisfactions even more empty? Why have we become technological gods and moral devils, scientific supermen and aesthetic idiots—idiots in the Greek sense of being wholly private persons, incapable of communicating with each other or understanding each other?

—Lewis Mumford, *Art and Technics* (1960)

In a Sense, This Is My Own Story

Nevertheless, this book is about four children, their families, and the professionals and others huddled at the edges of their humanity.

As a boy, I remember seeing a teacher trooping a group of children down the hall. What struck me is that they were all of different ages and sizes; they looked funny, walked funny, and were not in single file. We had, or wanted, or *needed* to get out of their way. I don't think I ever saw them again. It was 1965, and I was in sixth grade.

Something happened, and when I hear "retard," that image appears. Its power sways me. Did I look away? Did I see the shiny brown linoleum floor? Retard! Retard? Retard. "When we first met," wrote Philip Ferguson (1987), "Peter was 17 years old. For the last 16 of those years, he had lived in large state institutions. The labels used to describe Peter range from the laughably euphemistic to egregious slurs on his very humanity: medically fragile, vegetable, severely/profoundly retarded, idiot, multiply handicapped, custodial. Tomorrow's playground insults are always foretold by today's professional diagnoses" (51). I've come to know many people like Peter whose power riveted my attention, directed my gaze, and focused my career. Some I have befriended, some I've hated; I've written about them, spoken about them, talked about them, but I've always provided care and support.[1] But something happened in grade school that will not be shaken, and every time I meet someone who is different, and different in the ways that constitute what I think when I think "mental retardation," I am back in that hallway with brown linoleum floors.

I needed a job in the winter of 1981. I was a farmer and the U.S. agricultural economy was undergoing one of its washings-out of small producers that have occurred at tediously regular intervals since the mid-nineteenth century and beyond.

I went to work at the Center (a community-based agency that provided services for people with developmental disabilities "in a medium-sized Midwestern university town") as a weekend cook in a supported apartment building. The apartments were "supported," they told me, because the people who lived there had mental retardation and needed help, of what sorts I did not know. I was afraid to see them and meet them. I was also afraid to *cook* for them, but the weekday cook said, "They'll eat anything, don't worry."

The people who lived there were not much different than the kids I'd "encountered" in grade school except they were older. They drooled, talked too much or too little, spoke in ways I couldn't understand, peered suspiciously around corners and through small wire reinforced windows in doors, wet their pants, made funny and ugly faces, staggered like they were drunk, farted; finally one guy said, "Can I have a cup of coffee, hun?" He was repeatedly twisting strands of his hair while we spoke and pulling them out. We made coffee together.

Something happened, and I turned retards into people. We had fun in the kitchen, and I taught them to make pancakes and omelets. We had a system: One man who was particularly apprehensive would keep watch at the kitchen window just in case the Registered Dietitian would show. He'd yell, "Here comes the food bitch!" when she drove up in her white station wagon. We cleared the kitchen, and I put on the white hat and apron I was supposed to wear when I cooked. The "clients," as we called them, were not allowed in the kitchen because they picked their noses, didn't wash their hands, and were generally unsanitary.

Ten years later I worked in a classroom that was called "SPH." That stood for Severe and Profound Handicaps. These kids were aged 6-12, all

---

[1] The terms "care and support" as we shall see, become problematic, in that "care and support" can operate as masks for more portentous activities.

used wheelchairs, and had tubes hanging out of their stomachs so we could pump food and medicine into them. Their teacher told me that in the eight years he'd been teaching there, not one of his students had learned to say his name. One kid we "suctioned" by sticking a vacuum-cleaner-like device down his nose into his lungs to get all of the mucous out. They all wore diapers that we changed behind some waist high bookshelves at the side of the room. We wore surgeon's gloves when we changed the kids, the teacher's assistants groaned when there were bowel movements, and the air freshener we sprayed almost masked the odor wafting out into the hallway. When I first arrived in that classroom, I too, was back in grade school, and I swayed (when I began work in this school, I was confronted with colorful student paintings of the African American hero Malcolm X taped to the walls; the floors *were* brown linoleum, even though the social construction of who is and who is not a hero seemed to have changed). But I turned those children into little kids who were adorable and cute; I taught a blind boy how to play catch with me, and eventually, with some little blonde girls from Ms. Jenkins's general education class next door.

One time we were locked out of both classrooms and stood in the hall along the wall. I asked the kids from the "regular" class how we were going to get in. They told me to find their teacher, Ms. Jenkins, but I suggested that we use dynamite. Kait said, "Yay, then we could blow down the wall between our rooms. Cory said, "we could play with Nick and Shaleen." Bobby added Jimmy and Jenny to the list (Linneman, 1992).

Jenny, Jimmy, Nick, and Shaleen from the special education class drooled, soiled themselves, had seizures, and made strange sounds for no apparent reason. They had odd, discomforting behavior, ingested food through gastronomy tubes, and used wheelchairs, but the children next door still wanted them included in *their* classroom. What could have been interpreted as "gross" did not seem to dampen the enthusiasm of Ms. Jenkins's class reconstructing these children as "their own." Even if we were going to have to use TNT to do it.

Recently I talked with a friend about this people-making business. He said: "It's like those drawings they make with computers that are all over the place; like greeting cards and posters, little calendars to put on your desk. You have to stare at them, move them back and forth, strain your eyes, look at it again and again, then suddenly without warning you see a school of dolphins leaping before the prow of a boat."

The discovery of humanity is no small matter. Just the words themselves—mental retardation—imply some kind of absence, or partiality of that particularly (and problematic) human quality, the mind. The question of mindedness is so rarely considered in the field of mental retardation, so undertheorized, that once impelled into such a vacuum, one is forced into hopeless conundrums. Can a person have half a mind? Some years ago, Burton Blatt (1981) wrote an article called "How to Destroy Lives by Telling Stories." "Mental retardation," he said,

> is an invented disease. The only treatment possible for invented diseases are those which are themselves invented. And in that sense, all treatments for mental retardation are abusive. To be sure, lots of people have problems which can be treated, which a caring society will want to treat. And probably, people who don't read well, specifically, or don't think well, generally, would benefit from treatments to ameliorate their disabilities. But in each such instance, the "disease" is not mental retardation, but something else.... *The best way to cure an invented disease is to forget it....* Another way we can reduce human abuse is to be very careful about the stories we tell about people. Invented stories are like plays. In very good plays believable characters and situations are invented so brilliantly that even the actors believe the truth of the fiction they portray. In very good plays, not only for the audience but for the cast as well, invention replaces fact and, thus becomes truth. So, too, with ingeniously invented stories concerning mentally retarded...people (131, my emphasis).[2]

This drama found an unusual representation in Robert Bogden's (1987) "The Exhibition of Humans for Amusement and Profit." Bogdan drew our attention to the carnival Freak Show of years gone by. He identified motifs through which the Freak Show operated. Two modes of human display were common, the "*exotic*" and "*aggrandized*." Both were

---

[2] The current "zeitgeist" (Schalock et al. 1994) among researchers concerned with mental retardation would have us use "People First" terminology. Instead of nomenclature such as "mentally retarded people" a substitution, for instance "people with mental retardation" is suggested and in fact mandated by most journals in the field. Exceptions are made for "oldtimers," crusty curmudgeons like Wolf Wolfensberger who probably find the change troublesome or stupid (cf. Wolfensberger 1989, "Bill F.: Signs of the Times Read from the Life of One Mentally Retarded Man"; and Wolfensberger 1991, "Reflections on a Lifetime in Human Services and Mental Retardation."). The editor noted in both instances that "The author insists on the use of the terms retarded person, and the mentally retarded, although the official language policy of *Mental Retardation* (a publication of the American Association on Mental Retardation) is such terminology as person with mental retardation..." (1991, 369). In reviewing research, I will use terminology current at the time of its writing.

predicated on the rube's captivation with the bizarre and extraordinary: "The Wild Men of Borneo" (these wild men were "The Davis Brothers [who] were short and mentally retarded. They grew up on a farm in Ohio" [Bogdan 1987, 538]) serve as a familiar example of the "exotic." Public interest in the exotic waned as photography and ethnographic reports from far-away places like Africa became common in the nineteenth century.

Presented in "Aggrandized Status Mode," the crowd could step right up and behold, live on stage, a Freak, such as the midget, "General Tom Thumb," (Connecticut-born Sherwood Stratton affected an English accent on stage [Bogdan 1987, 538]) in a normal living room "set" in the company of his "wife" of normal stature, and at one time in his career, a baby. The allure, the seduction for yokels was the juxtaposition of an expectation of Freaky Life and the appearance of Regular Life. Emphasizing the collusion between Freak and Showmen (the Carny's insider term for this *espirit de corps* was "*with it*"—the mark and his money were not [Bogdan 1987, 538]), Bogdan used the aggrandized status mode of dramatic delivery and economic production as a metaphor for current practice in the field of disability and posed the question of whether "present attitudes represent real changes in what we think is proper for disabled people" (537). In his conclusion, Bogdan proposed that "[w]henever we study disability we have to look at those who are in charge—whether self-appointed, or officially—[and their telling] of...who the people with disabilities are and what they are like. Their versions of reality are presentations of people filtered through stories and world views.... When people are in the hands of charity and professional organizations the images created will be designed to most effectively reach their organizational aim. *In the professions, and in the human services, success often comes to be defined as survival and expansion. This can only occur with a proper cash flow, through charitable contributions, and public support*" (my emphasis, 548).

Although people with mental retardation have always been among us, the condition's study as an object of scientific investigation is a phenomenon of quite recent appearance. The face of the town fool was a familiar one among small town and rural citizens in America. He (the town fool in my mind is never a woman) had a name, a mother and a father, sisters, brothers, uncles and aunts, a face, a voice, a dream, and a story.

During the second quarter of the nineteenth century, superintendents of poor houses, poor farms, schools for the deaf and dumb, prisons, and other institutions for the destitute, discovered mental retardation among the human fallout of our increasingly urban and industrialized landscape. Since that time, practitioners and investigators have struggled to define the nature of mental retardation. The *scientific story* that emerges tends to focus on the traits of people who have mental retardation—their characteristics, their need for education, their medical features—but it is also a story of the definers (Trent 1994). This other, mostly unexamined story is perhaps the more important of the two because of how it has shaped and influenced the place and power of people labeled with mental retardation in society and others who provide for their care and support.

We are all familiar with theories of mental retardation, popular as well as scientific, that create it as an objective condition that people possess. These definitions are trait theories—normative and "functional" definitions of mental retardation, medically and psychologically oriented, that refer to a person's level of functioning (or more precisely, lack of functioning) in society.

Less familiar are theories of mental retardation that define it in terms of social transactions between people labeled with mental retardation and others with whom they interact. From this perspective, mental retardation fades as an objective study of psychological and physiological traits and reemerges as a subjective interpretation of how people ("with it" and "without it") go about the business of living mental retardation.

The notion that something as obvious as mental retardation is something "social" like social class, for example, is difficult for many people to accept. There is no denying that there are certain characteristics that many people labeled with mental retardation share, but, unlike disabilities such as vision and hearing impairment, there are no objective standards by which to measure its presence. For instance, when we say that a person who fails to hear a tone of a certain frequency and amplitude has a hearing impairment, we can be relatively certain that there is some correspondence between hearing and the physical world of sound. When a test is constructed to measure intelligence and a person misinterprets or reinterprets a proverb—"Tell me, what is the meaning of the expression, 'A rolling stone gathers no moss'?"—the correspondence is less clear. Over time, psychometricians have determined how the answers to these and other probes relate to what we call intelligence. While this example of the distinction (what the "mind" does, versus what the ear does) between theoretical standpoints is relatively simple to convey, my experience has taught me that it is difficult to demonstrate, to explain how the social construction of mental retardation operates in people's everyday lives. Moreover, some authors, confronting points of disjunction between functional and social definitions of mental retardation, have announced a paradigm shift (Biklen 1995; Hahn 1987, 1988; Heshusius 1989; Luckasson et al. 1992;[3] Skrtic 1991; Zarb 1992). Kuhn (1962/1970) challenged beliefs about progress in the physical sciences by arguing that "advances" in understanding do not happen as a result of smooth fillings-in of theory, but discontinuous leaps of understanding. When a paradigm begins to show its age, evidence and findings that don't fit amass as scientists go through the contortions necessary for them to sustain their faith in its underlying set of propositions. In some respects, at least according to some writers, such a process is well underway in the science of mental retardation, as evidenced by the patching, shoring up, and entrenching of its functional definitions. For instance, a language of reconciliation of unpredicted competence among people with mental retardation has evolved, including such terms as idiot savants, splinter skills (islands of capacity in a sea of ineptitude), hyperlexia (reading ability exceeds expectations), and so on.

Field Notes, May 9, 1994[4]

A couple of nights ago, I had a dream. I was leaning against (my thesis advisor) Janis Chadsey's car. The road was on a hill, and we were looking down into a wooded valley that sloped upward after about a quarter of a mile. The woods were lush with the first growth of spring. Janis was asking me about my research. From her inquiries, I become aware that I am studying turtles.

---

[3] I reluctantly include Luckasson et al.'s 1992 American Association on Mental Retardation's (AAMR) redefinition of mental retardation. Their work, *Mental Retardation: Definition, Classification, and Systems of Support* happily announced a "paradigm shift" in the organization's (and by implicit and explicit extension, "the field's") conception of mental retardation. Heshusius (1989) reviews work that indicates that Kuhn (1970) uses *paradigm* "in at least 21" (403) different ways to include metaphysical, sociological, and more directly concrete meanings. I am of the opinion that the AAMR "redefinition" fits nicely into the latter category. I'll include it among the others because of the AAMR's self-proclamation. The other references to "paradigm shift" are "focused [in the] metaphorical..., rather than equating it, as perhaps more typical within the social sciences, with a model of inquiry or with theory..." (Heshusius 403).

[4] During this time, I was writing the Methods section of a College of Education mandated "Early Research" requirement.

"What do the turtles look like?"

"Well, I don't really know, I haven't seen them." I wonder whether I said I saw them in my writing but not out loud.

"How do you know that they're there?" she asks me.

"There's little trails in the woods that the turtles follow."

"Have you seen the trails? What do they look like?" In my mind, I know exactly what turtle trails look like and I tell her.

"They are about six inches across, and they kind of look like gutters, almost. The grass is beat down, packed like baled straw, and light brown." My hand rocks back and forth in a curve, like a conductor of a symphony, showing her what a turtle path looks like.

"Have you really seen those trails?" I realize that I haven't, that I'm lying, but that I'm not lying, just making a simple inference because I've seen turtle turds.

"I've seen the turtle turds!" I say confidently. "They look like little brown cylinders, about the color of molasses, but a little smaller than pencil erasers."

"Dan, did you really see them?" I could swear that I did, but I didn't, now that she asked me. I am flustered. Later, a friend and me go back to the woods to look for turtles.

Case Study Method and Interpretation

Studying particular cases is useful, at least some of the time. Occasionally, the case is of such interest that it subordinates many related matters of concern and becomes bound intrinsically to itself, in effect, an integrated system (Stake 1994).

The problem here, as I see it, is to define those boundaries. The "asked and answered" rhetoric of mental retardation literature is insufficient to describe what I think is important about how we live and interpret mental retardation. The story of mental retardation is one mostly told from the perspective of those whose expectation is "to stamp it out" in both senses of the phrase; that is (invent), refine treatment for the condition or forge it from the raw material of human subjects.

It would be nice to say that I arrived at a decision to write about the children I did through careful consideration of the qualities of their situation, making a reasoned calculation that from these kids, among others, I could be tolerably assured that I would learn the most (Stake 1994). But as in many case studies of intrinsic interest, the youngsters were before me. Not unlike many teachers I was bound by an obligation to, well, teach.

The children fell under my gaze. It was directed by twenty years' commingling with people who lived mental retardation from both flanks of the diagnosis and lit by my academic study of disability, my life experience, the era when I grew up, and my personality—in essence, my biography.

With one exception, the kids and their families came to the Center looking for services. I'd known Woody (age 15) for a couple of years; he was a resident of one of the Center's children's group-homes. Eight kids with severe disabilities lived in that house instead of with their parents.

Cassie (almost four) appeared in November of 1997. Her mother and grandmother were worried about her inability to talk and exhausted by her histrionics in public places and at home.

I met Sean (age three) when his mother called the Center's intake person, wondering what to do with her son who'd been diagnosed with autism a couple of days before ("A '3' on an autism scale of '1-5'," according to the doctor) on February 2, 1998. I spent the late winter, spring, summer, and fall of 1998 playing with, teaching, and writing about the children.

Emily (who'd just turned four), the exception I noted above, and I have known each other since 1994. She and I played on a computer for about nine months then, and I wrote about our interactions as part of the requirements for my graduate studies. I see Emily from time to time, and we remain friends, although time and other interests have faded the intensity of our relationship.

My purpose in recording the events I cultivated with my young subjects was to provide you with some idea of what it's like *being there*, enough that could "...provide a maximum of vicarious experience to the readers who may then intuitively combine this with their previous experiences. The role of the...[writer] would then be to assist [others] in reaching new understandings, new naturalistic generalizations" (Stake 1982, 2).

The problem, of course, was to make public the task of "[m]oving from the field to the text to the reader..." (Denzin 1994, 501). He continues: "A situated, writing self structures the interactions that take place among the writer, the text and the reader. The writer presents a particular and unique self in the text, a self that claims to have some authority over the subject matter that is being interpreted." However, the rules for presenting this self are no longer clear. Denzin cites Krieger's provocation: "The challenge lies in what each of us chooses to do when we represent our experiences. Whose rules do we follow? Will we make our own? Do we...have the guts to say, '*You may not like it, but here I am*'?" (my emphasis).

I wrote to gain and give away understanding, knowledge, *and my experience* of the children's minds—and their interpretation by others—through these stories. Laurel Richardson (1994) interprets the act of writing itself as a method of inquiry. "Language" she said, "is a constituative force, creating a particular view of reality and of the Self" (518). "Narratives of the self" (521) Richardson continues, unchain the author, "...allowing the field worker to exaggerate, swagger, entertain, make a point without tedious documentation, relive the experience, and say what might be unsayable under other circumstances" (521).

A journey inward, knowledge; the gaze directed outward. As it says in the book,[5] "For *now* we see through a glass, darkly; but then face to face: now I know in part; but then shall I know even as also I am known" (1 Corinthians, 13 [my emphasis, not St. Paul's]).

Listen to me: I want to tell a story about mental retardation through the eyes of the beholder(s), and the beheld for that matter, "for we cannot order our speech by reason of darkness" (Job 37:19). And I found instances where families and others who lived and worked with the children did indeed order their speech for want of theoretical, and for that matter commonsensible, illumination that assumed mindedness in the children, and having done so, provided some evidence of mental retardation's social construction.

---

5 According to my family's folklore, for some time, there were few books in my father's house, the Bible, and some other Christian texts, although "upstairs reading" (magazines) was apparently condoned. This uncelebrated ambivalence toward things intellectual perhaps stemmed from my great-great grandfather's attending university at Heidelberg. There, in addition to, I assume, acquiring an education, he gained an appreciation for drink and carousel. The dreary provincialism of farm life must have lost whatever appeal it had, and he ceded his birthright to his eldest daughter's husband, and sent my disinherited grandfather's father to America, seeking their Old World neighbors, the Kufusses. They live about a mile and a half down the road from where I now reside. My grandmother, on the other hand, appreciated the benefit of education as an avenue to escape the drudgery of farm work, and farm life in general, and bought her children an encyclopedia. Although my uncle insists that he read the encyclopedia by candlelight in a dark closet, My Dad contests this: "We lived in Bloomington, for Christ's sake." Uncle Bill was "caught in the act"—my father asked grandma why Bill was up there reading those "Black Books?" grandfather overheard it, and asked, "What are these black books?" When this story is told grandfather always has a German accent, although he was born in America.

Chapter Two
Cassie

It was neither unusual or comfortable: trying to get a little girl to throw a fit while her mother, grandmother, and grandfather looked on. Nor was it difficult. They said, "She doesn't like to sit still." And that's exactly what she was doing, in a sense—that sense in which a larger body can control a smaller one.

She smelled like a little kid, little kid shampoo, fabric softener, school cafeteria food, a faint odor of diaper. "No, she's not potty trained," they said, as she screamed and squirmed and yelled.

Let go: She crawled away on her belly on the linoleum tile floor. She had shiny patent leather red shoes like Dorothy in Oz, except they were shaped like boots, boots that could be grabbed, to pull her back on her tummy, giggling. "Her grandpa plays with her like that."

If nothing else, her reputation is severe. The story I'd heard was that this little girl ran off in a cornfield with a teacher's assistant on her heels. They slid through the mud until the teacher sank into the Drummer Silty Clay Loam that lurks in the low-lying areas around Salt Fork. I'm familiar with this soil; it's common on our farm, and builds up on the boots (tractor tires, plowshares, etc.) like gooey concrete. I wrote a poem about it when I was in first grade. It went:

Spring comes with the mud;
Our mothers get mad;
Here we come,
Thud! Thud!
With more mud.

The assistant sank up to her knees in the stuff and had to wiggle her feet out of her shoes to extricate her legs, while the small girl danced merrily away. Her shoes were never recovered, but Cassie was.

If you fly over this central part of our state, you will notice that it looks like a chessboard. Roads run North-South, East-West in regular intervals, dividing land into sections, each a mile square, 640 acres. There are 36 sections in a township. Each section is numbered, such that it becomes possible to identify parcels of land by number. I live, for instance, on a 540-acre tract of land in Section 36 of Danvers Township; Allin Township lies across the road, and to the west, Tazwell County.

But I am far afield now. Somewhere, I heard that towns in the Midwest, the ones that are left, are separated by a convenient drive by automobile, as opposed, say, carriage or horseback-ride. There are ghost-towns here, if you know where to look for them. Those towns died out as farms got bigger, farmers fewer, and roads better. My dad brags that he and my uncle and some other farmers "tore down the town of Padua, Illinois." Somewhat of an exaggeration, since in actuality, all that was left in 1944 was a hotel.

They tell me the most interesting thing about the expedition was that they found two .45 caliber slugs embedded in the hotel's bar as they tore it apart. Another exaggeration, since the young men, Mennonites in name if not practice (my grandmother forbade me to bring my toy guns into her house; my grandfather, who passed away the year before my birth, had his boys practice close-order drill in the cellar with broomsticks at the outbreak of World War II), probably had little or no experience with guns. But I do believe they found some slugs in the bar.

They used the lumber to build some corn cribs, I think, now fallen into disuse, disrepair, and depredation as I look at them now, wondering whether they'll blow down this Spring, or next. The cupola will be the first to go and lists precariously leeward as I write.

The village of Salt Fork is what you might call a clean shot from my house, if you were from around here. The route follows township lines about forty miles due east, with a minor one-mile southerly deviation, at the end. The locals probably call it the "one-mile Y" on Route 9. Salt Fork is situated along the headwaters of the Sangamon River, nestled in a hilly area, moraine; the glacial formation makes the terrain seem heroic compared to the surrounding plains. The village thrives by small town standards ("Population 800" reads the sign), boasting a café known for its "goulash" (on Saturdays—but on this day, Cassie's grandfather told me the café had been purchased by a new owner and was under renovation. Unfortunate, in that my girlfriend had come with me that day, not only to play with Cassie, but to try the goulash. I myself, a vegetarian, had considered sampling the fare that day *if only* to absorb some of the local color), a hardware store with creaking oak-planked floors, and smells of wood, iron, and oil; and surprisingly, a video and craft store downtown named Serendipity. That's where all of this is going on, in the back addition of a row building on the town square which serves as a workshop for the craftspeople and a playroom for the little girl named Cassie with whose head I am messing.

At some point, Grandma tells me, "I wish I knew what she was thinking." Cassie is almost four years old on this dreary November day. Her birthday is December 7th. She has deep blue eyes, more indigo than the color of the old bottle of Bromo-Seltzer I found half buried in the part of my basement that is not finished but close to that. She is tiny and muscular and has "Fly, fly, fly away hair" (a phrase from some TV commercial I was exposed to as a child) that in my day, at her age, mothers would use some ozone-depleting product to control.

She was doing fine, Grandma told me, "talking—saying words like 'mom, bye-bye, go,' until she had a seizure. Then we took Cassie to Dr. Manley in Peoria, and he said she had Borderline Mental Retardation, and that it didn't have anything to do with the seizure."

"We didn't believe him," said Grandma, and knowing Dr. Manley (the only developmental pediatrician in our part of the state) from previous encounters, I was once again struck by the thought of a medieval town whose myopic headsman possessed smuggled motives. Cassie has a horse that she likes to play with; it's her favorite toy, and his hind legs are broken off.

The photograph in front of me must have been taken in the spring, but maybe summer; last summer it rained a lot. The grass is green. There's a small mound covered with grass in the background, along with what looks like some greening brush: One imagines mist, The Old Course at St. Andrews, leprechauns, banshees, and the Blarney Stone. In the foreground, an open-mouthed black dog chases a small barefoot girl in pink shorts and white shirt, translucent so you can see the outline of her belly as the sun pierces the white cotton. Her hair is flying, one foot planted firmly on the ground, her other knee at a right angle, her muddy foot poised for the stride.

Their shadows are long, as if the picture was taken in the early morning. The black dog's tail is outstretched, and his pink tongue, white canines, and shiny brown eyes are within a foot of the girl's bottom. The dog's left front and rear paws are on the ground under his chest, and his right legs are stretched at thirty degree angles fore and aft. He is going to get that little girl who smiles, gazing with delight at the ground about three feet in front of her.

Margaret (Cassie's Grandmother) Writes:

Dan,

Hey! Locals call it the three mile corner!

Smuggled motives? Do you feel the "*labels*" are self-serving to prove the authority or power of one's position? This is in reference to borderline retarded even before the seizure. Time out is a great technique when it works. Forcing a child to sit in a corner and sitting there until they regain control didn't work in the Doctor's office or at home. Further admonishment in a loud tone, finger pointing and finally a swat on the behind didn't help either (He had to send Cassie from the room, because she was so worked up). We used time out on our other granddaughter and it worked beautifully. By the way, Arianna, is *afraid* and runs away from ants. Cassie works very hard to catch them. Individuals are *individual* after all.

The technique of using fear of punishment as the discipline for behavior doesn't work for Cassie. She has no fear. Not with people, animals or events. Cassie doesn't respond to the technique of using fear. Although she "hides" her head behind her hands in certain parts of movies, it really isn't fear. It's a part of theater play. I have seen the greater change in Cassie's behavior using the softer tones and repeating messages.

Pink shorts? Your computer printout looks blue or purple. I don't remember.

Overall I love the descriptions! (but, what grandmother wouldn't?). It will be interesting to see further dot to dot connections with Cassie and her behavior plus the doctor and his smuggled motives, if you have further comment planned. Thanks for sharing.

Margaret

Three mile corner indeed! So I called it a one-mile deviation. I knew it was three, but I wanted it to seem like a *pure* clean shot from my house, and I think that three miles would be considered a stretch. Route 9 *does* turn off after a mile though, and you continue South on what locals probably call the "Salt Fork Road" into town.

Her shorts *are* pink! I am colorblind, for one thing, and Macintosh computers (which I use) handle color differently than Wintels (which *you* use). And besides, I want her shorts to be pink.

Singing, and Dancing in the Rain!

If there was ever a wet spring, that year we were having one. I woke up and had to call Mike 'cause I could hear something going on in the crib. It was early, like about 6:00, but I thought it was later. It sounded like a motor was running, the "off" switch made it sound worse, and the reset button did too. Mike came over and found the fuse box, pulled them, and the noise stopped. He said: "All this water...maybe a rat? What do you think?"

I said that I thought the crib was falling apart. "What're we gonna do when it falls down?" I asked.

"These ones (the ones on the Linneman farms) held out longer than the othern's."

"Dad says they made them out of cherry, and some wood from an old hotel."

"Too bad about the cupola" (pronounced "cupe-a-low").

"Yep."

My hands are feeling kind of beefy, I've been trying to set some posts for a fence to keep my dogs in so I don't have to watch them and they can be outside. They bug me whilst I try to write this book. "Our basset hound goes out in the field, and gets stuck; I didn't know what I was going to do, the other day," I told Mike, "maybe call the fire department?"

Mike said: "She don't have much clearance."

"Nope."

"Big feet though."

"Kinda like snowshoes," I remarked.

"Get a chopper in here for an airlift, maybe."

We talked about when he might be able to get into the fields again, which areas of the county got more rain, and so on. "Lotta standing water out near Salt Fork," I said, which is where I'm heading right now.

There are what we call "ponds,"[1] some covering 7-10 acres on many of the fields as I drive out there. I see a man and his son; the man is covered with mud up to his crotch, and his son to his armpits. They are carrying what looks like rope, but could be field trash. I glance over where they're walking from and see the freed-up standpipe sucking water like it

---

[1] According to my uncle, at least *some* of these are "buffalo wallers." These are areas that stayed wet when our land used to be prairie, and the buffalo roamed free. Over the ages, the wallers became so compacted from the buffalo, that they have defied even the legendary efforts of our *Gros-Grosvaters* to drain them.

should. They are slogging determinedly across the farm lot as I pass, and I can see a trail of mud across the highway.

Cassie and her grandparents are at the restaurant. I don't know the name of the restaurant and suspect that it has none. I do know the name of one of the waitresses whose name is Wendy, who everyone knows as "Windy." There's a five-gallon bucket holding open the back door, and some guy trips over it on the way out, looking at the bucket as if wondering, "How on earth did a five-gallon pail find itself positioned in such a manner?" Simultaneously, I am reminded of a drunk falling comically out of a bar in *Gunsmoke* and the noble work of Erving Goffman (1959), *The Presentation of Self in Everyday Life*. I don't think it was my knowledge of his work that caused me to avert my gaze as he attempted to assemble his dignity.

They're sitting at the back table, which is, problematically, round. Cassie is seated between Jake and Margaret, her grandparents. There is a vacant seat between Cassie and Margaret. The table can seat probably eight people. I dread my inevitable bout with the calculus of appropriate positioning.

Sit between Margaret and Cassie? No. The interpersonal space would be too small, and I hadn't showered, dirty from slogging around out at the farm with the dogs. On either side of Margaret or Jake? Then I couldn't see Cassie without leaning across either grandparent. The edge of the table opposite the family is somewhat jammed up against the wall, posing another problem; do I walk around Jake's or Margaret's side? Finally I wind up sitting across the table from them, on Margaret's side, spreading my arms on the curved surface as if I were not isolated physically and socially, which we all knew would cause a hassle. And, it did as Cassie squirmed in her chair trying to reach me across the expanse of the large table.

"You want anything to eat?" asks Jake.

"Naw," I say, but Windy, having magically appeared at my right side as I slid into appointed seat, is there with the coffee, which I don't refuse.

"Cassie likes bacon, real crisp. She's had about 10 slices..." The little girl is still trying to escape, and there's a little plate of what looks like a cut-up fried egg and some home fries. Cassie's looking at me with a Mona Lisa smile as she greases the table with the remaining third of what I suppose is the last of the bacon.

We adults were talking about something of consequence, maybe my plan to get Cassie to pee in a toilet today, and at some point it became clear that Cassie was finished eating, and she came over and I hoisted her into my lap. She grabbed a spoon and started stirring my black coffee, delightedly raising the spoon to her nose to inhale the rich aroma of the local brew (somewhat weak to my big-city sensibilities, which run to French Roast with a "shot" as I say, and which college-town café *serveux* seem to know means a shot of espresso). After everyone has told her at least two or three times, "Careful, it's hot!" she takes a sip from the spoon.

It's time to go, and rather than cruise the half-block back to the video store, Cassie and I walk. We proceed without incident, despite the fact that we had to make a left-hand turn, which could have caused problems, had Cassie decided, "Right."

Back at the store, we decide to sit Cassie on the toilet, just for fun, and she gets mad despite the sparkling play-dough I'd bought for her to pass the time on such occasions. Jake's back is hurting him; it has now for about a month or so, and it's hard for him to get up and down with her. I help, and Margaret offers to "unhook" the little kid potty that's attached to the toilet seat. I figure out how to do it.

Margaret gets us a bookbag with a diaper "just in case." I ask her if she thinks it's OK to take the little four-year-old girl into men's rooms, and she says, "Yes, all the men's rooms have changing tables in them now" (how *she* knows this I don't know), but I tell her that I'm going to get Cassie to pee in the toilet. I don't tell her that I have no idea how I will accomplish this, but I seem certain enough that it will happen. I grab the sparkly play-dough on the way out.

We stop at Casey's on the way out of town and get two 20-ounce bottles of Diet Pepsi, and start drinking. We drive down to the three-mile corner, and by then it is apparent that Cassie is not going to want to stay in the seat-belt. Trying to keep her in the seat-belt is going to cause an accident, and besides, she's talking. I don't understand a word she is saying but it sounds enough like English. As we round the Y-curve, Cassie tells me more.

In any case, I am balancing the therapeutic merit of the conversation in which Cassie and I are involved versus the risk of her bouncing around my truck like a piece of flubber should I err negotiating the one-mile corner. She talks up a storm, balancing adroitly against the shifts in equilibrium. I don't come to any conclusion, but I remember my mother holding me against the seat in the dark ages when only the Swedes thought it apropos to restrain riders in a car. Mom continued to hold me against the seat like that until I was 30 or so.

I drive a couple of miles east, and pull over and strap the child in, and bribe her with orange-flavored Tic-Tacs until we get to Bloomington. Actually, this is not the whole truth. Although she was *in* the seat belt, it would be better to say that she was tangled in the seat belt, for how else could one be standing up facing backwards, kissing the head rest?

We'd been drinking Diet-Pepsi the whole trip, and I at least had to pee. So we turned into a rather large gas station at the corner of Route 9 and Hershey Ave., a four-way intersection, choked with traffic at this hour on Saturday morning. We *run*[2] into the gas station, because I've had enough experience with Cassie wanting to go where I didn't in stores and go there quick that I figured if I ran with her, she'd at least think we were going somewhere interesting.

Unfortunately, there was a line at the men's room! So, we go to the candy rack at the front of the store; Cassie collapses in a fit, I pick her up and ask her what she wants, and she grabs some bubble-gum. I grab another pack, only because my special education indoctrination mandates that we offer choice whenever possible. Cassie picks the kind she wanted in the first place, pink. I have to pick up Cassie, who is screaming at this point, and put money in her hand to give the "lady."[3] Cassie is trying to open the gum, while I try to get one of her hands to give the money to the lady, while the lady tries to scan the gum, because they have to scan everything at this particular establishment.

Well, we made it into the bathroom, and I got the play-dough out of my pocket, helped Cassie with her gum, took her shorts and diaper off and placed her on the toilet, maladroitly, in that this bathroom is "handicap" accessible, and I smashed Cassie's head on the grab bar. She looked at me deliriously, started to cry, and I figured I'd wrecked this positive toileting experience, but there would be others down the road.

I'd been explaining that I would buy her big girl panties at Wal-Mart (in which, under any other circumstances, I would not set foot). Cassie was screaming and struggling on the seat, and I had visions of arrest for child abuse floating in my head, so I explained to her that we'd get off and try again later. I lifted Cassie off and banged her head on the bar again, and

---

2 "It was impossible when I took him with me to go on foot. It would have been necessary for me to run with him or else to use most tiring violence in order to make him walk in step with me" (Itard 1962, 23).

3 I call the women who handle money at stores "ladies." This is against my feminist leanings, but I do it anyway.

while she was standing there waiting for me to get my act together, she started peeing! I plopped her up on the toilet where she finished, and I got her off (this time without gonging her head on the bar), and babbled inane compliments (social reinforcement), like, "Good Girl! You did it!" "We're going to get you big girl panties!" and so on, meanwhile jamming her mouth full of bubble-gum.

Then, God help me, I danced her in her puddle (knowing from past experience that she loves jumping in puddles), singing, "I'm singing in the rain, just singing in the rain!"

I put on her shorts without the diaper, held one leg against the door so she wouldn't get out and run rampant through the store, and mopped up the urine best I could with the diaper. It's hard, by the way (although among parents I imagine this is common knowledge) to mop with a disposable diaper, because apparently, only the inner linings are absorbent. I understood the logic of this because of having watched a number of TV commercials in which fluids of various colors are poured into diapers to prove to parents that the outer layer stays dry.

Out we go, on the fly, to Wal-Mart. I pull into the wrong lane of Hershey Avenue with a wild child bounding ecstatically about the cab of my truck while the shocked citizenry of Bloomington attempt to scold me with their faces, and I attempt to get back in the right lane. I put the truck in 4-wheel drive and jump the divider in time to see the police pulling up across the intersection.

"*Cassie! Sit! Now!*" I scream as pleasantly as possible, and I lock her in again. We smile at the officer as we drive by.

We are in a big hurry when we get to Wal-Mart, of course, so we don't have to endure another scene together. "Where's the little girl panties?" I ask the greeter, and she gives us some incomprehensible instructions, while trying to put a smiley-face sticker on cute little Cassie, who is already on the move. We run. We find the panties. She grabs some, while I try to figure out what size to get. She's got some Sesame Street panties, and I of course have to get two other kinds with dinosaurs and Barbies on them so that later, we can choose.

We run to the check-out, and run smack-dab into my father's pet peeve. A woman is making a purchase, watching carefully as the check-out proceeds, and when the purchase is calculated, as if this, the final step in the oft-repeated procedure, comes as a complete surprise, fumbles in her purse for a checkbook, a pen, re-scrutinizes the total, and laboriously writes out a check. Cassie is screaming by now, and we are, in addition to the undies, purchasing some watermelon bubble-gum ("You got the pink kind last time," I tell her, helping her with an *informed* choice). We go through the money handling, gum unwrapping, scanning and paying, and yelling routine. *I* am ready with *cash*.

Into the men's room, and I am very excitedly telling Cassie about the "big girl panties," and she pees on the floor, and I put her on the toilet, blubbering more social praise that I hope will reinforce this operant behavior. We put on the panties and shorts and get the hell out of that den of iniquity.

Margaret Writes:

Dan,

This article tends to describe life as it really is—as it is happening. No social graces or formalities here. Parents/grandparents feel inept with raising their children anyway. Enter the stranger, a part time wetland farmer, and a four-year-old who learns "differently." It's my kind. I'm anxious to get to the ending, but don't want to miss the "how they got there."

Want to be published? You had said you were working on a book, I too, am in the long process of writing a book, the never-ending book. Not enough nerve to send in a couple of chapters. This is why we originally purchased the computer.

Margaret

Field Notes, June 18, 1998

He did not know why she pulled out the hair of the dead. Accordingly, he did not know whether her case was to be put down as good or bad. But in his eyes, pulling out the hair of the dead in the Rashōmon on this stormy night was an unpardonable crime. Of course it never entered his mind that a little while ago he had thought of becoming a thief.

—Ryunosuke Akutagawa, *Rashomon*

"Just between you, me, and the fencepost," said the older of two women working at Casey's in Salt Fork, "it'll be better for Cassie when Arianna's gone."

"Uh? Whaddya mean by that?" asks the space between me and the fencepost, "Like, people won't be comparin' Arianna and Cassie." I'm thinking all kinds of thoughts like, "People make unfair comparisons between Cassie and her equally darling curly blond-haired cousin

Arianna." Or that during a Individualized Program Planning (IEP) meeting Melanie said she wanted Cassie to go to regular kindergarten if only to keep up with her cousin "'cause it's a small town...and well...," she continued, "Arianna already thinks she's older than Cassie." Not that people talk or anything; I was on my way out of town.

"No," says the woman, "it's just that, well, maybe they'll be able to spend more time with Cassie."

Arianna's going off to Hawaii with her dad to catch up with mom, who's in the Army. Arianna's dad, Neil, is excited about going to Hawaii, as are many townfolk, and maybe the family. "Bet you're one of the ones who wants to hide out in one of our trunks," he asked me one time when I acted happy that he was going to live in Hawaii with his family, "but there's about thirteen lined up before you."

"I suppose I wouldn't mind," I smirked, thinking that I'd like to visit Hawaii, maybe. There are private schools now in Hawaii where they teach English as a second language in first grade.

I turn back to the women at Casey's, demonstrating the donnish quality that will prevent me from ever finding out anything about what these people think about Cassie, her mind, or anything else, and say, "I dunno, Arianna's prob'ly a good friend to Cassie, and maybe a good role model too." The women look at me. It's an academic question, anyway, as it were, because they're going to Hawaii, unless we get in a war or something.

"They're always holding on to each other's hands," says the younger lady.

Earlier that morning I'd rolled into town, and as usual, stopped at Casey's to get a Diet Pepsi, orange Tic-Tacs, and go to the bathroom. The older woman (who was working alone at that hour) asked me, "What are you doin' here on a Thursday?"

"I suppose," I speculated, "that I'm unemployed. Thought I'd come out and work with..."

"There she is, right *there*!"

"Where?" I say, spinning low and ready on my left foot.

"Right there," she says pointing at one of four jars on the counter. On each jar is a picture of a four- or five-year-old kid. I turn back to her.

"What's that for?"

"To elect the junior king and queen for the festival," pointing at a poster advertising a 4th of July party slated for the 28th of June.

"Like whatever jar gets the most money?"

"Yep."

I wonder some time later, what qualified Cassie's eligibility for the contest, and for the rest of the day, nobody tells me.

"*Orange* Tic-Tacs?" she chides.

"They're not for me!" I say, because in my mind, Orange Tic-Tacs aren't for adults.

"I know, I know."

We say our good-bye's; I put 35 cents into Cassie's jar, and head over to Serendipity. Trisha, the speech therapist, is getting her gear out of her car. She's got a barn, a large flat Rubbermaid container full of rice and toys, and a small, very new looking boom box. I am jealous of her boom box, because I want a nice small portable boom box with excellent sound.

I think I had a boom box before anyone did. My dad got me a Hitachi portable tape recorder, stereo, in 1970 or so. It was white. You could disconnect the speakers, and it had two plug-in microphones.

Trisha trundles in, and says "Hi" to everyone. Jake, Melanie, Margaret, and Cassie are present. Cassie freaks out for some reason. Trisha offers Cassie a cherry twizzler that she doesn't want at that particular moment, laying on the floor, screaming and kicking the way she does. I take it and break off a little piece and offer it to her, she screams, "Nooooo!" so I eat it.

Jake tells us that she likes Tootsie-Rolls the best, and Trisha oooo's and ahhh's. We look at Jake, and he says, "I mean Tootsie-Roll pops, orange flavored," but he adds defiantly, "sometimes she gets *cherry*," shooting us a challenging look.

Margaret tells me that Cassie let her cut her bangs the other day. With no trouble at all, "Cassie just sat on my lap and let me cut 'em."

Trisha opens the Rubbermaid rice vessel, and we begin to play. Cassie calms down for some reason. Trisha knows sign language (American Sign Language—ASL) and she signs every significant fragment of her sentences. While we are playing in the rice, Trisha turns on the boom box, and the sound is just as good as I'd imagined. There is a song going about a farmer, something about grandpa's farm, and the kinds of animals he owns. The therapist makes signs for cow, horse, and sheep. The sign for sheep is making snipping motions with your index and second fingers of one hand on your other forearm. I, of course, recognize that Trisha is setting up a transition from rice to barn play. When Cassie hears the word grandpa, she looks at Jake.

Trisha breaks out the barn, and we play with it for a while, and I make hay about grandpa the farmer, much to my amusement. I can't see Jake, but hoped he enjoyed it as much as I did. Then Trisha begins to sing the clean-up song, and we start to put the animals away. Melanie bought Cassie some crocodiles (three—a small, medium, and large one) and they're parked in the hayloft. I make some crack—"if it keeps raining like this we're all going to have crocodiles in our lofts." Melanie says, "Cassie, show them what happens with the teeth," but Cassie doesn't respond.

We've put up the barn, and Trisha had a small broom and a dustpan, and I help (hand over hand) Cassie sweep up rice. If I don't prompt her like this, she sweeps with the bristles in the air. Trisha packs up to go, and, I believe, at my instigation, we all go out to her car with her. I say, "at my instigation," because I kind of led the charge. I felt like I was doing the 'wrong' thing, because this, I knew, and I bet everyone else knew, would probably have behavioral consequences for Cassie. But, why all the fuss? Is it not my place to bring understanding to her tantrums?

After Trisha leaves, Jake points out his dazzlingly beautiful stand of hollyhocks, and just as I am about to tell him that I am a lover of hollyhocks, that my uncle wrote a poem about them that burlesques Psalm 23, Cassie darts through the flowers and runs past the swingset and around the lilac bush.

Those hollyhocks that huddle underneath that picket fence,
Have so done so for years.
In the spring they huddle, cower,
But when summer comes they'll tower,
Wave their heads and toss their flower
Over all the other alley boundaries,
Making purple lanes of hollyhocks
For garbage trucks and vagrant boys
With fishing poles and swimming fins.
But why all the fuss?
Those hollyhocks have so done so for years.
And on a lazy,
Hazy,
Summer's day so long ago,
They made such fine and pretty ladies,
Like Dolly Madison
Or someone equally fragile
Pressed between the pages of a favorite story book.
Holly, holly, hollyhocks in free.

—"Hollyhocks," Bill Linneman (1955)

I engage her in the chase. In the alley, she attempts to climb up a gravel slope to an adjacent driveway. There are easier ways to get to Casey's, where I assume she's going, but she always tries to crawl up the 3-foot gravel slope, and I always catch her there.

Why not go to Casey's? I sit down and hold on to Cassie's hips, ask her to look at me, and repeat the mantra 3 times: "We will go into the store. I will give you a quarter. You will go get a Tootsie-Roll pop. You will go up and give the lady the money. You will wait for the change. We will walk out of the store together."

"Cassie's here!" says the younger woman. "Time to run around Cassie?"

"Not while he's with her," says the older woman.

And Cassie more or less does what we've rehearsed, except that she started unwrapping the sucker, which is not really a problem, just not in my script.

We walk back the way we came. Cassie stops at the swingset to play. She lays her sucker on the ground in front of the ladder that leads up to the slide, stands up, then bends down and says "good bye" to the lollypop, giving it a little wave. After we play for a while, Cassie picks up her orange Tootsie-Roll pop and we go back to Serendipity.

I am invited to lunch. We go down to the restaurant, me, Neil, Arianna, Melanie, Margaret, Cassie, Jake, and the little baby. The baby is a girl. I can't remember her name. Margaret tells me the name of the restaurant, but I can't remember that either.

The special: goulash. It's good. I order cottage cheese and potato salad with mine. Jake gets iced tea and orange juice, and Arianna finds that odd. I sit in between Cassie and Arianna, after some negotiation with Melanie. There is a lot of discussion around the table concerning the logistics of some stuff I don't understand about a boat, someone named Tim, cleaning a boat, a contingency plan for rain (why clean the boat if it's going to rain?), a truck that Neil wouldn't drive around town, let alone to Alabama, kids falling while getting in or out of the truck, a "train car" (apparently Arianna's word for van), going to Alabama in the morning to pick up Neil's wife, getting a rental car, "you can go swimming all the time in Hawaii, Arianna, but look out for those waves," who's going to take care of Cassie and when, which kid is eating more (the baby), how when Cassie eats good, Arianna doesn't, and vice versa. At some point, I pat Arianna's head and lift up her curly locks and say, "You have such lovely hair, young lady." Cassie's hair is "up" in a ponytail like thing that I've never seen. Melanie comes over, because "it's coming loose," and tightens up Cassie's ponytail.

When Cassie finishes eating, she starts squirming, and Jake tells me she likes two different men, and always goes to see them when they're in the restaurant. Cassie runs to the back where one of them is sitting. Melanie follows her. The cook comes out from the kitchen and asks one of her customers, "Whadda you want?" Jake says, "No wonder they keep you in the back." The poor man says, "I just want a cheeseburger... " Jake says, "Don't ask her to put anything on it," and the man says, "I'm afraid to...I *thought* I was risking it, asking for a *chee*seburger."

Jake picks up the tab.

We go on out, and I walk with Cassie and Arianna who hold my hands. We swing our hands back and forth. Arianna trips on the curb, and falls on the street. I pick her up and simultaneously restrain Cassie. Arianna is already crying big tears, and I hand her off to Neil.

Back at Serendipity I make arrangements to come back on Monday. Jake lets me have *Jungle Book*, and *Toy Story* so I can make some pictures for another kid I'm working with. He says, "Those three are *Cassie's favorites...* " I feel guilty for not taking them to make pictures for her.

As I'm pulling out, a stranger drives up looking for some country club. I am baffled by the mere idea of a country club in Salt Fork, and say, "I don't live here, really..."

Melanie comes out of the store, and I tell her he's looking for some country club and she starts explaining, and pointing east.

When I left Casey's on the way out of town, I put a dollar in Cassie's jar.

Margaret Writes:

Dan,

I'm not familiar with Rashomon, the Japanese story. Just the old Indian .story is familiar; The three blind men telling about different parts of an elephant! Yes, I know about the comparison thing. I do it too. Like Cassie is more observant about the things around her. She saw the moon and stars long before Arianna. And she notices the birds and wildlife in addition to bugs, which she enjoys immensely. The girls each have their own special qualities that endear them both to me. They enjoy each other—holding hands and playing ring around the rosie and racing down the street.

I noticed you have written "They always *hold* (missed a word) on to each others hands."

However, I'm not sure if we spent more time with Cassie that *we* can make the difference. That's why we want all the help we can get from our group of professionals.

Qualification for the fourth of July in this small community is difficult. You have to bring in a photograph of a child between the ages of 3 and 4! Thanks for asking.

That was a nice boom box. I'd like one for classical music to see if there is any noticeable difference in Cassie. Maybe Trisha could play some Mozart for Cassie.

I think you missed part of what I said about Cassie's hair. "If you sit on the bench in front of me and let me cut your hair, we can play on the computer afterward," I told her. Her only response was "OK." She has used the word, infrequently. There she sat perfectly still. I was so nervous. I didn't have to grab a strand or two, then wait until later when I could catch her again. We did play 'Jump Start Toddler' afterward. She sat very still on a chair beside me. I held her hand to move the mouse. It was like she felt big and proud. Just another one of life's little miracles. See, I do learn from what you are doing with Cassie. That was the first time I have observed Cassie understanding the consequences of good behavior. I said to myself, "she knows, she knows!" Melanie has always said that Cassie doesn't understand the consequences of her behavior—like being bad or running out into the street. I could have cried for happy. She could mentally put the two actions together and give me an appropriate response.

Thanks for letting me read the latest. It doesn't disturb me what people say. We both know the comparison thing will always be there when Cassie is among her peers or classmates, teachers or community.

Margaret

Field Notes, June 24, 1998

I stopped at Casey's in Salt Fork, got a Diet Coke (they were all out of Diet Pepsi, and when it comes right down to it, I don't have a preference), and put some change in Cassie's jar. There are more entrants, maybe six or seven now. I removed some child's jar from atop Cassie's, and surreptitiously glancing about, put hers on top of the others.

Margaret and Jake met me at the desk at Serendipity. They have a tanning salon there, and each time I walk in there, I see the display of tanning lotion, wonder why, and go on about my business. The tanning lotion display is so incongruous that eventually, my mind loops back in reflection, and I remember the tanning parlor.

I was about a half an hour late due to circumstances, depending on one's sense of self-efficacy (or judgment thereof in others), which were or were not under my control. Jake said, "I thought *we* were going to be the ones that were late."

I explained the reason why I *am* behind schedule. Schedule is my middle name now, Behind my first. I went into the back room, and Cassie was hiding under a blanket. Toys of all sizes were strewn across the floor. She laughed and smiled when she revealed herself to me.

I gave my newly upgraded consent form to Margaret and asked her to read it and have Melanie read it and, hopefully, sign it. The current revision was necessary because of Sean's dad's insightful critique. I renamed the project "Mindedness and Children," said that I was interested in children who 'learn differently' and that I expressly didn't want to add to any stigma that they might experience as a result of my work with them (in my role as special educator).

Cassie had thrown her blanket on the floor, covering many of the toys. She started walking across the blanket, comically stumbling over the horses, pigs, crocodiles, dinosaurs, and so on lurking just beneath. I picked up the blanket, folded it, and Margaret took it from me. Cassie was working her way toward the books, which are kept in a box on top of the VCR. I suggested that Cassie help me "Clean up, Clean up!" (I actually tried to sing it but felt too dumb). I got the toy bucket out, and she helped me put about 2/3 of the toys in there, which was about a bucketful. We'd at least cleared an area large enough to set down the box, and peruse the volumes. We're sharing my Diet Coke.

Cassie helps me get the books. The box probably weighs 20 pounds, and I always give out a healthy groan (or unhealthy—really it's a pretend groan—I can lift any old twenty pound box), which for some reason beyond me Cassie will imitate. "Ummmmph," she intones.

The mystery, you see, is that she'll imitate my "aarrgs" and "ummmph's" but not words like, "OK." Maybe it's the act of helping. I think that Cassie likes to help.

We get the box on the floor, and after tossing a few books helter-skelter, I got Cassie in the habit of placing them in a pile on the couch, positioning them neatly with two hands. This took no amount of work on my part. I just took her hands, held them on each side of one book, helped her place the book on the couch, and I said, "ahhh, that's better."

She only looked through about 10 books, placing them neatly on the couch, and then walked over to the computer. Margaret helps us find a CD, I can't remember what it's called. It is a simple program that mostly teaches (or at least allows for the possibility of teaching) basic mouse skills, including pointing, clicking and dragging. There's, for instance, a screen that comes up that's covered with leaves and you must move the mouse around to, in a sense, sweep the leaves away. When you get the last leaf out of the picture, there's a cow or some other animal who sings a little ditty.

I sneak a peek at my watch, and it's 10:10. Cassie stays with this activity for 20 minutes. She does OK with the mouse, but I'm prompting her quite a bit. She seems to enjoy watching enough, but maybe, and I mean just maybe, she's not too interested in the mouse. Personally, I can't imagine why a person wouldn't be, but that's Cassie's business for now. She broke away at 10:30 and went to get a dinosaur and a crocodile, and put them in front of the screen, and we continued for about seven more minutes.

Cassie was sitting on my lap, and I knew that she didn't have a diaper on. Margaret had disposed of it when I'd arrived, muttering something about her daughter. I thought that we could try the potty. Jake got Cassie into the bathroom, I brought a book that she'd looked interested in, and grabbed some play-dough. She threw the play-dough at Jake, and he'd pick it up, and say, "No, Cassie." They repeated this activity several times. Finally, Cassie threw it into the garbage, and Jake said, "Fine, leave it there."

She's kicking and screaming, but with great enthusiasm (on my part), I give her the book. There are little doors on the pages that you can open and look at the pictures on the inside. Cassie works at this, calms down, and sits on the toilet calmly for about three minutes but didn't pee. After this, we let her down, without raising a stink, as it were.

Jake and I put on a new diaper, and I had to leave.

Field Notes, June 26, 1998

Today, I would spend most of my time interviewing Melanie. Melanie appeared tired and, as she put it, not very talkative.

The most remarkable thing about Cassie was that she worked/played on the computer throughout the entire interview, which lasted approximately 45 minutes. She and Margaret sat together quietly talking. I could see that Margaret was having trouble "getting" Cassie to hold on to the mouse.

I asked her about this later, and she said that she'd whisk away some of the obstructions in the peek-a-boo game, those on the outside of the screen, and then have Cassie complete the job. I wonder privately about just why this strategy to teach Cassie to use the mouse "worked."

In a way, it's the age-old problem of mouse repositioning that people seem to learn in the same way as riding a bike: there's a long period where "nothing" happens, and then, suddenly and permanently, a person divines that if you pick up the mouse and put it back down, the cursor remains in place, and you can move it to the desired position.

I don't know why Cassie doesn't want to use the mouse. Margaret says that she just wants to watch what's going on in the program. The important thing is that she is sitting there absorbed in a task for a prolonged period of time.

Reflection on Cassie's "attention span" brought back memories of a squabble Melanie (and I) had with the school district a month or two ago as the school year drew to a close. Melanie wanted Cassie to go to summer school. The district didn't, and that was that. They didn't think she'd benefit from it—she'd be able to recover any educational losses she might suffer due to lack of instruction over the summer within a few weeks (besides, they'd have to bus her ten miles or so every day). Melanie had a part-time job and didn't have insurance or money to cover diagnostics for Cassie that might provide some additional information to the district. I thought the school used this paucity of assessment against Melanie. I encouraged Melanie to use her due process rights guaranteed by IDEA, the Individuals with Disabilities Education Act, and we got a mediator from the state to come up and negotiate some sort of compromise. After meeting for couple of hours with the district's administration, we got Cassie two one-half hour sessions per week with a speech therapist for nine weeks.

We talked about whether the speech therapist was "doing any good." Melanie and Margaret thought that Cassie *might* be getting something, but the therapist hadn't been there enough to really judge. The transmission in her car went out, and she'd missed a few sessions. I looked at Melanie and wondered out loud if we should have tried for more at the mediation hearing. She kind of shrugged. I'd have took 'em to the mats—we would've prevailed—but Melanie didn't want to make a big fuss in her little town (I suppose I have smuggled motives of my own).

"It's like those big drivers, and the PGA," I said to blank stares.

"You know, like "Tiger Woods" or Big Berthas, I don't know. They're oversized golf clubs or something that are supposed to improve one's drive."

Dawning recognition.

"Well, you see, the PGA (Professional Golf Association) banned them because they might give someone an unfair advantage, but the companies that make the clubs, now they're in the position of saying, 'Well, we make good woods, but they don't really give anyone an unfair advantage.'" I tell them the manufacturers cite statistics that say the *average* golf score has stayed the same since their introduction.

"It's like Cassie's attention span, and all that crap the school was giving us. They say, 'Well, if Cassie's attention span is so short, then she really won't benefit from extended time with the therapist.'"

"At this point in the game," I continue, "We can't really say that 'Cassie has a wonderfully long attention span' because that's what we've been hanging our hat on. If we say that it's *real long*, her attention span, then they'll say that, 'Weehl then, *she* should be able to make up what she loses over the summer when she gets back to school.'"

This "regression/recoupment"—that's the official terminology—criterion for summer school is a devil's snare. I pack up and leave after saying good bye to Cassie and the assembled adults.

Field Notes, June 29, 1998

Over the years, I get dreams. In these dreams the children, adults, young adults who don't talk, speak to me. I know that this is not an uncommon experience for people who are friends with or work with people who don't talk, that is who are alingual—at least in the common sense of the word (if there is a common sense of that word).

It is astonishing to have these folk speaking, and I ask them all kinds of questions, but I can never remember what they've told me. This is not to deny that everybody is always involved in speech acts, performances of some sort that are wonderfully expressive after their own fashion. After all, I am drawn to them like a bee to nectar.

I choose this metaphor carefully. The "sting," as it were, is the fact that I can't resist finding ways to make their performances more meaningful to the world at large. I don't know what to think about this, although normatively, I understand that it's the correct thing to do. Still, people may have their own reasons for remaining "silent." For instance, one time at a rather informal Individualized Program Planning (IPP—the adult equivalent of an IEP) meeting for a young man who I'll call Mark was, for a change, responding with nods of affirmation and denunciation. "Do you know what autism is?" I asked. He nodded an emphatic yes. "Do you think you are like that?" Again, a resounding yes. "Would you like us to learn ways to help us understand you better?" I conjectured. "NO!" and that was the last he said to me during that meeting.

When I drove up, Margaret and Jake were in their van. Cassie was sitting in Jake's lap. He opened up the window and Cassie said, "It's Dan!"

It was 87 degrees at 9:30 in the morning, and the chill started somewhere in the upper center of my spine, crawled up the nape of my neck, and slithered out my arms leaving me with goose flesh and the feeling that, had I some, the hair would be standing up on my head.

I stood there with my mouth hanging open while Margaret told me that "she'd" said "Cassie" a couple of times the day before. After what we (special educators) call perhaps an inappropriately long latency, I managed to say hello to Cassie.

Jake told me that they were heading down to Peg's (I finally figured out the name of the thus-far-unnamed restaurant) because her "other teacher" was coming at 10:00. Cassie held my hand from the truck to the restaurant, and when Jake got the booster seat and tried to set her up at the end of the table, she wanted to sit next to me. So there we were—Jake and Margaret on one side of the table, Cassie and I on the other. They order some bacon and orange juice for Cassie; I get coffee, as does Margaret, and Jake gets tea.

Margaret tells me that Cassie was trying to form words with her mouth while she was playing along with the computer yesterday, but nothing was coming out.

"But I was singing along with her." She's been playing with a dirty diaper recently, Margaret said, there's an awareness, at least. Margaret's niece (unnamed, and at an uncertain time in the past), took a dirty diaper, and wiped it across a screen door. That was the same two-year-old that ran a car into the garage door, because her mom left her in there with the car running, according to Margaret. The cause and effect are not completely obvious, but I could see how leaving her in there would set the stage for such an occurrence.

I have my tape recorder playing, and Cassie grabs one of the tapes and quickly unreels about three inches. "She's fast," Jake tells me. I reel the thing back in with my key, and Cassie takes my key and begins digging it into different ports in my recorder. I tell the adults that it's the kind of tape recorder that reporters use and meant for heavy duty use, and not to worry about it. Cassie takes the key and sticks it into the tape reel and tries to imitate my winding action. We practice putting the tape away. We practice taking the tape out. We practice trying to keep Cassie occupied. She has one of her alligators, and I show her how to give the crocodile a drink.

"Does the alligator need a drink?" I ask.

"Yaa," or something like that.

"I guess they had the fireworks, during the rain," Margaret is talking about the 4th of July celebration (on June 28, 1998—the one, I hate to say, that Cassie was not the little queen of). "I didn't go."

They'd been telling me about how Melanie was having a rough time with Cassie and the diaper incident, which I now learn happened last night while Melanie was watching the store for her parents.

"She had her in tears on Wednesday," Margaret tells me, "Melanie said that, 'she'll mind everyone but me!'"

I wonder about this and ask why.

"Because she knows she can get away with it. And she knows that momma won't swat her butt. I don't swat her hard, just a little swat. And I raise my voice. Mainly raise my voice. Even with my own kids, I used to raise my voice. Not much, but I did," Jake tells me this with some authority.

"Sent one down the road crying," says Margaret.

"That was 'cause he was doing something he shouldn'ta."

"What was that?" I ask.

"Well, he was trying to, uh, kiss Melanie and stuff, wouldn't leave her alone. So I yelled at him. I don't even remember what I said now, but he went down the road. They called, his parents, and I said what he'd done, and they said they'd take care of it. I said, 'what am I supposed to do, hit 'em between the eyes?' But he went down the road. Came back, too, and apologized."

"I mean, she throws her tantrums with me, too," Jake continues, "but I just have her sit in my lap until she calms down, and she knows that she ain't getting down until she calms down."

"But I usually don't have her unless he's around," Margaret laughs, "so I don't have to do anything."

We laugh. Margaret goes on: "'cept read to her, and play with her."

"She's smart. She's smart as a whip."

"Um hum," I say.

"She just don't talk," Jake says.

"And she'll get *away* with what she *can* get away with."

"Do you think she understands what we're talkin' about now?" I ask.

"Ohhh..."

"I don't know; I don't think she's paying any attention to us, now," says Margaret.

"I don't think so right now, no. It's what you're dealing with at the time, that she knows what's goin' on."

"Like what the, what the, uh, social situation is?" I say cringingly, looking at the adults for some understanding, even though I'm not sure what I'm talking about either. Simultaneously, I'm thinking about John Searle saying that all language is about people waving and yaking at each other, and when the metaphors and symbols have died a pleasant enough death, comes understanding.

"You know...uh," I continue.

"Well, she..."

"Well, she listens to our conversations," says Margaret.

"What do you think about us calling you 'she,' little Ms. she girl?"

Jake says: "Well that's true, now that's true. I can go on sayin' she, and as soon as I say 'she' whether she understands it or not..."

"She can *say* Cassie now," Margaret tells us.

"She said that yesterday; we have this little game where I stick my arms in the air, and say *'Cassie!'* two or three times, and then all a sudden, she comes a runnin' and jumps. But yesterday, she started out by sayin', 'Cassie!'"

"She wanted to play the game."

We talked and laughed for a little while longer, tried to keep Cassie's hands out of glasses, napkins out of her mouth, and left the restaurant for her speech lesson.

Trisha, the speech and language therapist, had missed most of last week, based on car trouble. I think the transmission had gone out of her car. There's a little *ding-dong* that announces the presence of a customer at Serendipity's door, and this particular ring heralded Trisha. She apologizes for her busted tranny and goes to work on Cassie:

"Hi Cassie, can you take the rubber band out of your mouth please. Come here, I need you to tell me what you want to play with today."

Cassie attempts to go over to the computer. Trisha has four cards with objects fastened to them, including a Tootsie-Roll, a bathtub, some rice, and a cassette tape. Above the physical object is a line-drawn ASL gesture for the activity. Thus, the Tootsie-Roll is the physical representation of the line drawn ASL gesture "candy;" the plastic bathtub is the physical representation of a sign for "house," in this case, a Playskool fold out house, and the rice glued on the cardboard is the physical representation of the ASL "rice." Trisha has a big tub of rice that kids can play in, and some toy cups and other objects designed to dump it all over the place.

She has a toy watermill that you fill at the top, open a hatch, and watch the rice drain down through the wheel. I bet by now you know what the cassette is all about if you've been reading carefully!

"How are you, Dan?"

"I'm fine, Trisha. I've got a tape recorder going, is that OK? Not an invasion..."

"That's fine."

"What are you going to pick, Cassie? But what about all these other things? You want the rice? Have a seat. OK, let me go get it!"

"Trisha, what's the sign for wait?" Cassie is screaming in my lap while I wait for the rice. Trisha shows me.

"Cassie, look, this is what you picked...oh, oh, oh, oh!"

Cassie: "No, No, No, ahhhhhh, ahhhhh."

"Cassie, do you want something different? Oh, you want the house! What do we need to do to the house? Do we need to open it? What's that? A boy. Where's the baby, Cassie? Can you find me the baby? A boy and two girls. I'm looking for the—baby!"

Cassie: "A bath."

"That's right, Cassie, a bath. Do you think the baby needs a bath?"

Trisha uses a sing-song voice when she's teaching like this. Every word or at least nouns and some verbs are paired with signs. I find it impossible to talk like this. I come up through this 'hood in the world of adults, and you would not believe how many people will still talk to full-grown 50-year-old men with a kiddy-kiddy voice, and I grew to detest it so that I can only use it with sarcasm. In Trisha's case, I do not throw the baby out with the bathwater.

"Good eye-contact today, Cassie, I like the way you're looking at me. Do you want some candy? First we have to clean up the toys!"

> Clean up, Clean up,
> Everybody everywhere!
> Clean up, Clean up,
> Everybody do their share!

"We need to close it! Cassie, Cassie, wait, *I* will go get it."

Dan: "You're doing very good."

Trisha: "Cassie, do you want some candy? Uh oh! What are we going to do? Should we *open* the bag? That's good thinking! That's the way to open the bag."

"What are you going to do with the wrapper?" asks Margaret.

"Cassie, come here, I need you to pick it up. Grandma says to put it in the *blue* basket? Cassie, ask *Dan* if he wants some candy..."

"Cassie, maybe you need to ask Grandma if she wants some candy."

"Open," says Cassie.

"Open for who?" interjects Trisha...

"What are we going to do next, Cassie; what's your choice? Oh, you want the rice! Remember, we have to clean up whatever mess we make!"

"Oh, Oh!" I say, thinking that there must have been incidents.

"Umm hmm. That was a big trick last time, wasn't it, Grandma?"

"Cleanin' up," I say?

"And throwing the broom!"

They play with the rice while I look on, wishing I was a farmer, not because of the rice per se, but the mechanical action of the "water" wheel reminds me of grain-handling equipment, especially those old, falling apart cribs on our farm. They work the same way as Trisha's toy, except in reverse.

Trisha and Cassie are filling the bin on top of the toy again, together:

"I like it when we work together, Cassie," and Trisha once again is moved to song:

The more we work together,
Together, together;
The more we work together,
The happier we'll be.

"Scoop! Thank you, Cassie! I think it's full! Shall we *open*? Cassie's being much more careful than she was last week. Remember, we have to clean up whatever we get on the floor."

"You're gonna be cleanin' rice for the next two years," I say to Margaret.

"Naw, Jake's going to mop the floor after she leaves." I'm not at all convinced.

Trisha says she's going to leave the house for Cassie to play with, maybe because Cassie signed "open," or maybe just because she likes Cassie. They play with the house some more. Trisha, according to the stipulations set forth at our mediation hearing, only has to stay for 20 minutes, but Trisha's spent at least 30 by now. She and Cassie continue to talk about what the people and animals (there's a dog) are doing in the play house.

But now it's time for Trisha to go, and we have to clean up, clean up.

"Noooooo!, Noooooo, ahhhhhhh!!!!" says Cassie.

But they get it cleaned up.

Cassie gets another piece of candy, and I say: "Let's see that, let's figure this out."

"What do you want Dan to do with it?"

"A candy!"

"Uh huh."

"What should I do?"

"Help!"

"Ya, that's fine Cassie," she hadn't signed it, just said it, "I'm always happy to help you out."

"Cassie, it's time for me to go."

Trisha again: "Has anyone talked to you about Therapeutic Riding Programs."

"No."

Trisha explains the Therapeutic Riding Program to Margaret and me, who eventually figure out that she's talking about riding horses, and not writing to gain, perhaps, a better understanding of one's self.

"You always hear about kids that really have a lot of problems, and I never think of Cassie as being eligible for those..."

"And I don't think you have to prove that she's *so bad* to get the help. But I saw those horse books and something clicked."

After some time, spent disorganized, in various attempts to get Cassie's shoes tied, figuring out where to put the house, our bodies, and so on, Trisha gets ready to go. Whilst we bumble about, I notice Cassie on an overturned bucket using ballerina-like motions with her hands, a beatific expression on her face.

Trisha tells me in a confidential tone that she's going to remove the physical objects from the card next week. She wants to see if Cassie can associate the sign with the activity. Jean-Marc Gaspard Itard (who we shall meet in Chapter Five) used a similar method to establish correspondence between object and symbol in the early nineteenth century: "*What a difficult step I had overcome! I was convinced of this when I saw our young Victor fasten his gaze and successively, upon each object, choose one, and next look for the drawing to which he wished to bring it, and soon I had material proof by experimenting with the transposition of the drawings, which was followed on his part by the methodical transposition of objects*" (Itard 1962, 40).

I try to get some time where I can interview Trisha. We spend an ungodly amount of time doing this because she is just so damn cooperative that the opportunities open up to me like a field of clover to a bee. We figure something out, and Trisha leaves, as do I, after a certain amount of formality.

Field Notes, Cassie, July 3, 1998

"Dan! *Cassie's Drowning!*"

Wendy, my sister-in-law, said this some with urgency. I turned my gaze from the shoreline where the dogs were running unrestrained among the abandoned fishing tackle that I was sure would get caught in their paws, tongues, eyes, hides, wrapped and embedded around their necks, and other negative fantasies.

Cassie's pearlescent skin formed an exquisite backdrop for the swirling bits of decaying wood and other debris in the water. Her eyes were wide open, as was her mouth, head pointed skyward beneath the water, arms reaching for the surface in front of her head. I grabbed her under the arms and hoisted her quickly to my chest, her diaphragm on my ribcage. She was sputtering and choking, so I was fairly certain I was not going to have to use extreme measures as I placed my right forearm under her ribcage and locked my left hand on my wrist and gave her a sharp squeeze, inward and upward. I felt warm water gush over my back, Cassie's breathing became more regular.

Only when I was certain that she was OK did I head to shore. My back was turned from the girl for only a second or two. And she'd sunk like a rock.

"Wendy, thank god you told me about Cassie," I murmured, soothingly, unnecessarily because the small girl in my arms was screaming, kicking, slapping, arching her body, and generally doing anything to get back to the smelly water. Her shouts echoed deep through the forest, disturbing, in my imagination, the people on the bank fishing and those on the trails hiking.

"I didn't say anything about Cassie drowning," Wendy told me.

"Oh?" That memory remains the most vivid of that day.

"Look," I said to her, "here's what's going to happen. I'd like for you to get the dogs on their leashes, I'm going to take Cassie out one more time, then we'll take the kid and the dogs up to the truck, and I'm going back to Salt Fork." Rachel, my niece, had emerged from the muck, and said: "*I* want to go with *Dan*" as if someone was going to stop her.

Cassie calmed as we got deeper into the water, and she splashed happily as I held to her hips with both hands, bent over in a way that I reckoned would cause me to suffer with a bad back for a few days. She was talking to me, screaming with delight about "Waaaaaaar! waaaaaaar!, gooooooow!" I told her it *was* time to go, and she began to panic and fight me all the way to my truck. She managed to knock off my Wayfarers. Somehow, Wendy had corralled the dogs in the back of the truck, and I manipulated the despairing and protesting child into the middle seat. Rachel had to go back down by the lake to get something, and I told her to hurry as I pinned, as gently as possible, Cassie to her position on the bench seat. Rachel got in the truck, and we took off. My brother Kurt flagged me down and asked, "How do we get back to Bloomington?"

"Head west!" I yelled spewing gravel and dust in his bewildered face.

The day had started placidly enough. We took the truck, and Kurt and Wendy drove their rental car. Bobby, my nephew, and Rachel rode with me. I'd explained, as well as I could, about Cassie: That she understood what we talked about but didn't talk. "Why doesn't she talk, Uncle Dan?" asked Bobby.

"Don't know, just doesn't say much now."

"Where do you teach her?"

"I don't know, stores, at her grandparents' video store, just about anywhere."

"Are you going to teach her today?"

"Hope so."

When we got close to Salt Fork, Rachel said that she was going to be friendly to Cassie because she's *so* shy. I smiled.

Jake was at the front desk, and Margaret was in the back with Cassie. "Who's that?" they asked, but Cassie just grabbed my hand and tried to lead me to the back room, but I had to resist so that I could introduce my family. They were all happy to meet each other, according to what they said.

I got some directions to Moraine View State Park, a route that would take us down remote country roads where farmers in their pick-up trucks would wave to us as we passed. I would wave back, as is our custom. Margaret gave me Cassie's backpack with some fresh diapers and her passy (pacifier) if she got into trouble. We piled into our vehicles, and as had been previously determined by the toss of a coin, Bobby had to ride with his parents.

Rachel talked quietly with Cassie while we drove and tried to teach Cassie the names of my dogs. "You're petting Chauncey's head," she would say, and Cassie would say "ooooooooh, a dog!"

"There is Petunia, see, she's lying down." Rachel pointed out farm animals, and said their names distinctly and correctly, and Cassie would say them back: "A Cow! A Cat!"

We stopped at the entrance to the park, where there was a horse stable. Rachel needed to change into her swimming suit and go to the bathroom. I showed Cassie the horses and she ran around the corral, trying to get in, grabbing my hand in an attempt to make it open the gates, but she had no luck with my clumsy appendage and contented herself by running around, climbing the fences, and petting the towering, gentle creatures. Wendy had to help me round her up, and Cassie didn't seem to get too mad; I don't know why, and somewhat sexistly, I considered the value of a woman's touch, or perhaps that of a stranger, or perhaps the magic of Wendy.

Then Bobby decided he needed to go to the bathroom. It was hot outside, and the adults could only scratch their heads, or in my brother's case, lean the seat back further in his car. I worried about the dogs and the heat, Cassie and the heat, and what would happen next.

We drove around the lake, and Cassie became progressively more excited. The official swimming area at the park didn't look too dog-friendly, so we landed in another spot, got the dogs out to get some water, and those unfamiliar with the strength of a headstrong (and physically strong) Dalmatian were dragged from one doggy point of interest to another. He finally ran loose and got in the way of a few cars, whose drivers looked at me with exasperated eyes.

Cassie took off down a trail, looking at me with her "You can't get mee-ee" eyes, but I did and carried her out of the woods, set her down, and tried to catch the dogs again. I got 'em, and went after Cassie, who'd run back down the trail; Wendy stopped me, saying that she thought it was a game Cassie was playing, that we should just wait to see if she came back up the trail. We did, and she did. This was great fun for her, and I found myself wondering how this would work in a store. I haven't done one thing that I've been wanting to do which is get her a brooch that says "Cassie."

We finally wandered down to the water, where I almost lost Cassie.

All this happened in two hours; I reflected that it was a rather long two hours. Cassie was inconsolable on the ride back, and Rachel experimented with different ways to bring her back to us, finding paper for her to draw on, letting her play with the Bob Marley and Frank Sinatra tapes, and finally putting them away when Rachel was certain that there was no way to convince her charge that it is not a good idea to pull the tapes out of their cartridges.

My part of Illinois is not known for its cool, clear waters, and we were all soaked to the bone, smelling like anaerobic fermentation and dead fish. Rachel and I wondered out loud if we were going to get in any trouble for bringing a water-rat home instead of a grandchild.

Rachel said *she* wasn't going to go into the store, and I said that's OK, Cassie's my student. But Rachel did come in to face the music, and I honestly thought that she'd done this as an act of responsibility, to help me through my ordeal.

I stood there telling our misadventures to Jake: I'd figured we were going to be gone all day, and here we were back at 12:45. They seemed to take the near-drowning, or what I perceived to be a near-drowning in stride. Somewhere I lost the passy. They had a spare, they said, and they toweled off their crying and suffering grandchild while I told them that next time I go swimming, I was going to be a little bit more organized.

They wondered, mainly, if she had had a good time. That surprised me somehow, and I said *yes*, now that I think of it. That before we lost it, Cassie was chattering with Rachel, petting my dogs, got to see some horses, did some hiking, and *loved the water!*

Rachel and I stopped at the park on the way back, and she found my Wayfarers, and I picked up a dirty diaper off the ground that Cassie had lost during her last swim.

Margaret Writes:

Dan,

The position you wrote about at the lake doesn't sound possible. If she was facing you—your right arm under her ribcage and you locked your left hand on your wrist. Unless you squeezed from the back or someone else held her against you. Jake read this one. He said reading this scared him more than when you first told us. I guess I more or less expected this action after pulling her out of the water.

You said, "and she began to panic and fight." Not panic but probably an outburst of anger about being taken away. I doubt that she was afraid. Also, what are Wayfarers?

I'm glad you wrote that you smiled "I smiled." Good. This is an all-knowing smile, because Cassie is not shy! Right!

"A Cow!" This reminds me I thought Rubic Cubes were named Arubics Cubes because the "*a*" was always added. Does Cassie think a cow is acow? Or a cat—acat? Or a barn—abarn?"

As much as it might have been with the horses, I believe you had success with this event. In keeping her out of the corral yet she could enjoy petting the horses.

You said that Cassie got "progressively more excited." Was she trying to talk and point at the water? How did she display her excitement?"

We've let her wander off by herself and it's worked a few times outside for us. But it is not good to let her go when she's in possible danger, i.e., crowds or cars being close by, to see if she will come back. Or perhaps this is something we should practice more often.

I've seen Cassie in a near-death situation (before and after she died). She is quite a fighter. I'm hoping this will be a part of what causes her striving to speak and get along in the world. It just doesn't seem to be helping in the potty training. Or maybe she is fighting not to be trained.

Cassie is one of those free spirits that people talk about—no fear and loving every minute of life of whatever *she has chosen to do!*

Margaret

Dan Writes:

Margaret,

I was holding Cassie so our stomachs were together so my arm was across the *back* of her ribcage, and I'm sorry if I didn't adequately express the fear I, at least, experienced. You're right, the panic that I was describing was not fear of drowning, or fear of anything else except having a rather large man tear her away from the water. Maybe I said panic, because I was projecting, but another word, such as hysteria would have described her emotional state more adequately. Wayfarers are sunglasses, expensive ones.

I smiled when Rachel said that Cassie was shy, because I never said she was shy, just that she didn't talk. My smile was born of personal experience, attempting to find some way to explain to children the behavior of others who might not act in a predictable way. Who might act in majorly unpredictable ways. I've heard kids, sometimes after twenty minutes of tortured discourse say, "Oh, you mean he's *shy?*" Like, why didn't you just say so?

I had to laugh when you called into question my use of "progressively more excited." I believe that's what we would call a gloss, as in a glossing over of some important details, or an idea that one hopes to convey by merely throwing out a word.

As we drove around the lake, Cassie would get glimpses of the sun shining on the rippling water she forgot about the dogs, plastered herself against the passenger seat window, said "ooooooohhh!" and "waaaaaaa," pressed both hands against its surface, and I think she even licked it. Rachel watched in amusement, and held the little girl close to her so she could look for water. Rachel said, "Where's the water, Cassie?" I said authoritatively that "Cassie *really* likes the water."

I don't know what to say about Cassie using the article "a" in front of her words. I really don't.

Dan

I Interview Trisha, July 8, 1998

After a certain amount of dealing with who we know, what doctors take Medicaid, and so on, I talked with Trisha about her initial impressions of Cassie:

Dan   You've been working with Cassie for about 4 weeks, right? You wanna tell me what your initial impressions were?

Trisha   Initial impressions were that there were a lot of behaviors that we had to get past to get to what she could really do communicatively. But it seemed like she used the behaviors to replace some of her communication needs. It seems like if we can come up with some alternative means for her to communicate, not relying only on the verbal, she seems very successful. And today is what I would base that on, she used a picture symbol, not just a concrete object but a representative symbol, to tell me that she wanted to play with the rice first, and then she was able to tell me that she wanted some candy. It seems like the symbols are supporting her verbalizations, because she then verbalizes what she wants after she's had that visual symbol to scaffold, or support, her communication. I feel that the behaviors aren't as intimidating as they seem on first impression. She's screaming and yelling and not telling you anything, she's just moving, but once you get past that surface...

Dan   Like the Tasmanian Devil—eeeeooooeeeeooooeeooo!

Trisha   Constantly on the move.

Dan   But she sits quietly, fairly quietly, at least with you.

Trisha   Mostly though, her attentiveness is better with activities that she's been able to choose herself. When I introduce the activities that I want to start with, that attention's a lot less. But it seems that you can shape her attentiveness in a more positive way within other activities, like if she wants the rice and she gets the house, if I let her find something in the house activity that she wants, still giving her choices, then we can kind of build from there...I think...that's an encouraging thing. But even just like the progress of sweeping, the first day I did that, it was the most horrible thing I'd ever done to Cassie. Today, she asked for the broom and swept up the rice because it was bothering her where she was sitting. Without me asking. So it seems that the structure, when it's given to her, helps her to be able to move toward more appropriate behavior. The other thing I wanted to tell you in terms of first impressions, was that her social needs were pretty significant. She didn't make much eye contact; she wasn't interested in taking turns, getting her to share things. But today, she was grabbing my hands so she could pour rice on my hands, and I'd open them and pour the rice out. It wasn't the parallel play that we saw so significantly in the first and second sessions. I think that we have a long way to go. Again, it's not that all or nothing principle...

I asked Trisha what she meant by scaffolding, and she said that there was a lot of literature out there that "talks" about it, but that it mainly means that one builds on the skill that the child has in order to produce a "more sophisticated communicative end." For instance, running away is a skill Cassie has; she uses it for escape. The idea here would be to build upon that skill, using augmentative means, to indicate that she wanted to do something else.

Trisha   It will be interesting next week because I'm going to introduce some other activities and remove the rice and the house, and use cards that do not have physical representations on them to see how much support she needs to learn the connection between the symbol and the event.

Dan   What kind of goodies are you going to bring?

Trisha   I think Tootsie-pops will be our candy, and I'll bring the Fisher-Price Garage—she seems to like that kind of toy—and the sand for her tactile experience. I want to give her candy to replace that "toys in the mouth stuff"; something that's more socially appropriate. Those are things that we can use to learn more about Cassie, and it all can be done with play. That's the important thing I don't want anyone to forget; play offers a lot of opportunities to learn from Cassie.

Dan   Heh, heh, that's what I've been doing with her, but I'm way less structured than you.

Trisha   And my setting in this room lends itself to structure. But I do think that for me to achieve the ends that I want, knowing whether or not she can understand the representations of symbols, knowing if she's got those social prerequisites, eye contact, and turn-taking for example, I need to give her a little bit of structure. It would be really hard for me to accurately assess those behaviors if I didn't have her in a controlled environment. You probably know a little bit more about Cassie that you can take her beyond the controlled environment that I have her in right now.

Dan   Well, for a long time, I never took her out. We'd stay in here and I'd pretty much follow her lead, and oh, I guess I had some of the same goals in mind, but I was more interested in developing a relationship with her, and seeing what the outcome of that would be. But she still...I'm not, in terms of the outcomes, I think I've got a good relationship with her, but on the other hand, I don't think I've been able bring out, uh, the same kinds of things that you have.

Trisha   I think that it goes back to that scaffolding thing. I've got four different things for her to do, and she's got to make a choice. It's a social behavior she's going to encounter at school. There are, I don't know how their Early Childhood Education (ECE) environment is structured, but there's probably housekeeping, block area, sand and water play, and maybe one other area, a motor area, and she's got to make a choice during work time. I assume she can't just wander around aimlessly...I want her to be able to transfer what she learns here to what she has to do in school, it's just going to be a bigger area (laughs). I will say on a positive note that her speech therapist at school wants a lot of feedback...

Dan   So you've been in contact with her.

We talk about how her current speech therapist, and how I hope she's able to enact what Trisha's doing, because her speech therapist is of a "pull-out mentality," meaning that Cassie gets pulled out of class and gets taught something or other, and the expectation is that she will carry that back to the classroom.

Trisha tells me that she is fortunate in that she is able to do all of her work in the classroom, and that her relationship with the ECE teacher is a collaborative one. They team teach. Trisha thinks that a visit to her classroom would be a very positive one for any ECE teacher and speech therapist, not that they do everything right, but that she thinks that they have a good handle on how children learn through play, and that there's not that opportunity in her "therapy box" (her words).

Dan   How would you convince someone of a "pull out" mentality the merits of your in vivo speech therapy philosophy.

Trisha   For one thing, I don't have to waste ten minutes of my time taking the child down to the speech therapy room, and for another, there's another adult there to help with the behaviors. Before you get burnt out on a kid, you can trade off...

Dan   What kind of advice would you give me? I mean, you've seen me interact with Cassie.

Trisha   I have a question about how the Tic-Tacs work.

Dan   The Tic-Tacs. Ummm, I use them when I'm out in a store with her, and if she, like goes into a fit, I try to give her a Tic-Tac to try to break her out of it. By giving her a Tic-Tac as a reinforcer (I giggle).

Trisha   I don't know if it's a concern, but I don't know if she's getting reinforced for the behavior because she gets a Tic-Tac whenever she misbehaves, do you know what I mean?

Dan   Well, uh, people ask me that a lot, and if you want my pat response...

Trisha   I'll take any response...

Dan   You know, I always try to reinforce good behavior, like if she's holding my hand, I try to buy her a coke, or play with her when she's sitting quietly with a toy. Tic-Tacs are emergency measures, and I did use the term reinforcer inappropriately, it's really an emergency measure, not a reinforcer, but most people don't know the difference. I call them Tic-Tactics. I wouldn't use them if there wasn't a grand scheme in place to improve her behavior...But, tell me, who's going to learn anything when they're lying on the floor of Toys-R-Us screaming their fool head off?

Trisha   And that makes sense. About the signing, I'm very interested in augmentative communication, and some children, if you support their hands while they sign, it won't generalize, and you wind up having to prompt them all the time. Cassie seems to have some imitative skills so I think, for everyone, we should avoid physically prompting signs, and really, I'd hate to stick something in there that's unnecessary that will actually inhibit her acquisition of communicative skills. Just model them, and if she uses them, great, and if she doesn't she'll have to find some other way to express what she wants.

Dan   I suppose that's some kind of comment on my physical prompting of signs.

Trisha   I have another student, and he won't sign unless I'm there to help him, and everyone says, "How do we know that it's him making the signs, and not you?" And I'm comfortable modeling for Cassie, because as I said, she seems to have imitative skills. It's going to be really hard to say good-bye to Cassie. Someone jokingly said that Melanie's dating someone from LeRoy, so maybe she'll wind up with me after all. It's those times when she comes up and touches my cheek, like today, that lets me know that she thinks I'm more than some lady that comes over and makes me touch pictures.

I hit the pause button while I explained some of the details of the mediation hearing and then asked Trisha what kind of advice she'd offer teachers who would be working with Cassie.

Trisha   I think Cassie, educationally, is going to require teachers who are going to have to adapt a lot of their thinking. Just like even the computer. Not every child has to use the mouse, and hopefully those teachers will acknowledge that there's other ways for Cassie to do something. They're supposedly trained to do that, and this will give them the opportunity to use those skills. And maybe if Cassie has a hard time at calendar, they don't expect her to go up and touch the numbers, they modify their expectations so that maybe Cassie just has to stay in circle. Their expectations have to modified to meet Cassie's needs.

Melanie comes in, and talks about swimming the night before. We talked about going out to Dawson Lake (Moraine View), how Cassie *chose* to go swimming, how I wished I'd had a chance to get the wallet, cigarettes, money, pacifier, lighter, and keys out of my pockets before I had to chase in after her.

Trisha said that the autism diagnosis doesn't fit Cassie, and borderline mental retardation doesn't fit either, because her social skills would be more advanced.

Trisha   I am sorry that you (Melanie) haven't had a good experience with ECE, because there's so much positive that can happen in that environment. Not that it would be appropriate to move to LeRoy, or anything...

Melanie   Someone's been talking...(looking at her mom).

Trisha   Does your boyfriend have a brother named _____.

Melanie   No. But his mother changed her name to _____.

Trisha   Oh! Mrs. _____, I love her. The tape recorder's on so I'll leave it at that.

We talk more about who knows who and that kind of thing. I ask if Trisha's been able to get a hold of Cassie's teacher, and she hasn't. I say that every time I call the number the school gave me, I get some business, and no one ever calls me back. I say that maybe Cassie's teacher is a little mad at me cause I raised a little ruckus. I look at Melanie and say, "or maybe I should say that Melanie raised a little ruckus." Trisha asks me to pause the tape, and after a while, we continued:

Dan   Based on what you've seen over the last four weeks, where do you see her in four months?

Trisha   I see that we could expand the number of symbols that we use to communicate, and I don't see any reason why her classroom environment can't be adapted so that she has symbols...If you put a housekeeping symbol where they do housekeeping, and you put picture symbols on all of the different things in her classroom to give her one more way of talking, and I'm using the word talking loosely, what she wants to play with, what she wants to use, to share; that's nothing to do. The research says that that's a basis for reading, long-term we need to think about what we're going to do for Cassie in terms of reading—that's really important, how she's going to express her thoughts to other people, not just by talking or using symbol sets, but expressing her ideas...Cassie's entitled to the same experiences as other four- and five-year-olds.

Dan   You could be invited to an IEP meeting, couldn't you?

Trisha   Of course. And then the district would have to decide whether they'd give me release time to do it, but that's never been a problem before...It's real hard to know where my different lives lie, because I'm an employee of the school district, and that makes it difficult. But I don't think I've said anything inappropriate, and I would say everything that I've said to you to them...

We chatted for a while, and Trisha and I headed off, toward home.

Field Notes, Cassie, July 10, 1998

Today is a beautiful day here in Central Illinois, provided you are not allergic to corn pollen. The smell is heavy; the wind is not blowing, and it hangs like the smell of good cookin' over an old farm house when there's not much wind. The corn has grown probably two feet in the last week or so, wasting no time. I could go on about this, but only if you are interested. There is much that I could tell you about sugar metabolism, crop ecology, and so forth. But mostly, as I head toward Salt Fork, I wonder what the place would look like if our great-great grandfathers hadn't drained and plowed the land and killed off the natives or even if it had remained as it was when I was a boy.

I go over a bridge down the road where I used to see snapping turtles resting before the road was paved and before I had any formal education. My dad used to tell me, "If one of those snappers' gets hold of you, it won't let go till sundown." They used to sit out there, and when we passed in his truck, they'd lop into the water like pancakes off a griddle. The creek's been straightened now, and the road paved, and I never see any snapping turtles. And now what I hear from my dad is stuff like, "Why do you write about marching in the basement with broomsticks?" I could go on about this too, but you are not interested. But I do know that the creek straightening began sometime around the time I was fourteen or fifteen, and it struck me as strange. Creeks in the old days were beautiful; they meandered like snakes, made oxbow lakes, and I suppose, generally took up too much room.

Of course I'm on my way to see Cassie, and I know I missed her speech therapy. But we are going to go to Moraine View State Park, and we are going to swim in the area reserved for swimming. It will cost us a dollar a piece. I have to stop at my old bank to get some money. I have yet to close my account there, but I'd better, just like I'd better do a lot of things. But right now I have better things to do.

At Serendipity, I say "Hi!" to Jake and Margaret. Cassie is watching a video and comes to get me. Melanie arrives, and says, "I'm here, I was just in the bathroom." Margaret gives me a piece of paper that has her comments from the last batch of field notes. Somewhere along the line, I've picked up Cassie and am twisting my body back and forth, stimulating her vestibular system, and with a sing-song tone of voice, intoning "Cassie, Cassie, Cassie!"

Margaret tells me that Trish left me some books, one called *Communicative Alternatives to Challenging Behavior: Integrating Functional Assessment and Intervention Strategies* (1993) by Joe Reichle and David P. Wacker and another called *Breaking the Speech Barrier: Language Development Through Augmented Means* (1996) by Mary Ann

Romski and Rose A. Sevick.

I know the former two authors, both colleagues of my mentors at U of I. I've sat at a table and cracked jokes with Reichle and made jokes about a child psychologist named *Wacker* (whacker—get it?). I'd taken a kid who was thrown out of school, and practically out of the Center to see him, and an incredible number of professionals at a "large childhood disability clinic in a middle-western state."

He did a functional analysis of the kid's behavior in a half-hour, the results of which indicated the very helpful information that his "challenging" behaviors (like slugging us, biting us, kicking us, throwing soup cans at us, puking on us, and, as I labeled it on a data sheet, tie-sliming. For some reason, when in a room with a man with a tie, he would lick his hand and rub it on his tie, until someone could stop him, which was not easy) had their basis in his desire to escape noxious situations. He needed to learn functional, appropriate language to express his needs, wants, desires, and so on. Ho hum.

The latter book "originated with a feasibility study to determine whether the teaching approach (including the technology, symbol set, and instructional strategies employed with Lana could be adapted for use by individuals with mental retardation who had not learned to talk" (21). Lana was a chimpanzee (*Pan* troglodytes).

I think about a cartoon I once saw that depicted Vicki the chimp, stumping the chump. A scientist was holding up cards while Vicki indicated she was an *existentialist*. In reality though, as the caption reads, she was a *logical positivist*.

I look gratefully at the books and ask Melanie, who's got Cassie at this point, whether I can borrow *Jungle Book* again.

Melanie shows me how to get Cassie's diaper off before we go swimming. She tells me that Cassie can't go swimming with it on because they fill up with an unbelievable amount of water. An incredible amount. I say, "I know, I know," wisely. Melanie also tells me that her bathing suit will go right up her crack, and that it's a constant battle to keep it where it belongs.

It turns out that Cassie was swimming yesterday at Melanie's somewhat new boyfriend's mom's house. He is very much interested in teaching Cassie water safety, or at least he is very aware of water safety, because his dad drowned when the boyfriend was eight. He said that he didn't know if Cassie would be able to learn to swim because her arms are not that coordinated. Melanie said that he was really good with her, that she'd had a tantrum because they wouldn't let her walk around the edge of the above-ground pool, and that it took her about 20 minutes before she calmed. I asked how long she swam before either a) it was time for her to get out; or b) she got out on her own, and Melanie said that it was about 45 minutes.

After checking the bookbag for diapers, clothes, towels, sunscreen, *and* the passy, we head off to the park. Cassie looks out the window, and I point out the various attractions, horses, barns, cats, dogs, but Cassie is quiet, and she holds on to the dashboard, looking out the passenger window.

We get to the park, and I show Cassie the horse stable. I say, "Cassie, after we swim, we'll go see the horsies! The HORSIES, Cassie!" But she does not appear interested. I drive around until I find the official swimming area, and it looks inviting and festive enough. I remove Cassie's diaper using the method Melanie taught me. I throw it in the trash.

There is a wide grass area that leads down to the beach, which looks like it had been raked by some mechanical means. We stop on the grass. Cassie is "waiting nicely" for me, holding on to my hand, and when I say, "We have to wait," she holds a finger in the air, and says, "Wait," with patient-looking eyes. She permits me to get her shoes off, and "waits" while I get mine off (I position myself between her and the water to facilitate this).

The water is brown and smells like a lake but not a festering swamp. Children are playing in the sand in the bright sun, swimming with all kinds of inflatable toys that will probably wind up in one of our landfills at the end of their vacation. Older girls are acting like nurturing moms to siblings who they probably detest in real life; one looks at me from her perch on a chartreuse vinyl "inner tube," winks slyly, and says, "I'm getting some *help*," rolling her eyes somewhat as she says this so I am painfully aware of the torture she endures as her little brothers and sisters gaily push her around the lake.

Cassie and I entered the lake calmly enough, hand in hand. She wanted to go out deep, and I didn't really care. I discovered right away that if Cassie lost her footing, she'd go down even in two feet of water, even with her legs kicking. She'd come up wide-eye'd, wide-mouthed, and wide-nosed, sputtering water, and scared enough that she'd cling to me for a second or two before seeking another thrill.

I was trying to get her to hold her breath. The difficulty, or at least one of them, was to get her to look at me. "Cassie!" is probably an indication that something probably unpleasant is coming, although this is changing, according to Margaret and Jake, who've helped her invent the "Cassie" game.

How do you get a kid to hold their breath under the water? I don't know. Babies can do this, I think. I don't know if they teach them this or whether it's some sort of instinct.

Actually, until moments ago, I didn't know any of this but now I do, after a visit to the World Wide Web. There are no mysteries to life anymore, I swear.

It turns out that babies are nose breathers. They reflexively close their mouths when immersed in water and hold their breaths. Babies gradually lose this reflex until it disappears by the age of eight months. Waterbaby instruction begins at three months when instructors start pouring water over their heads until they stop trying to breathe it in. Then they get them in the water, count to three, and blow on their faces, which reflexively makes them hold their breaths, and dunk them. The babies soon learn that "1, 2, 3!" means a dunk. When they've mastered that, they teach them to float on their backs, which most babies resist and which causes most parents anxiety. The baby will finally quit fighting, or give up, or something, and learn the acquired taste of back floating.

Cassie continues her water fun, and so do I. I experiment with slowly lowering her into the water, holding her by her armpits. When she gets to about her chin, her paddling-like but purposeless motions get more frantic, and when she gets her mouth in the water, I can see her start to suck it in. I try all kinds of ways to get her to hold her breath, including holding my hand over her mouth and nose, but this just makes her suck harder on my hand, increase efforts to rid my hands of her body, and then, sink.

We go on like this for some time. She wants to get away from me desperately but can't because she'll drown if she does, so in controlled combat, we passed the afternoon. She learned how to dunk me by putting her hand on my head and pushing. She would scream in a high-pitched little girl voice, and up I would come.

Eventually, Cassie got up on the beach and ran away. I let her go, and slid like an alligator along the shoreline in foot-deep water. There were a lot of people around, and I noticed to my puzzled relief, that she respected people's interpersonal space and their tempting possessions. She would run and then look for me. I've wondered, sometimes, about her eyesight (not for any particular reason, symptom, behavior, etc., just curiosity), but I'll tell you, she can pick me out of a crowd in glaring water at 25 yards.

We got back in the water, and I started preparing her for going home. I said, "Here's what we're going to do, we're going to swim for about 10 more minutes, and then we're going to go see the horsies, and then go home. I am going to bring this up about every minute or so, and then I'm going to count to 10, and we'll go."

That's more or less the way it went. She protested and tried to drop to the ground but just once. I said, "We're going to go see the horsies!" We (I added a step) got an orange pop, got in the truck, put on our shoes, and drove down to the stables. I freed Cassie from the truck, and she ran around pretty much like she did before. I tried to get her interested in feeding the poor things some pigweed, but she'd tear up a leaf until it was about the size of a dime and give it to these animals whose heads alone looked as big as Cassie herself. Her hand would disappear inside the mouth and let go, Cassie said, "Ow!" and then petted their heads, saying "awwwwww, awwwwww" in a deep voice that I don't recollect hearing before.

I told Cassie that we'd be leaving soon but not right now, and she ran harmlessly south along the fencerow. I knew she'd be back, because there were more horses up my way. She came back, and I started counting to ten, and I think she was repeating some of the numbers. At least she was saying something. She tried to drop to the ground once, but that's all, and walked quietly to the truck.

We got in the truck, Cassie had some orange pop (all of it really), and looked at me and said "pa." I said, "You want your passy?" She said "pa," and I didn't make her say something like yes. She was nodding and asleep by the time we got back to Serendipity.

Melanie was headed out but brought Cassie in with her I guess to change her, and so forth. Cassie practically slept through the whole ordeal, which I watched with detached interest (while I talked), because I think that I should change to regular clothes when we go next time. I figure we'll be swimming a lot this summer.

Jake brought me the books, and I said I appreciated them and all, but really what I was doing when I was talking to Trisha was setting her up to talk about communication and its relationship to behavior (aberrant or otherwise). "I studied that stuff 'til I was blue in the face," I said, but not that it finally blew me away. I said I didn't know whether it was ethical or not, but I wanted to "get it on tape, what she had to say about Cassie and her behavior and her communication." Margaret said whatever you gotta do, you gotta do. I told Melanie if the IEP is reconvened in the fall, as we'd agreed, it would be a good idea if we could invite Trisha.

Then I collected Trisha's books, the *Jungle Book* video, and drove home.

It's a clean shot, more or less from Salt Fork to my house in Danvers. Oh, there's a three-mile northerly deviation down to the three-mile corner, but for all practical purposes, a clean shot. Driving home in the evening, the sun's in my eyes, but I've got a nice pair of sunglasses.

I'm thinking about a little girl that lives in that town, someone I know who loves the water. It's been a long time since I swam much, I think I gave it up when the cops shut down this gravel pit outside of Bloomington ten years ago.

The water felt good today, and I think I'm going to teach that little girl how to swim.

Margaret Writes:

Dan,

Melanie finally took Cassie boating with Tim and another couple. She fussed while waiting for the boat to be put in the water. However, when they put the lifejacket on her she quit yelling and she was willing to wear it. She swam for a while and loved it. Melanie noticed that she never used her left arm. It was limp at her side. They couldn't figure that out.

She climbed the ladder into the boat. They would count to three and throw her back into the water with Melanie. Cassie would head back to the ladder to do it over and over. She would go down a couple of feet and bounce back up and not sputter. She holds her breath—Thanks to your trips this summer at Dawson.

Also she had a small toy that floated. Melanie would throw it and Cassie would go get it. Soon Cassie would throw the toy and go get it. Later they let her go naked with the life jacket because the swim diapers broke her out. Picture that? They spent the whole day with an afternoon nap in the bed below deck. It was a great outing. Melanie came back very happy with Cassie's behavior.

Melanie wanted to tell you about it, but she's been working all week. I thought if it isn't too late you could use this information to help with your dissertation. Good luck with all you have to do,

Margaret

Chapter Three
A Mind Is a Terrible Thing to Waste

People write the history of experiments on those born blind, on wolf-children or under hypnosis. But who will write the more general, more fluid, but also more determinant history of the 'examination'—its rituals, its methods, its characters and their roles, its play of questions and answers, its systems of marking and classification? For in this slender technique are to be found a whole domain of knowledge, a whole type of power. One often speaks of the ideology that the human 'sciences' bring with them in either discreet or prolix manner. But does their very technology, this tiny operational schema that has become so widespread (from psychiatry to pedagogy, from the diagnosis of diseases to the hiring of labour), this familiar method of the examination, implement, within a single mechanism, power relations that make it possible to extract and constitute knowledge.?

—Foucault, *Discipline and Punish:*
The Birth of the Prison (1977/1979, 185)

And so Cassie will undergo extensive medical, psychological, and educational evaluation as she matures. The professional argot that describes her condition will be transcribed into a file that constitutes her "case." She will forever be an actor in the scientific narrative of mental retardation.

Shortly after swimming season, Cassie was taken by her family to a notable children's disability clinic for what is known as an "arena assessment." In tight choreography, pediatricians, psychiatrists, psychologists, neurologists, physical and occupational therapists, social workers, and educators administered their evaluations. The family was invited back weeks later for the "staffing." Sequentially, each professional presented his or her findings represented in succinct reports followed by a summary statement from the clinic's lead physician: Cassie has moderate mental retardation with autistic features. For years to come this proclamation will be a fixed point of reference to guide professional treatment, educational programs, and the guidelines by which Cassie's conduct will be interpreted.

"Normal" and the calculable quantity of "normalcy" make quantifiable departures—abnormality—possible. The word in its new conceptual garments did not become commonplace in European language until the mid-nineteenth century (Davis 1997). Until then, the word "norm" signified a carpenter's tool used to measure perpendicularity. As bourgeois industrialists and public health officials became engaged in directing public policy, the "political arithmetic" of statistics emerged. Startlingly enough, the early fathers of the science—Sir Francis Galton (Sir Charles Darwin's cousin), Karl Pearson, and R. A. Fisher—were early eugenicists (eugenics being the science of improving the human race through selective breeding), at least according to Davis. "Eugenics," Davis noted, citing the words of L. A. Farrall, "was in reality applied biology based on the central biological theory of the day, namely the Darwinian theory of evolution (55)." At the very least, the political, social, and economic preoccupations of the Social Darwinists created the primordial soup from which statistics emerged. "Feeblemindedness" was one of statistics' early and lasting concerns.

Since that time, formal diagnoses such as mental retardation and autism vector their prophecy well beyond the afflicted. The twin reifications of deviance (Becker 1963), and stigma (Goffman 1963/1986) have helped to organize and index the preponderance, if not all, of research about people with mental retardation and disabilities in general. The two themes have been implicit in practice-oriented, often quantitative and positivistic research (Danforth 1997, Ferguson 1994, Guess and Thompson 1993, Heshusius 1989, Skrtic 1986), and explicit in most qualitative, interpretive-oriented research (Danforth 1997, Barnes 1992, Oliver 1992, Zarb 1992).

Positivistic research in the social sciences is directed at finding lawful, generalizable relationships between various social phenomena, for example, that of "mental retardation" and "social skill deficits." In an attempt to match the promise of the natural sciences, the emphasis and intention is to quantify relationships. Although positivism practically dominates the field of mental retardation (Danforth 1997, Guess and Thompson 1993, Heshusius 1989), positivism, at least in its extreme forms, "is dead," according to John Passmore, writing in the *Encyclopedia of Philosophy*, "or as dead as a philosophical movement ever becomes" (1967, 56).

The Science of Mental Retardation

Practice and epidemiologically oriented positivistic research on people with mental retardation *implicitly* examine deviance from identified, socially consequential norms of body, mind, behavior, and so forth. Without belaboring the point, investigators involved in the study of definition and remediation of disability assess individual deficiencies and implement or develop methodologies to diminish or eliminate the effect of particular or assembled abnormality. "When such repair is possible," Goffman remarked, "what often results is not the acquisition of fully normal status, but a transformation of the self from someone with a particular blemish into someone with a record of having corrected a particular blemish" (1963/1986, 9).

It is important to note that "abnormalities" are quantified as personal attributes defined and diagnosed by medical, psychiatric, psychological, and other human scientists, along with social workers and practitioners in the field. "The judges of normality" said Foucault, "are everywhere. We are in the society of the teacher-judge, the doctor-judge, the educator-judge, the 'social worker'-judge; it is on them that the universal reign of the normative is based; and each individual, wherever he may find himself, subjects it to his body, his gestures, his behavior, his impulses, his aptitudes, his achievements" (1977/1979, 304).

Diagnosticians and practitioners in the field of mental retardation operate have been provided the tools with which they operate by positivistic science. Instructional methodologies—for example, those focused on correcting disability—are for the most part based on Applied Behavioral Analysis (ABA), a method derived from the principles of behavior modification developed by the likes of J. B. Watson and B. F. Skinner. Theory and law governing, say, the relationship between contingency and reinforcement represent "[t]he attempt to study men and animals on the basis that they do not have minds, but only patterns of behavior..." (Bullock, Stallybrass, and Trombley 1988) based on the give and take of environmental variables. Human action is reduced to observable and quantifiable descriptions that lend themselves to alteration by manipulating stimuli in the social and physical milieu. This "diagnostic, prescriptive, remedial paradigm presents itself not as an option to other paradigms or models, not even as a significantly modifiable education approach (other than further refinements of its procedures); it is, to the contrary, offered as the sine qua non for the education of students with severe disabilities" (Guess and Thompson 1993, 392). Disparate methodologies, according to research presented by these and other critical investigators (cf. Goode 1994; Heshusius 1989; Trent 1994), including cognitive and developmental theories such as Paiget's, and movement-based approaches such as van Dijk's are "perceived by the majority of university teacher-trainers as both unimportant for classroom teachers to know, and...addressed little, if [at all], in personnel preparation programs" (Guess and Thompson 1993, 394).

In fact, a 1997 article published by a befuddled Stephen Mitchell (a self-confessed "newcomer to the field of providing clinical services to persons with various developmental handicaps" [141]) in the journal *Mental Retardation* called "Flying Blind on Purpose? Thoughts on the Banishment of Developmental Theories from Clinical Settings" directly addresses this theoretically and semantically confusing situation. He can't seem to comprehend the taboo on developmental theory in clinical settings for people with mental retardation (a *developmental* disability). Aside from his very real fears that "the old prejudice [that] mental retardation [is] a 'forever' condition—frozen and unalterable—still reigns under our more humane and optimistic surface attitudes," Mitchell also hypothesizes that "developmental theories (either of a certain school or in aggregate) just raise too much personal anxiety in those of us who are service providers for individuals with disabilities.... To truly apply a theoretical scheme to others, we must first or at least simultaneously apply them to ourselves. This application to self is nearly inescapable and may be very unpleasant, for it is a task that, if sincerely pursued, surely unmasks our own 'retardation'—our own developmental glitches and failings" (142).

Harlan Hahn (1988) also suggested that our own anxieties contribute to the discrimination (let alone the "banishment" of potentially effective treatment) that people with mental retardation and other disabilities experience. *Aesthetic anxiety*, he said, evolves from fears that once disability is acquired or "discovered," a person will individually experience the sanctions levied on those who deviate from normative standards of beauty. Further, Hahn identified an experiential component, *existential anxiety*—"*THAT* COULD HAPPEN TO ME!" Beset with these worries, behavioral scientists (and their audiences) risk losing their objectivity and, before long, their efficacy.

The Sociology of Mental Retardation

On the other hand, researchers concerned *explicitly* with stigma and deviance as *social constructs*, for the most part, explore the relationships between people with mental retardation (and disability in general), and those "without it" using various qualitative methodologies. This perspective represents observable human differences as productions created by social groups. Difference is regarded not as an attribute of a person, but a consequence of society's application of standards or rules (Becker, 1963). When the difference has negative social value attached, the personal attribute emerges as a stigma, and in Goffman's words, people become "*not quite human*" (1963/1986, 5, my emphasis).[1] The successful application of a stigmatizing label creates a "deviant" (Becker 1963). Stigma can be conceptualized as the difference between a person's (expected) virtual[2] social identity and his or her actual identity (Goffman 1963/1986). For example, our society "anticipates" normal intelligence. When the stigma of significantly subnormal intelligence is detected, a deviant label put to use, such as "mental retardation."

The study of devalued groups from this perspective is not unique to persons having mental retardation; according to Mike Oliver (1992): "Some 30 years ago, much sociological research was criticized for its underdog mentality, and caricatured as being the 'sociology of nuts, sluts and perverts'." Nonetheless, the examination of deviance has provided four general insights into the study of disability in society (Taylor and Bogdan 1989). First, disability is a social and cultural construct, not an objective condition. Second, labels are applied to persons with disabilities, and these labels carry a stigma. Third, labeling a person with a disability

---

[1] Goffman's (1963/1986, 5) oft-cited phrase—"not quite human"—(Bogdan and Taylor 1987, Hahn 1988, Taylor and Bogdan 1989, for example) can be misleading to the casual reader, who risks the assumption that his only intention was to emphasize the distinction between human and other-than-human. However, Goffman's suggestion reaches far beyond this apparent gloss of what is and what is not. Placed in its context, the quote reads, "By definition, of course, we believe the person with a stigma is not quite human. *On this assumption we exercise varieties of discrimination, through which we effectively, if often unthinkingly, reduce his life chances.* We construct a stigma-theory, an ideology to explain his inferiority and account for the danger he represents, sometimes rationalizing an animosity based on other differences such as those of social class. We use specific stigma terms such as cripple, bastard, and moron in our daily discourse as a source of metaphor and imagery, typically without giving thought to the original meaning. We tend to impute a wide range of imperfections on the basis of the original one..." (5, my emphasis). Goffman is telling us that stigma is deadly.

[2] Goffman actually uses the term "virtual identity"—as intriguing as it is prophetic in an epoch where many of us adopt a silicon interface, subsequently transcribing ourselves onto the circumspect world of instantaneous autarchic communication.

creates a self-fulfilling prophecy because social roles carry such powerful expectancies (Wolfensberger 1972). Finally, social institutions designed to care for people with labels create or reinforce behavior that further distances people with disabilities from the broader community, socializing these people into a kind of deviant identity (Wolfensberger 1972).

But if deviance can be socially constructed, so can friendship. "Acceptance sociology" stands in opposition to the "sociology of exclusion" described above (Bogdan and Taylor 1987; Oliver 1992; Taylor and Bogdan 1989). In an article entitled, "The Social Construction of Humanness," Robert Bogdan and Steven Taylor (1989) interviewed people who had ongoing, "long-standing [relationships]...characterized by closeness and affection" (278) with persons who had attributes that one would expect to challenge their "humanity." Yet the participants in Bogdan and Taylor's interviews viewed their partners as "*full-fledged human beings*" (280, my emphasis).

This standpoint contrasts to Goffman's (1963/1986) notion of the "wise" (19)—people who share knowledge of particular stigma because of their particular social position (say, professionals and para-professionals who work with people among mental retardation), who may, through what Goffman calls "normalization"[3] show just "how far [they can] go in treating the stigmatized person as if he didn't have a stigma" (1963/1986, 31). In a way, as Taylor and Bogdan (1989) affirm, this perspective has the potential of casting those with accepting relationships with stigmatized people into a deviant category themselves, "the cult of the stigmatized" (Goffman 1963/1986, 31).

Regardless, four dimensions of accepting relationships seem to contribute to the social construction of humanity: "Attributing thinking to the other; Seeing individuality in the other; Viewing the other as reciprocating, and; Defining [a] social place for the other" (Bogdan and Taylor 1989, 280). Each of these dimensions becomes problematic when projected against the glare of prevailing attitudes toward mental retardation and its treatment.

The difficulty in discovering humanity as described above, particularly among people labeled with mental retardation and other disabilities that severely compromise our taken-for-granted intersubjective "evaluations-

---

3 There are at least three interrelated but apparently academically sequestered definitions of 'normalization' of which I am aware: Those of Erving Goffman, Michel Foucault, and Wolf Wolfensberger.

embedded-in-experience" (Goode 1980, 195) goes beyond, or is at least limited by expectations imposed by stigma and subsequent labeling. Additionally, people with mental retardation and other disabilities have been historically set apart from the rest of us socially, if not physically. Furthermore, pragmatic and even philosophical obstacles present themselves to those engaged in the search for humanity. Philip Ferguson (1987) states that "The weakness of the constructivist position in disability studies emerges at those examples where culture seems beside the point; where physiology has gone so far awry that it threatens to overwhelm the social context.... The challenge of profound retardation, however, is precisely how close it seems to come to the absence of agency. It is not just the passivity of limbs that do not move or environmental barriers that trap the individual physically. One reason for the almost total absence of qualitative research with profoundly retarded and multiply handicapped individuals is the difficulty in conceiving the social world of someone whose experience of concepts and communication is so uncertain for us" (54). For instance, authorization of "thought," due to "communication...so uncertain for us" (Ferguson 1987, 54) appears particularly problematic. Thought and language, in most people's minds, are predicated on the assumption of *the other's* having a "mind."

The Non-Human "Other"

Animals, it can be argued, are "not quite human." A method of study, according to Sanders and Arluke (1993), in an article titled "If Lions Could Speak: Investigating the Animal-Human Relationship and the Perspectives of Nonhuman Others,"[4] must be predicated on intimate familiarity with the nonhuman other, in such a way that the researcher's "disciplined attention to his or her emotional experience can serve as [a] source of understanding" (378). The authors argue that the human/animal distinction with respect to mindedness is nothing more than an anthropocentric ideology that obscures discovery, in the same manner as androcentric ideology obscures and silences the experience of woman. The authors describe encounters of pet owners and animal trainers that led them to believe that animals are minded and do not adhere to the traditional view that "[t]rapped in the here and now, the nonhuman animal

---

[4] The authors inform us that "The title is taken from Wittgenstein who observed that 'if lions could speak, we could not understand them.'"

habitually or instinctively responds to stimuli presented in the immediate situation."

Sanders and Arluke propose that the study of nonhuman/human interactions as the interplay of minded creatures holds the possibility of transcending the current status of sociological theory, and contributes to notions of how the mind is constructed. They point to the research of investigators such as David Goode, Robert Bogdan, Steven Taylor, and Jaber Gubrium (1986) who study humans but have in a sense, the same kind of problems demonstrating mindedness as those who study animals. Our understanding of mind, according to Sanders and Arluke (1993), could be expanded by "[e]mpathetic, disciplined investigation of the routine social exchanges between people and their nonhuman companions necessarily [focused] on how human actors construct, (*or avoid constructing*) an understanding of the animal-other's subjective experience" (384, my emphasis).

Theorizing animals as minded creatures brings other questions into focus, such as "... how does the central activity of 'taking the role of the other' proceed apart from conventional linguistic exchanges? What methods do actors use to define situations so as to contextualize interactions and thereby imbue them with meaning and order? What is the role of emotional experience in the structuring of intersubjective encounters?" (Sanders and Arluke 1993, 384).

The Will to Intersubjectivity

Research conducted by David Goode provides a rich body of method and data for interrogating just these questions. Goode's first field experience, under the direction of Robert Edgerton and Melvin Pollner, took place at a local "State Hospital and School for the Retarded." One wing served as an exhibition through which visiting doctors, nurses, and researchers could descend, observing the various forms of developmental disability people experience. The ward, like Dante's seven circles of Hell, was contrived to deliver one closer and closer to the ultimate anguish and revulsion humanity endures under the defilement of disease, trauma, and other transgressions of human development and misfortune.

Goode entered one room and beheld an "unreal monstrosity" (Goode 1984, 230). He "[i]mmediately became nauseous and broke out in a cold sweat. [He] grabbed the bedboard for support, felt faint and tried to keep [himself] from 'letting go of the cookies.' A nurse must have seen [him]. She miraculously appeared, grabbed [his] arm and talked in a calm and reassuring manner."

Fortunately, the neophyte but disciplined researcher had his tape recorder operating because given his indisposition, he was, outside of the nurse's encouraging tone of voice, largely unaware of what she was talking to him about. After his descent, in the asylum of his office,[5] Goode listened to the tape and heard what the nurse was trying to tell him: "Oh, I see you've found Johnny, my favourite. I've been here three and a half years and he's my special favourite. He's eighteen and I'm his mommy during the day. I wake him when I come on shift, wash him and dress him. We have our routines...He loves rock and roll, I usually open the window up so it's bright and put on the music loud. He loves when I take his hands and clap them to the beat. He has his likes and dislikes, you know. He loves his red flashlight" (Goode 1984, 230).

Goode and his mentors, Robert Edgerton and Melvin Pollner, pondered the discrepancy between the 'Johnny' he'd encountered, a "...profane object, monster or object of disgust" (Goode 1984, 231), and that of the nurse—her "favourite." In a chapter titled "Socially Produced Identities, Intimacy and the Problem of Competence Among the Retarded," Goode (1984) describes the process by which he discovered that in addition to multiple disabilities people who lived in the state hospital, had multiple identities as well.

The significance of Goode's attempt to reconcile his épater les bourgeois[6] to the nurse's rapport with Johnny led him to one and one-half years of fieldwork in the early '70's at a State Hospital and School for people with mental retardation in a ward designated for children born with rubella syndrome. From among the inhabitants of the ward, Goode, after serving several months as a "direct care staff," decided to concentrate his research efforts on a nine-year-old girl named Christina. She had "bilateral cataracts, functional deafness, clinical microcephaly, central nervous system damage (a low-grade diffuse encephalopathy), abnormal behavior

---

[5] "It is as if fieldwork is an extension of our anthropological, academic everyday life, a deformation of the outer skin of our Western culture that never breaks. The skin does not rupture. In the field we are still academics, safe behind the membrane, we keep the same hours, do the same sorts of things, or do different things temporarily in order to advance our life chances back home. In brief, in the field we work. In the office we work. We work and we write" (Rose 1993, 196).

[6] "...disconcert [of] those with conventional tastes or beliefs. —Attributed to Baudelaire." (Webster's II Riverside University Dictionary, 1984, p. 1529).

patterns, and severe developmental retardation" (Goode 1980, 188). These are some fairly significant disabilities to "forget about."

Goode became increasingly dissatisfied with the adult-authored institutional identities of Christina and set about formulating a methodology by which he could understand Chris on her own terms. He used prolonged observations (some up to 36 hours), allowed her to structure their interactions, remained passively obedient while he was with her, and mimicked her behaviors. In addition, Goode attempted to experientially simulate Christina's deaf-blindness. He gauzed his eyes and utilized wax ear plugs to restrict his hearing.

Goode found that when he moved in the way which Christina was accustomed (stereotypic side to side head movements and rolling her head on her shoulders), he could produce a "beatlike quality" (Goode 1980, 198) to ambient sounds in the environment, and "what one observer called a 'light show.' By light show I mean that the head rolling, which Chris performed with her head back and her eyes facing the overhead fluorescent light, provided an overall effect something like the following: Alternative musical beats, occurring when the head was accelerating from one extreme position to the other, were culminated, when the head came to rest, in either light stimulation (*when the head rested on the left shoulder, thus directing her good eye toward the light*), or lack of light stimulation (when the head rested on the right shoulder, thus interposing her nose between the light source and her good right eye). Chris was providing her otherwise impoverished perceptual field with a richness her eyes and ears could not give her" (Goode 1980, 198-199, emphasis in text).

Activities like those Goode described above are not part and parcel of the usual, remedial orientation of special education programs, but, "[t]hese changes in our relationship, and its documentation," Goode notes, "allowed me to produce a competent identity for Christina" (1984, 243).

Interestingly, but not surprisingly, hospital staff had their own interpretation of this friendship. Goode reports that at one staff meeting, an administrator commented on Christina's ability to "wrap [Goode] around her finger" (1980, 192). Goode does not state this explicitly, but I, at least, was impressed by the administrator's recognition of the expression, implicit though it may have been, of any social competence at all by Christina.

As Goode neared the completion of his research at the State Hospital he began to feel that the ward staff "began to resent [his] presence there"

(Goode 1980, 206). Staff were, in effect, envious of his position as Christina's "superplaymate" and acted out their jealousy by intimating that Goode's activities were interfering with their own educational activities with her.

Observing staff at times when the hospital's remedial, educational regime was not in effect, when staff were "playing" with the children, Goode observed a marked change in both the staff's and the resident's repartee. At these times, the hospital's normative rules for interacting with the children were deferred, and educational goals for the children were suspended. "[S]taff were afforded the opportunity to experience the residents in nonidiologically defined activit[ies]. Play activity, for the sake of itself, transcended the institutional goals of remedialization and provided for the staff a time when they could 'meet the residents on their own grounds.'"

The notion of "remedialization" is central to Goode's work with Christina and the other children and adults he has researched. "Remedialization" implies that there is something wrong and must be fixed. Goode uses the notion of "fault-finding procedures," one he adopted from his academic experiences with Harold Garfinkel to explain how disability professionals tend to interpret the behavioral displays of people with disabilities as failed attempts to live up to normative standards. Adaptive Behavior Assessments are a concrete example of fault-finding procedures. For instance, if a child of six years is unable to communicate basic needs ("my head hurts"), her behavior is at fault; a remedial stance is adopted, goals written, instructional programs developed and carried out.

Blatt's (1981) insight into this situation was that although people may be in need of help in certain areas, a label such as mental retardation is harmful and unproductive. In David Goode's work, we can see that "forgetting about it" can lead to different understandings (the creation of competent identities for instance) of people who otherwise are at risk for dehumanization. He literally closed his eyes (and ears) and found Christina.

Minding Alzheimer's Disease

Some kinds of disabilities have similar sequelae of developmental disability but occur after the "developmental period." These we might call "disabilities developed." Alzheimer's syndrome is one of these, and here there is a rich literature of mindedness. I don't know why this is so, but I suppose that people make the assumption that an Alzheimer sufferer once had a mind, and the task at hand is to find or somehow preserve the mind, which is not necessarily taken for granted in developmental disabilities like mental retardation.

For instance, I have a book called *Self-Determination Across the Life Span: Independence and Choice for People with Disabilities* (Sands and Wehmeyer 1996). I tried to look up 'mind' in the index, and it skipped from "*Mills v. DC Board of Education*"[7] to "Mobility skills, training in." A similar search in Hickson, Blackman, and Reis's *Mental Retardation: Foundations of Educational Programming* (1995), Heward and Orlansky's *Exceptional Children* (1992), Barton's *Disability and Society: Emerging Issues and Insights* (1996), L. J. Davis's *The Disability Studies Reader* (1997), Begab and Richardson's *The Mentally Retarded in Society: A Social Science Perspective* (1975), Brown and Lehr's *Persons with Profound Disabilities: Issues and Practices* (1989), and Wright and Digby's *From Idiocy to Mental Deficiency* (1996) disclosed no mention of mind. Bogdan and Taylor (1989), as I've mentioned before, consider the attribution of thinking, which I believe I can confidently link with mindedness, as one of the four important factors in socially constructing the humanness of people with severe disabilities. A quick look at mindedness is in order here.

Generally, most people will go along with the idea that mind originates and is modified by social experience. Gubrium (1986) quotes from Mead: "Mind arises in the social process only when that process as a whole enters into, or is present in, the experience of any one of the given individuals involved in the process. When this occurs the individual becomes self-conscious and has a mind..." (37).

Its capacity for social modification suggests that in certain ways, your mind is not your own. The degree to which this is so, and subsequent implications, is unsettling. Consider the extent to which our minds have been commodified. We pay psychologists to interpret our minds for us. Sometimes, we pay them to help us find them if we lose them (Gubrium, 1986).

Jaber Gubrium (1986) presents evidence gathered from his observations of a day hospital for the care of Alzheimer's patients and support groups for the "other victims of Alzheimer's"—caregivers, family, friends,

---

7 A landmark case leading to the right of all handicapped children to education in the 1970s.

and so on, that the mind in many ways can be considered a "social preserve." Gubrium raises the question, "while the victim's outward gestures and expressions may hardly provide a clue to an underlying humanity [Gubrium, here, seems to equate humanity with mindedness], the question remains whether the disease has stolen it all or only the capacity to express it, leaving an unmanifested, hidden mind" (40).

Others, then, are confronted with the responsibility to recover, discover, preserve, interpret, and, in effect, realize the mind of the Alzheimer's patient.[8]

A patient's spouse wonders "what to think or feel. It's like he's not even there anymore, and it distresses me something awful. He doesn't know me. He thinks I'm a strange woman in the house. He shouts and tries to slap me away from him. It's not like him at all. *Most of the time he makes sounds, but they sound more like an animal than a person.* Do you think he has a mind left?...Am I being stupid? I feel that if I don't do something quick to get at him that he'll be taken from me altogether" (my emphasis, 41)

Gubrium concludes that mind [humanity?] is "experientially tied, in the final analysis, to the faith of those concerned and to the social preservation of the assignment.... The working sense of mind found in the Alzheimer's disease experience is, at once, individual, social, and discursive" (42). In the sense that they must be spoken for, minds camouflaged decry questions of personal agency.

"Speakers for the victim's mind," Gubrium (1986) affirms, "are a motley set" (43). Think of psychiatrists, psychologists, doctors, nurses, personal care attendants, the police, the neighbors, your wife, husband, children, the dog, social workers, the crisis team—and you get the sense of what Gubrium is getting at. Mind can only persist to the extent that it is experientially preserved, and who will uphold, articulate, and

---

[8] Like mental retardation, diagnosis of Alzheimer's disease, versus such conditions as "senile dementia" is based on mental status examinations and questionnaires similar to adaptive behavior scales. "Recently," as Golander and Raz (1986, 273) point out, "the controversy throughout the century over presenile and senile dementia is historically based on 'anecdotal clinical observation'[and]...competition among universities was one of its underlying determinants. Further, Golander and Raz state that "medically undecided, 'dementia'—whether Alzheimer's type or other—becomes a matter of description and labeling. It enters the realm of public culture, defined as a 'social problem,' prescribed with procedures of care and institutionalization in order to provide practical answers for worried families and busy caretakers" (273).

authoritatively assert, "Yes, this person has a mind?"

In "The Mask of Dementia: Images of 'Demented Residents' in a Nursing Ward," Hava Golander and Aviad E. Raz (1986) present some compelling stories of how people act out 'minding' as a social preserve. Shimon, for example, wandered the ward aimlessly, entering other patient's rooms and sat for long periods on their beds with wet pajamas, talked loudly and incoherently, walked about ignoring the fact that his pants had fallen down, and would periodically disappear, only to be found cold, wet, and (even more?) disoriented by the police or other authorities. On one occasion, after his recapture, he said, "What is all this turmoil? Have they caught the Arabs sneaking over the fence? What did the greedy scoundrels do this time?" (275).

In the morning, Shimon was sitting thoughtfully in an easychair, remarking, "If only I could, if only I could ..."

"If only you could what?" asked another resident.

"Find a buyer for my cow," replied Shimon confidently.

Golander and Raz present several hypotheses generated by Shimon's caretakers for his apparently unexplainable behavior (as it turns out, Shimon's wife had admitted him to the hospital, "neglecting" to mention that he had a tendency to wander off). One was that he was out looking for his wife. Hospital staff tested this assumption by asking his wife not to visit for a while, but Shimon's roving ways continued. Hospital staff were convinced that he was just confused, and said, "senility strikes again!" (276).

At the same time, though, other residents spoke in respectful terms about Shimon. They, unlike the hospital staff, had constructed a positive social identity to explain what was going on in Shimon's mind. He was an early settler, a *Halutz*, a respected breaker of the soil, a giant of the earth in Israel. His *distaste* for confined spaces was predictable and reasonable. "Shimon's speech, which preserved the distinct vocabulary and diction of the pioneers' language, contributed to his social persona" (276). The never-finished tasks of a farmer—milking and selling of cattle, breaking and harrowing of the land—accounted for his behavior (at least to the other residents), who exalted and humanized Shimon, despite his wet pajamas.

Minding Mental Retardation

"Jimmy used to be in that ward. *He ran the place.* They brought him up to us though—he was pulling out his cock and chasing women.... Man, he didn't pull that shit anymore"
> —Anonymous attendant at a state school for the mentally retarded, cited in Bogdan et al. 1974, 147, my emphasis).

Hidden in the statement above is a treasure—that is—the impotent acknowledgment that people with mental retardation have the capacity to control their environments and the people around them. I've made the claim that mental retardation is a social construct, and as such, I implied that there must be instances where as a reification, it wavers and dissolves like a mirage before a thirsty seeker of knowledge (like the "self-evident" truths of the Declaration of Independence of the United States), or, in mental retardation's incarnation as a scientific paradigm, it collapses like a black hole under the weight of its own illation[9] or unravels at the edges in border skirmishes.

Examining the attendant's statement above from this faithless perspective leads one to believe that people with mental retardation, despite low IQ scores and aside from other limitations, are capable, very capable, of exerting extensive control over their environments. Few researchers have gone so far as to study people with mental retardation as "full-fledged human beings," people who by their personal characteristics,

---

[9] Albert Einstein and I struggled under common the burden of a day job, but he was able to write a three page paper in 1905 called "Does the Inertia of a Body Depend on Its Energy Content?" which proposed that the relationship between energy and inertia is governed by the equation $E = mc^2$. This brought the science of physics as it was then known to a dead halt. He did this without citing any previous work in the field. Einstein was also a socialist who wrote in 1949 that "There is no provision that all those able and willing to work will always be in a position to find employment; an 'army of unemployed' always exists. The worker is always in fear of losing his job. Technological progress frequently results in more unemployment rather than easing the burden of work for all.... Unlimited competition leads to a huge waste of labor and to a crippling of the social consciousness of individuals" (Schwartz and McGuinness 1979, 169). Hahn (1987) relates the industrial reserve army to people with disabilities by way of their vocational limitations in an postindustrial economy (standardization of production and output assumes normalization of the working and consuming population). John McKnight, in the article "Valuable Deficiencies" (1977) sees people with disabilities as valuable additions to a service-based economy that in many ways, "needs people in need." In fact, he proposes that our very economic growth "depends on our capacity to identify more deficiency" (37).

their presentation of self, their relationships with others, challenge our assumptions of what it means to be human.

Thirty miles down the highway from where I live is one of the oldest institutions for people with developmental disabilities in America. Founded by Charles Wilbur (one of the fathers of the Association of Medical Officers of American Institutions for Idiotic and Feeble-Minded Persons) in 1867 as the Illinois Asylum for Feeble-Minded Children at Lincoln. It was later known as the Lincoln State School and Asylum, Lincoln State School and Colony, and currently, the Lincoln Developmental Center. At one point in its history, 5,000 Illinois residents lived there. The years 1945-46, brought 96 persons per month to its gates.

Now there are 400. During the Seventies, "deinstitutionalization" dramatically reduced its population. Exposés, litigation (much of it driven by parent's concerns that their children have equal opportunity in education and related supports), sociological and more traditional scientific work in the discipline of mental retardation, and state funding restrictions (Ronald Reagan once referred to California's system of state operated institutions for people with developmental disabilities [a nd prisons] as "the biggest hotel chain in the state" (Trent 1994]) drove the depopulation of many such state schools. Although considerable research and best-practice-oriented literature exists to guide special educators and community service providers, there is, as I have strived to demonstrate, considerable lack of any kind of work concerning the mindedness, be it a social preserve or otherwise, of persons with mental retardation. The question begs itself: "What is the relation between mindedness and mental retardation?"

The belligerent attitude of the attendant quoted above is hard to miss. The notion of a mentally retarded man "running that place" is a haunting scenario; empowering, as I pointed out, but not with the same sensitivity David Goode lent to the descriptions of his interactions with Christina. Both though, acknowledge the mindedness of the people with whom they worked.

Chapter Four
Sean

In the midst of a six-year battle between Caterpillar Manufacturing Inc.'s management and labor, a baby boy was born. To say that he was accidental would be accurate, but unwanted, he was not. One supposes that it would be hard to support a husband, wife, two college-age kids, and a newborn on strike pay.

One also wonders how many of *us* gave up the notion of bringing children into this world because of pollution, threats of nuclear annihilation, plastic trashbags, plastic dreams, and plastic *Weltanschauung*. Mary did in sixth grade, at the same school her son Sean will attend, if they can provide a semblance of education for him.

Have you ever thought about what it takes to embrace motherhood? To become "*mom?*" Mary said what did it for her was three-and-a-half years wandering between pediatricians, ophthalmologists, neurologists, speech and occupational therapists, child developmental specialists, developmental pediatricians, and finally the special education system in her town. You see, Sean was always slow, and *something happened* about a year ago to make him slower. Now she is *Sean's* mom.

Jargoning, July 2, 1998

When students, clients, and sometimes daughters and sons who are talking in a way we don't recognize or don't understand, the teacher, therapists, and parents-in-the-know often label the speech "jargoning." We read in notebooks that teachers (especially special education teachers) and parents use to relate the events of a child's day at school and home and find that our little student spent a large portion of the day *jargoning*, for instance.

I arrived at Mary's at about 11:30, as did Janice, Sean's teacher, and

Danielle, his speech and language therapist. Sean was watching TV and eating lunch as we talked about him.

Danielle was telling us that she had purchased an easel to hold Lego-type toys which attaches to the wall at an adjustable angle, "...with Sean in mind," because the occupational therapist said that things that "...go up, or slant, are better for 'visual.'"

"For visual," Janice emphasizes.

"And I got my book today, my *Language with Toys* book," Danielle told us.

Mary said that Dr. Petard, an adult neurologist who specializes in eyes, said that Sean doesn't have nystagmus; only in his right eye. "So, either he did, and it's getting better, or he never did, I don't know."

Danielle says: "So it *can* get better?"

"Evidently, and the doctor thinks he can grow out of it. I wouldn't stick your fingers in his mouth, Dan."

"Yeeow! Ha, ha, ha!"

"Did he bite?"

"Yup." I'd been shoving the noodles that were hanging out his mouth to where they ought to be.

"They're sharp, his teeth."

"You want some peaches?" I ask the little feller.

"Mmmmmmmm, peeeeeeeaches." we say.

Janice tells us that they had trouble getting him to eat anything at school or to put his hands in anything, even the rice where they'd cleverly buried his favorite cards. They'd even gave him some soft cookies at snack time.

"It must be the *tactile thing*," Danielle tells us.

"Yeah, the tactile thing."

"Does that slant up, or is it just a cover?" Danielle asks pointing at a Playskool desk that Mary'd bought for Sean, probably at Wal-Mart in Lincoln.

"It slants it's like an easel I got it 'cause of that, or, I don't know why, but I got it. I thought we'd draw on it, but we never got a chance to."

"He might surprise you," Danielle says, "just like that little stacking toy," looking at Janice who nods, "you'd put it in front of him, he'd never touch it, never touch it. One day, he started stackin' em."

Mary tells us that when he first got to school, he wouldn't do anything, not even hold her hand, and that she wanted me to explain how I "...*got* him to do..."

"Some of the things..." Janice interjects.

"You got him to..." Danielle finished.

Janice and Danielle talk about school. They said at first, they couldn't get him to do anything. Although he didn't at first, he wound up liking the gym. He *loves* the gym. The kids play a game in there called *Duck-Duck, Goose*, and the time is unstructured compared to class time. "Sean got to where it'd ruin his day if he couldn't go to gym," Danielle said, "and finally when we were playing *Duck-Duck, Goose* he'd follow the kid around, whoever was doing the *Duck-Duck, Goose* bump, he wouldn't sit *down* or anything. I mean when we first started, he'd just *'go off.'* But then finally, he'd run around following, then when someone got bumped, he'd turn the wrong way, and run into the other kid!"

"We had another kid just prior to him, that was like him, uh, he had some of those same behavioral things—well he had PDD (Pervasive Developmental Disability), actually he was pretty hyperlexic. I mean at three, he'd just go down the hall and label all the letters; he couldn't read or anything, though. We just grabbed his arm, and he followed us."

Janice: "Of course that was always to the gym, it got to the point ..."

Danielle said that "... when he first came in to do the testing we couldn't do, as long as I was chasing him, or he was chasing me, we were OK."

"Why do you suppose he loves the gym so much?" I inquire.

Janice: "Could be anything, with all the noise in there, it could be the '*auditory thing*,'" looking at Danielle, who said that yes, it could be the "...'auditory thing'. He doesn't like going outside—too quiet? I don't know."

"At least for us, he won't imitate like a babble, or uh, so if you have any ideas, we're trying to get like gestures, pointing, giving a high five, all those precursors to language."

Mary directs our attention to Sean, who is at this point, tuning in the cable box on top of the TV, I suppose because he doesn't want to watch the video anymore. "He just now started using the buttons [on the TV cable box], he uses his little tiny fingers, and just presses hard enough..."

"A duck!" says Sean. He always says things while he is not looking at you and quietly enough and unintelligibly enough that I never know he said a damn thing until I get home and listen to the tapes.

"A duck," say I.

Mary: "He's pointing now..."

Danielle looks over at Sean, and asks, "Did he just do something with the VCR?"

Mary said that he was pressing the VCR button so he could fast forward it.

Looking at Sean, Danielle asks, "Do you want to press 'Play'? Push it so we can see."

"We're waiting for the monkeys," I state with all the authority I can muster.

"Oh," Janice says, "he likes the monnnnkeeees."

"Push play," says Danielle, continuing, "push play so we can see ..."

"OOOPS, Sean, I think we're going the wrong way! That Tiger's not supposed to be there yet, I don't think, or maybe it is, I don't know, what do you think?"

"Play," says Sean.

"What do you think, you need some help, kiddo?" I say.

"I've never heard him do that before," says Danielle, "make statements."

"I wonder," Janice says, "what he'd do if I was holding him like that?"

"He's tired," Mary replies.

"Doobie-do-do-do-wah," I sing, anticipating the scat vocals of King Louis, voiced by Louis Prima *"I wan'na be like you: The monkey song"*, (Sherman and Sherman, 1966), and Baloo the bear.

"I wonder if we got one of those old heads, you know the old heads like they had?" Danielle wonders, "I had a Farah Fawcett one when I was a kid. You could suction cup it to the table and do whatever you wanted to it."

I giggle quietly.

"Would you like that Sean? Plastic eyes and lips?" To us, "he's so fascinated with faces."

"On, On, On!" Sean tells me.

"I wanna see the monkeys," I tell him.

Janice says that "...he doesn't seem as adamant with him," referring to Sean and me. I'm forcing him to wait till the monkeys start, although they're midway though their routine at this point, and he's mildly protesting.

"That's because of the noise level," Danielle warrants, "it's so loud at school."

"Sean, I hear that jungle music! Do you want to show your teachers how you can dance? Where's that jungle beat, Sean? I can hear it!"

"On, On, On!" Sean tells me.

So, King Louis of the Apes grabs the "mancub" Mowgli and makes a thinly disguised play to nab the boy's secret that separates the child from less noble beings.

Sean stretches out his hands to me, and we start jitterbugging.

"I don't think I could do that," Janice allows.

"Neither could I," says Danielle

Mary: "It's real hard, I try it every once in a while..."

"He won't have to work out tomorrow!"

"That's good for *the sensory!*" Danielle offers. "Can he dance without you?"

"Sure," and I let go of Sean...

King Louis of the Apes: *Now I'm the king of the swingers,*
Ohhhh, the jungle VIP,
But I reached the top, and had to stop, and that's what's botherin' me!
I wanna be a man, man-cub, and stroll right into town,
And be just like the other men, I'm tired a monkey'un roun.'

"Ohhh! Sean, you are gooo-ud!"

Sean is dancing on his tippy toes in front of his teachers, clapping his hands and singing.

"Ewwww...good one, dance!"

Mary asks, "Is that a characteristic of autism, to be on your tip toes?"

"Yup," I say, "but all kids do it. And ballerinas too," I think to myself.

"Wheweeeee! Go Sean!"

"That's hard work I guess," Janice says looking at me sweating and panting.

"You betcha. But we can invent a new jazz therapy!"

"Go, Go, Go Sean!"

Baloo, the bear: *A zop-on-aroni!*

Danielle starts dancing with Sean, saying, "We're gonna invent a new craze, aren't we?" They're swinging, man!

King Louis: *Doodley-bop do boppa...I wanna be like you-ew-ew, I wanna talk like you, walk like you, do-oo-oo-oo-oo!*

Evvverybody is swinging at this point!

You-ew-ew, I wanna be like you-ew-who!

I wanna talk like you, walk like you, do-oo-oo-oo-oo!
Yes it's truuuue, an ape like me-ee-ee,
Can learn to be, hu-oo-oo-man too!

"Take me home, daddy," I sing.

Yes it's truuuue, someone like you-ew-who!
Can learn to be, like some one like me-ee-ee-ee-ee

"He's found it now!" someone says. While the scene plays out, I ponder whether the human authors enjoyed the final irony of the beasts jazzing it up; the untrammeled delirium just who *is* learning to be who?

"Do you wanna do it again?" I ask. "Are you going to be able to wait? Getcher blankety-blank finger offa the button!"

"Have you heard any *p*s or *b*s?" asks Danielle?

"A lotta *d*s," Mary replies, all around the house, like when the duck comes on in *Toy Story...*"

"And probably from that," according to Janice, who is gesturing toward the TV.

"What do you want, Sean, what do you want? Gimme some words!"

"On! On! On!" Sean tells me.

"Alright, alllllright baby!"

King Louis: *A bop-bop-bop boppy-dew, bop-bop-bop!*

Seizures, June 9, 1998

This morning Mary called me at 8:30. She said that Sean had been having seizures all weekend. She said that she'd contacted Sean's doctor and that he'd recommended seeing a neurologist. A nurse had found one Monday afternoon (presumably one that the insurance would cover), but by the time the nurse called, the neurologist was out of the office. Mary was waiting around this morning for the nurse to make the necessary connection and wanted to let me know that there wasn't any point for me to visit Sean today.

I asked about the seizures. Mary said that they'd started Friday night, and that she'd felt him shuddering against her while she was sleeping. They'd been increasing in duration, frequency, and intensity since then. Now he was getting them about every two hours, and they were lasting one-half to one minute long. I suggested that she take Sean to the emergency room.

She said that his left arm seemed to be going numb. I asked, with as much bedside manner as I could how she knew this. She said that he was banging it into things, getting bruises and scratches, and not seeming to "hurt."

Mary said that once he recovered from the seizures, he seemed to be somewhat more alert, that he was paying more attention to herself and Harry. I said Electro-Convulsive Shock therapy works for people who are depressed sometimes, and that Sean was probably getting the equivalent every two hours. I said that probably she should take him to the emergency room.

Did I know anything about seizures? "Not much, but I'll tell you, if one of the kids at the group homes I used to supervise was having seizures every couple of hours and hadn't had them before like that, I'd discipline whoever hadn't taken him to the ER."

Mary said that she thought that maybe she'd pack up and go to the emergency room. I said to "just go there and get in their face or sit on them till somebody does something."

20%, July 23, 1998

Before I took off to Dixon City, I made a copy of Sean's MDC/IEP (Multidisciplinary Committee Report/Individualized Educational Program) and in the process, read it. I'd had it for weeks sitting there on my desk.

It turns out that Sean is "Unable to say words and only a couple beginning sounds." He was untestable using the Stanford-Binet. He doesn't appear to understand concepts of color or body parts. His communicative status/general development appeared to be that of a 16-month toddler, although *he was uncooperative and no formal evaluation was conducted.* He had an unusual tilt to his head at 8 mos. and a "neurological" (MRI) revealed no abnormalities. Subsequent referral to an ophthalmologist produced a diagnosis of nystagmus with compensatory head tilt. His primary diagnosis, according to the MDC team, was "Developmentally Delayed." His language, motor, social, and self-help skills were destined to have an adverse effect on his educational performance, the document reports.

Sean spent last school year in Special Education, to the tune of 1440 minutes per week, including 150 minutes of *group* speech and language therapy (although the report indicated his need for 1:1, small group language-based instruction). An Occupational and Physical Therapy evaluation was recommended (but not conducted, because, Mary said, the therapists said he was "not ready, or something like that").

Sean's delays in motor, social, and self-help skills, along with his age determined his placement: segregated Special Education, 100% of his school time. Of course, as I've mentioned, according to his teacher and speech and language therapist, Physical Therapy is unavailable to students unless the therapy will help them "get around the school." Ho hum.

Oh, the ice here is soooo thin! These teachers seem to be friends of Mary's. She told me once that she didn't expect any problems with the schools because she knows all the teachers and they are friends of hers, and they wouldn't do anything bad to Sean. I know better, but then again, I know better than to make Sean's battle my own: But all work and no play makes Dan a dull boy.

All work and no play makes Dan a dull boy. All work and no play makes Dan a dull boy. All work and no play makes Dan a dull boy. All work and no play makes Dan a dull boy. All work and no play makes Dan a dull boy. All work and no play makes Dan a dull boy. All work and no play makes Dan a dull boy. All work and no play makes Dan a dull boy. All work and no play makes Dan a dull boy. All work and no play makes Dan a dull boy. All work and no play makes Dan a dull boy.

I would like to get the principal of that school to say at trial, "...but your honor, we don't give Physical Therapy to students unless we deem it necessary for them to get around the school! And we don't give OT/PT evaluations unless the student is ready." Enough!

The wind had been blowing from the East South-East (of all things) for a few days, and everybody looked like they were going to drop dead. Finally, we had a storm, a relatively small one, that blew like a demon from due West, filling our house with the seemingly irreducible smell of pig shit from our mile-away neighbor's manure lagoon. Then it blew clear from the North, rendered the humidity de-humidified, and the air breathable. I was heading to Dixon City.

Mary met me at the door and invited me in. Harry was in the kitchen, and I peeked in there to say, "Hi!" He smiled.

"We didn't have such a good time at speech therapy today," said Mary, and I asked her what happened. She said that Sean was screaming and crying, but they did get him to bounce on a beach ball for a little while, and he was making word sounds when he was on that. She said that

Sean has been making a lot more word sounds since Harry's been home on vacation, and she thinks it's because he enjoys having both of them home together. Things must have calmed down, maritally speaking, because I think that Sean could sense tension.

Thinking about the characteristics and diagnosis of Landau-Kleffner Syndrome (LKS) prompted me to ask a couple of questions about Sean, before I "got started" with him. First, I wanted to know when the EEG was going to happen; Mary said the doctor was going to call with an appointment on Monday or Friday, depending on when he got back from a conference in Phoenix. Second, I wanted to know Mary's assessment of Sean's receptive language. I asked, "How much of what you say to Sean do you think he understands?"

She said, "I think he understands about 80% of what we talk with him about." I didn't ask for any for instances, but I've seen him look for his milk tippy-cup when Mary's asked him if he wanted some chocolate milk.

Then Mary said, "I only think *we* understand about 20 percent of what he is telling us." Again, I didn't ask for specifics, like, what do you think he's telling you? But I'm certainly aware of the frustration of not even knowing where to start.

Sean was watching his televisions. One, the one I think of as "Sean's," had been rearranged so that it is flat against a wall, the end of a couch some 3 or 4 feet from the screen, pillows stacked against the end of the couch. Previously, the TV screens had been positioned at either side of the room, forming an angle such that if one were situated in the middle of the room, both could be observed.

Toy Story is playing on Sean's TV, and the usual allegedly educational programming occupying the other. He dragged his attention away from the TVs long enough to greet me by opening his arms in such a way that I knew that I must grab them and dance with him! We spun, we twirled, we came together, and pushed apart. We were cool.

"You like to dance with Dan, don't you, Sean!" Mary exclaimed. I can only hope that Mary and Harry, his stepbrother and sister dance with him.

Sean and I continued to play. He always holds his hands in either a fist or a flat open position. We hold hands like this, but today I tried something different. I made it so our fingers interlocked. Why? I don't know. Just try something different? Something like that. I wanted to see how much he would object, I suppose, and also, it would give me greater control as he tried to walk on my stomach, a favorite activity of ours. I figured I could position his arms in a way that would simulate a person trying to maintain balance that way. Somehow, it seems like he doesn't have much of a *protective reflex*; he's not throwing his hands forward when he falls forward. I've noticed this when I hold him upside down by his foot. He only very tentatively lowers maybe one arm toward the floor, and only grazes it with one or two of his fingers.

I asked Mary about the protective reflex, and she said that he "did it" sometimes, and sometimes not. To me, it looks like he simply does not like to touch things with his hands.

Sean is very talkative. The words he uses are the usual ones he uses, like "eeyhh, eeyhh," but he's using them in a context. So, if you ask him if he wants to dance, he says, "eeyhh," or if he wants something, like for me to turn on the "other TV" that I turned off because I considered it a distraction, he'd make some sort of demand, at least I supposed it was.

By now, lunch is ready. They'd made me a cheeseburger, and Sean got a bologna and cheese with mayo. He came up to the table and Mary moved to feed it to him, and I said, let's see if he can eat it by himself (for christ's sake). I discovered I didn't know right offhand how one holds a sandwich; kind of like my mother who can't remember her network password without her hands on the keyboard. I grab half of the sandwich (Mary cuts them diagonally) and ascertain that I hold a sandwich cut in this manner with my thumbs underneath and my fingers on top. I position Sean's hands like this, and he goes in the TV room and eats the thing on his own, with some help from me repositioning his grip on it from time to time. We bring his plate in front of the TV and put it on this little plastic desk he has, and I situate him under it and pull the plate closer. He toys around with the macaroni and cheese (Mary's given him a fork again) and gets up to reverse the *Toy Story* video. He watches the introductory part of the video where they advertise a computer game that follows the plot of the movie in a "Mario Brothers" motif. Mary tells me that she wants to get a bank loan to upgrade their computer so it can run Windows 95, get a CD-ROM, a sound card and a faster processor, so that she can get Sean that game. I eat the cheeseburger.

At some point, Sean gets off the video game jag and starts watching the part of *Toy Story* where Buzz tries to demonstrate that he is not a mere toy by taking flight. During this sequence, he dives from a platform of some sort and lands on a rubber ball and bounces to a platform where he lands on a toy car, *et cetera, et cetera.*

Sean gets in front of the TV, puts his head on the floor, puts his butt in the air, and watches Buzz hit the rubber ball. He does this about 9-10 times. Is he bored?

I make ready to go. On the way down the street, there's kids playing outside. Mary has always told me that she wanted to form a play group, and I think, why doesn't she just take him down to this corner in the shade of some old maple trees. There are always kids there, at least 4-5, sometimes many more, ranging in age from toddler to maybe 10-11 years. There are always two women there, who appear to be the parents of the kids. It's crossed my mind that they could be lesbians, and maybe that's the reason Mary doesn't take Sean down there, but it's not a very good one, in my opinion.

Harry disappeared at some point after he made me my cheeseburger, and came in sweating as I left. He had a magazine.

On the way home, I stopped at the Mackinaw River, which I cross three times although I only have to turn twice on the 35-mile trip to Dixon City. Someone is shooting a gun down there, so I can't go down and look at the water. I go home and sit out front in the shade with the dogs.

I Get a New Bank Account, June 10, 1998

Today, I called up Mary's, and Sean's stepbrother answered the phone. I can never remember his name. I am not good with faces or names, unless I can connect them with text. Sean's stepbrother said that "they" were still at the hospital, that they'd gone to Peoria. He gave me the telephone number of the hospital, and said that you have to say "you want patient something or other."

I got through to Sean's room, and Harry answered. He said that they'd come here from Lincoln's, and that they were going to do some more tests, and they might be able to go home tonight, or the next day. Sean was still having seizures. After he'd given the phone to Mary, Sean had another, and she went running down the hall so the doctor could level his gaze upon the patient. Sean had two seizures while we talked on the phone.

The medical professionals were attempting to stabilize Sean on depakote. In the background, I heard the nurse say something and heard Mary repeat something about "blood levels," meaning that the Depakote has to get up to a certain dilution in the blood before it will start to work.

I was wondering whether "they" needed the worthless "multidisciplinary" report Dr. Juke wrote, and Mary asked the nurse whether they did, and the answer was an emphatic "yes." This is why I wound up with a checking account at the Minier Farmer's Bank.

I grabbed the report and ran out to the truck, stopping to say "Hi" to Uncle Bill, who was out checking the crops. Bill said I might be able to fax the thing from the bank in Minier. So I drove to Minier, went to the bank, and asked to fax this medical report they needed at St. Francis Hospital in Peoria, "'cause this kid was having seizures; it's kind of an emergency." She tells me that the first page costs $3, and each page after that costs a dollar. I reach for in my wallet, and I have $3.00, and a couple of paper clips in my pocket. Upon a rather thorough examination of my checkbook, I detect that I only have a check from a month ago for $26.37 that I, for god knows what reason, and to heaven knows what party, I never completed writing.

"Can I use this to pay?" I ask waving the check in her face. I get a look, and the information person goes to talk to the woman behind the tellers. She comes back to me and says they can't fax anything, or cash my check unless I have an account.

It's about 12:00 PM, and I have yet to get any writing done for the day, because I've been dealing with shit like this. I say, "Well now, I'd like to open an account here."

I'm taken to an office where a harried functionary clears her desk of Avon catalogs, newspaper coupon clippings, and so on. I sit there while she goes through the options—the variety of accounts available. The bank is cool (temperature), and I find myself actually thinking about the different possibilities lying before me; engaging the friendly operative in a discussion of the worthiness of a basic vs. economy account, service charges, VISA debit cards, and so on. I'm thinking that I've been wanting to get an account at this bank for a while, even though the thought has only occasionally crossed my mind (I hate my current bank because they have incomprehensible rules about just about everything).

Tapping my finger on my upper lip, I decide on the "Economy Account," whilst minutes tick away, and Sean gets regular scramblings of his brain. This kind of account, the functionary had explained, was her own personal choice. There is a $12.00 per year service charge, and a 50-cent charge for each check; but you get a free VISA/debit card that "you can just about use for *anything*," she'd said.

Once I'm signed up, I can cash my check, and I ask to fax my document. The bank functionary says I should go to Ringler's Welding to fax the damn thing because it's less expensive there. Ringler's modified a cultivator for me once when I used to be a farmer. With sparks a flyin' we faxed the report, which consisted mainly of the tests which Dr. Juke attempted, but was unable to complete due to Sean's demonstrating "a great deal of distress in response to any movements made by the examiner."

I called Mary later that evening, about 6 or 7, to see if she'd got the fax, and she said that she hadn't checked, and that Sean's seizures had failed to stabilize; that he was still convulsing for about a minute every hour and a half or so. The MRI was canceled until 2:15 Thursday, 11 June. I said "Good night, hope everything goes OK."

I never did find out whether they got that fax.

The Day Started Innocently Enough, June 5, 1998

The day started innocently enough. Mary was outside either burning trash, barbecue or something. I drove up somewhat late because I'd gotten lost down there (they live in Dixon City, south and west of our farm). Somehow, the Mason County country seems less prosperous than our own, only because it must have once been more so. There are falling apart hotels, roadhouses in want of paint, windows, and post-1960 beer signs—but not patrons. On Route 136, there are signs that inform: "Bridge Out" "Free Ferry, Expect Delays," and so on. The thought of ferries, the sprawling Illinois River, and bridges being out makes me feel as if I am entering a land of adventure.

There's a "river town" near where I'm headed, Havana. My girlfriend got a job at the high school there which she fled after only three days because of teachers' talk before school commenced about "Nigger Lake" into which apparently, unwanted African Americans were, at least at one time, discharged. She got her "little Jewish hide" out of there.

My uncle calls Havana a "river town" and refers to river towns as in muted tones as if to imply they were places that good young boys such as himself and my father could become debauched by any manner of mysterious, unfathomable means. I don't know whether this is truth or whether it's another of my uncle's fictive utterances; he was, is, and remains a romantic scholar of the works of Mark Twain and medieval philosophy.

Mary leads me into their house, which they've rearranged since my last visit. What was once the master bedroom is now the family room, sporting two large TVs. This is so Sean can watch his videos, while his father, Harry, watches the stock car races. Harry is a machinist at Caterpillar, and has been working, striking, and generally suffering through management's vagaries for the last six years. He's "on" again with a UAW contract which for the first time since Sean's birth three-and-a-half years ago, includes an insurance agreement that is likely to last longer than a month or two.

Sean is smiling and watching both of the TVs, wandering in between them. Mary and I talk for a quite a while. It turns out that the speech therapist that she's been seeing weekly with Sean at the hospital is only partially covered by insurance. I ask her for the twentieth time whether she's eligible for SSI (Supplemental Security Insurance), and she again tells me that her family makes too much money.

"It's a bill I wasn't expecting," she tells me, and to my way of thinking, it's a big bill. There's got to be some way around this, and I ask for Sean's IEP (Individualized Educational Program), which turns out to be a MDC (MultiDisciplinary Committee) assessment combined with an IEP. The school has been holding up their end of the agreement, but the other therapist is the family's (and their insurance carrier's) expense. The insurance is only paying part of the bill, it turns out. I believe Mary's been trying to tell me this for a while, and I'm just not getting it. I look at the MDC and can't really read it because my glasses are in the truck, and I say I'm going out to get them, where I sag for a second or two.

I try to think of some different ways of funding this speech therapy. You'd think there'd be some way, and that I'd know it, given my vast experience in this field (from which I know that funding will be a problem).

I ask about the consent form that she and her husband were to sign, and she said that Harry's "against" it; that it was titled, "Mindedness and Mental Retardation," and that he didn't really want "to get involved in all of that" and wouldn't sign it or, I assume, let Mary.

I wanted to know what "all of that" was. Wouldn't you? So she told me: She said that Harry doesn't think that Sean is mentally retarded and that Harry thought I: (1) was only there because I thought Sean has some sort of mental retardation or disability; (2) that I was "only in it for the money," so to speak; and (3) that for some reason, if Sean gets involved in all of this (my doctoral studies), it will somehow make "things worse" for him, by which she means he will somehow become more disabled. I flatly deny the second allegation.

The other two are, of course, problematic. I conceptualize Sean's difficulties to be disability related, in a practical, if not theoretical manner. I have to ask myself about Harry's common sense pragmatic; after all, I do believe that disability is socially constructed, and I am part of that particular construction crew. Mary returns the consent forms, and I resolve to go back to the drawing board, hoping that this will not cause problems with the Institutional Review Board at the university.

Sean has been standing there watching the same three-minute segment of *Toy Story* the whole time I'd been there, and now Mary asked me, "You don't think he's autistic, really, look at these criteria," (she had the American Psychological Association's [APA] Diagnostic and Statistical Manual [DSM] IV 1994 list).

I said, "Well, he certainly doesn't have echolalia..." (he can't say a word, really). Fortunately she got the joke.

Then she said, "He doesn't perseverate." I was watching Sean watch the new robot land in the *Toy Story* kid's room for the 49th time.

Me: "I don't know, I'm not a diagnostician, just a teacher, but to be brutally honest with you, he's perseverating."

This family is really messed up about Sean. I really don't know if he has autism, but he might as well. I told her that it didn't really matter, at least in the way I would teach him.

On a previous visit, some neighbor kids were staying with Sean's family. I walked in, and one kid asked me if I was going to make him talk. "And I'm the hoochie coochie man," I thought to myself.

I told the kid that I just might, you never knew. He told me that he hadn't said a word since they'd been there. Then he turned to Mary and asked her why Sean was so hairy. Sean has more hair than usual on his neck and his arms. Mary told them that's just the way he was. Sean then proceeded to play with the kids by rolling around in their sleeping bags with them, neglecting the TV, which on that day, was in "his" room. I assume this is the master bedroom now.

Mary told me about how Sean had been having laughing spells at night, that he'd just double up and laugh for no apparent reason, for about 15 minutes. I said that sounded like psychomotor seizures to me.

"What are they?"

"I don't know, really," I said. "I knew someone that used to have them at the Center. She just did weird things every once in a while and laughed like crazy, and somebody told us she had psychomotor seizures."

I told her I'd look them up when I got home.

Sean and I played for a while. He was watching *Toy Story*, and I lay on the floor on my back and grabbed him and made his legs straddle my stomach, so his trunk was braced on my knees which would suddenly, with the warning, "Open!" would spread slowly apart. Sean had to figure out what to do about this so he wouldn't fall. He put his hands on my knees to close them, and I said, "Close!" and my legs came back together again, only to "Open," again.

I try to play games like this with him. Anything to get him rocking and rolling. For about the last half-year, according to Mary, Sean's been watching the Walt Disney animation (not to be confused with the newer version populated with real people and animals) *Jungle Book*. This is practically the only video he will watch on TV. Sean stands close to the TV, and when the camera angle (if there is such a thing in an animation) changes, Sean will stand on his tip toes or crouch, moving from one side of the set to another in order to assume the point of view of the "camera" or whatever. I hypothesize that Sean likes *Toy Story* so much because the angles are so different in the film; it's all from a toy's point of view.

But I digress: Sean seems to like what we (Harry, Mary, and I, call the "Monkey Part." In his inimitable, or shall I say predictable way, Walt has cast a orangutan as a modern-day Prometheus. The Orang, King Louis, is the self-appointed king of the Jungle, and the only thing keeping him from the status of "Man," is the ability to make fire.[1] Mowgli has been raised by wolves, a Sauvage so to speak, and knows nothing of fire. Anyway, King Louis proceeds to kidnap l'enfant and coerce him, actually in an informed manner, into teaching him the secret of fire by singing the song, "*I Wanna Be Like You: The Monkey Song.*" The song, by Louis Prima, really swings, and the monkeys do the jitterbug as the King scats like the coolest of cats.

One day, I just grabbed Sean. I think it was Easter Sunday? Around that time. His cousins were around, and I was telling Sean he should be dancing with the girls because it'd be a whole lot more fun than dancing with me, which is what we were doing after I grabbed him. Let me tell you, generally, 44-year olds should not jitterbug on their knees with kids one-fifteenth their age, unless of course, the therapeutic demands of the situation make it absolutely necessary. Especially when the kid seems to know *all* the moves. We were spinning each other around, passing under each other's arms—*just like the monkeys in the video.*

Toy Story is just an adventure and lends itself to more sedate activities. After a while, I said my good-byes, that I'd be back on Tuesday, and left.

---

[1] Jean-Marc Gaspard Itard carefully observed the Sauvage of Aveyron's use of fire. The boy threw potatoes into the flames, left them long enough for the skin to get hot, and then ate them.

I got home depressed, but then I thought I'd call around and I talked to a nurse at the Child Disability Clinic (CDC) at Carle Clinic in Urbana, and she confirmed that they do multidisciplinary assessment there, but the social workers weren't around. After all, it was a Friday.

SIU supposedly did a multidisciplinary assessment with Sean in February, but all that happened was a talk with mom for an hour by one doctor, and she made the Dx. (diagnosis), nailing him at "3" on the 1-5 informal autism scale!

I called up Mary and told her the name of the social worker at the CDC, and she told me that the SIU doctor said that her assessment was a multidisciplinary assessment. I said something like, "Ya, right."

Oh well, Mary's going to call Carle Clinic on Monday, and we'll see what happens. I gotta warn her though, 'cause most insurance policies have caps on them for kids with disabilities if you can believe it, so even at age three you have to start playing poker. For instance one must, at some point consider, "What if he gets in a bad accident when he's fifteen, and we spent $2500 on a worthless assessment when he was three?"

It Does Not Escape My Attention, June 25, 1998

Today, I had my cards along. Last week, I'd unsuccessfully attempted to load the *Toy Story* document on the family's hopelessly underpowered computer. It's a 486, running Windows 3.1. This is an opaque operating system that somehow manages to combine the worst aspects of DOS and Mac's OS. I'd labored fruitlessly on my last visit to get the thing to display my document, which had pictures of *Toy Story* that I'd captured from the video on Melynda's computer and incorporated into a MS Word document. Somehow, although all the graphic filters are installed on the machine, the graphics refuse to show up.

What I did was print the thing out on card stock and cut the pictures with their descriptive text into something resembling 3x5 cards. I'd thought about laminating them but ran out of time before my appointment.

On my way down to Dixon City, I thought about how I would "introduce" the cards to Sean. Sean does not like new things, new toys, new foods, new anything. I wondered whether his mother should give him the cards, whether I should spread them out, stack them in front of one of the television sets, between the television sets, next to the computer, or where? I finally decide that I'll just give him the stack of cards, and let him figure out what use they could best be put to.

So I took it as a good sign that he took a few cards and gazed at them thoughtfully. He was carrying around a book that he laid down on the floor. He placed the cards in a neat stack on top of the book. I sat down and arranged the pictures so we could see them, but apparently he didn't want them spread out (I stacked them back up). I'd cleverly numbered them (on the back) so that keeping them in the order in which they appear in the movie would not present a problem should speed become critical.

Mary told me that Sean's seizures had stabilized but that he was still stumbling around some, and his legs have some large bruises on them. Apparently, Depakote "thins the blood" and makes it harder for it to clot, congeal, coagulate, or whatever.

We eat lunch together. Mary is still having to hand-feed Sean, and we took turns doing this. "We" (the interpreters of Sean's actions) don't know why he doesn't feed himself and wonder about it out loud. Probably it's related to some kind of what "we" (in the special education community) call tactile-defensiveness. I think that Mary told me once that Sean had begun to eat on his own, and then stopped for unknown reasons.

The tape recorder is rolling as I simultaneously interview Mary, eat, and help Sean eat. We talked about whether it was OK—talking about Sean. Mary seemed to think so. We were careful to include Sean in the conversation. It doesn't escape my attention that at the chocolate-milk-making counter, Mary has set up magnetic letters spelling the word M–I–L–K. Itard, as we shall see, would be proud.

I listened to the tape on the way home. Between Sean and his mother was an unmistakable intimate dialog—delicate, sonorous—while the three of us talked. I wasn't tuned in while we ate but the tape recorder was. Sean answered when Mary asked him questions. He commented while his mother and I spoke and at other times when their attention mutually focused on some task such as mixing chocolate powder with milk.

He's Moving in Time to the Music, June 30,1998

Sean was watching his televisions when I arrived. He was standing in front of "the other TV," as I've come to think of it. He's watching some show on PBS that Mary tells me the name of, and I immediately forget. They are Moon Creatures or something that pop up across a mountainous landscape, say things, and do things that make Sean laugh.

I wonder about my *Toy Story* cards. They're not in evidence, so I don't say anything. Mary was going to put clear contact paper on them, and I wish she had, because they would become soaked with Mackinaw River water, where later in the week, I would take my brother, his wife and kids, and the dogs for a swim. I was supposed to take them home and waterproof them. But that, dear reader, is another story.

Sean bounces around in front of the TV, balancing precariously on his tippy-toes. Mary wonders if that is a characteristic of autism, and I say a lot of kids do it, but that yes, if you look in the DSM IV (1994), you would find it listed as a symptom there. Sean turns his attention to "his" TV and the *Toy Story* tape that is playing. I am watching to see what parts of the film he will be into today, and it seems like the big hits are the commercials at the beginning, and the theme song at the end. These are sung, I believe, by Randy Newman. "Is he dancing?" Mary asks.

"Think so," I say as I watch the boy leap delightedly about in time to the music.

"He's moving in time to the music," I say with as much authority as I can. Sean is very sensitive to my touch, until I mess with him enough, then he enjoys it. He will come up to me and stand there until I do something to him. I reach behind me and turn off the TV. He doesn't notice at first.

Mary has a large ball that I've seen physical therapists use with kids. They roll them on it, sit them on it, and bounce them around on it. I figure that this will be good for him, both to develop his musculature and to stimulate his vestibular system and provoke language.

So after we're comfortable, I begin. He didn't seem to like to be rolled on his tummy as much as sitting and bouncing. We watch *Toy Story*, and bounce. Sean babbles excitedly and beats both of his hands on the ball. He has a habit of grabbing his shirt near his crotch, bending at the waist, and squeezing. He'll do this with the kinds of things he likes to hold, such as video tapes and an occasional book. Mary thinks that he developed this habit when he had an operation to correct his undescended testicles. He squeezes so hard that when I pick him up, I can feel the muscles in his chest. Beating the ball is something like this habit of Sean's.

Sean tires of bouncing, and he dismounts as gracefully as we can manage. He goes over to the other TV, notices that it is turned off, and comes back to me, and grabs my hand. My hand doesn't know what to do, apparently, so I ask him: "Sean, what do you want me to do?" He says "eahhh." I repeat my question, and he says the same thing, so I go over to the TV with him holding my hand. He is yelling loud now. I worry that Mary will think I am being mean to him, but I am not. Just trying to get him to do something; show me something.

My hand gets closer to the TV, and I demand, "What do you want?" He says "eahhh." I say, "On, Sean, on!" and gradually he gets it, I think, and says "Ohhn, ohhn." I turn on the TV, and he is happy, even though the wrong station is on, and I don't know what the right station is. So, he helps me find the right station, although he looks curiously at the different channels.

Mary brings out some food, and we start to eat. She's made tuna sandwiches and some kind of noodles. Sean likes noodles and the sandwich. Mary feeds him like she does: she holds the sandwich in front of him, and he takes bites out of it like, according to Dr. Juke's report, "a little bird." Mary is telling me that the other night Harry was using hand-over-hand assistance to feed Sean, and we try it. I get Sean to take a few bites from the fork like this. Then, I remember that we are supposed to start with a spoon, when teaching children to eat, and ask for a spoon. Sean doesn't like my hands on his, or at least I'm getting that feeling. So, I dig out a spoonful of noodles and leave it on the plate. He approaches the plate, picks up the spoon in his fist (his thumb is pointed toward the business end) and takes a bite. Mary and I cheer him on, and he continues to eat like this until Mary takes over, explaining that it is time-consuming to have him feed himself.

After we finish eating, it is time for me to go, and I say good-bye, that I'd see her Thursday, when I am to conduct the interviews with Sean's speech therapist and his teacher.

I Learn That, Indeed, Sean Does Not Smoke Cigarettes, July 31, 1998

I arrived with Sean's MDC/IEP in hand, and an article that Nicki, Tess Bennet, and a doc student wrote about Emily's successful inclusion in regular education. Mary was feeding Sean a grilled sandwich of some sort, a little piece at a time. Sean sticks out his head "like a bird" and accepts the morsel.

Mary had a neurological report, two pages, not the extensive report that she wanted and been promised. Interesting, the second paragraph said that "this three-and-a-half-year little boy, with the above noted problems, has not yet started smoking cigarettes or using tobacco products." I laugh when I read this. I tell Mary, "Jeez, you'd think he'd be smoking at least a pack a day by now. Yet another developmental delay?" I speculated.

I'm somewhat concerned because the doctor stated that Sean presented with developmental delays characteristic of Pervasive Developmental Disorder (PDD). This is kind of a grab-bag syndrome that indicates that "they" don't know what in the world is going on.

Mary tells me that she hasn't called about the EEG that would rule out LKS.[2] Actually, the doctors were supposed to call her and schedule an appointment last Friday or Monday, but I at least, figured that this was not going to happen. She also wants to schedule a new IEP for Sean, preferably before the school year starts. The likelihood of this happening is also remote, because teachers, therapists, and the like are contract workers who start and end their school years on particular days. But sometimes, they'll start before the students come back, and maybe we can squeeze it in then.

Rosemary Crossin (from a nearby university), it turns out, charges $500 for an "Educational Assessment and Recommendations" report. I say that maybe I could write one, that Janis, my thesis advisor, suggested that I was qualified to do this. I tell Mary that I could maybe perform this service but that it might not carry the same "weight" as one of the heavy-weights, like Crossin.

Mary is going to make some phone calls whilst Sean and I are "messing around." I am not sure what to make of her labeling my teaching, "messing around," but I don't hold it against her.

Right now, I am holding Sean against my chest with his back to me, "playing" with his arms. OK, so it's a game, but what I'm really doing is knocking him off balance and assessing how he compensates. I have his arms stretched out side to side so I can determine, by way of pressure changes, whether he is using them to regain equilibrium. I'd like to see him use his arms more when he walks and runs, and just use them in general. When he holds something, he clutches it to his chest.

Sean seems very talkative today, making what seem to me to be new sounds and an increased frequency of his older sounds. Some of them apparently serve new communicative functions. For instance, he's making growley noises to protest commercials on TV, some of my teaching maneuvers, and one time because his mom was doing something he didn't want her to do. We couldn't figure out what that was, exactly. She had said that she was going to the store and then started talking to me. Sean growled and then pushed her. She ventured that "Maybe he just wants me to get to the store," Later, when he was watching TV, an ice cream cone came by, and he made lip-smacking sounds, like a kissing sound. Mary

---

2 I'd done some research on the World Wide Web in search of diagnoses, and Landau-Kleffner Syndrome was one among several that seemed to fit Sean's current difficulties.

says that he had a good speech therapy class yesterday and ascribes his vocalizations to that.

He screamed and tantrumed through 'his' own speech lesson, but then two children arrived for their session, and Sean changed "like that" (Mary snapped her fingers to emphasize the dramatic change). Cody (not Sean's Cody who he "follows around" and imitates—to the point of using playground equipment like slides) and his little sister named Misty. Cody, it turns out, has trouble with making "th" sounds and some difficulty with social skills. Mary said that she is going to ask Cody's mom if they (Mary and Sean) can join on a regular basis, not a bad idea, based on the 'progress' Sean is making in his regular speech. I don't know why he's getting speech. It is not specified in his IEP.

Sean and I developed a new game, a social game. I would roll him like a log and then back away with a look of terror on my face, and he would come and get me using his new growl. He actually stops watching the TV for a few minutes.

We go through our usual routines, dancing, holding Sean on my shoulders. I ask Mary to write down all of Sean's word sounds, and she doesn't know how to write word sounds, like "chsk" or "e-i-e-i-e-i." I suggest that she label these sounds with a recognizable name, so then we could have a list. This is also beyond her. I finally ask if they have a tape recorder, so she could just say the words to the tape recorder, and I'd figure out what to do with them, and it turns out they don't have a tape recorder, but that they might get one. She wants to play classical music to Sean at night because he has been having trouble sleeping. He's been getting up at 12:00 AM for an hour or two. But not last night because they had such a "busy" day. She said she'd heard that they taught little kids how to play violin, and it changed their brains (for the "better" I assume), and that maybe listening to classical music would do the same for Sean.

There's also some anecdotal research of some sort out there that says kids diagnosed with autism develop language skills at a more rapid rate when they are "exposed" to classical music, but I don't tell Mary this. I toy around with the idea, and finally give up, after thinking of another anecdotal story related to the world by Marc Gold (a paradigmatic rebel) via video tape. Gold died in 1981 or 1982 at a young age from pancreatic cancer. He was about on his deathbed when he told this story that went something like this:

"I don't know if this is true, and I certainly know it was not what we would call a controlled experimental study, or anything resembling that.

But, in the back ward of one of our institutions, an enterprising worker set up inmates' cribs with large switches on each side, including the head and foot of the bed. Each switch controlled a tape recorder that played a different kind of music. Available for the 'vegetable's' listening pleasure were rock 'n' roll, classical, country, and some kind of other music, maybe elevator music. In this way, people could roll to one side of the bed and listen to the music of their choice. Anecdotally, we can say, 'vegetables' prefer country. There's something about this story, its power, that appeals to me," said Gold.

I've never been able to find that tape or any indication of such research, but much is lost for various reasons, maybe the status of this worker was such that no one would listen to his clever "experiment," except Gold.

Mary makes us some sandwiches and starts to feed Sean, and he strolls up and grabs mine out of my hand and takes a bite.

I help Sean finish it and eventually leave.

The Ride Home was Mercilessly Uneventful, July 17, 1998

Somewhere, I heard about a book called "Blue Highways," not so named because of their association with blues music:

> I'm gonna take that lonesome ol' highway,
> somebody you know is gonna need my help someday...
> —"Sweet Home Chicago," Robert Johnson

but because of their color on road maps. These are the hard roads, the old state highways, in this case, Route 136, which stretches from Danville, Illinois, on the east, across the state to the Mississippi River and beyond. Even though the road does not appear in blue on my map, the chicory flowers that grow in abundance alongside give the phrase some meaning. Blue skies, blue flowers, look pretty; makes me wonder why they call 'em the blues when they fall down so hard.

I'm heading to Sean's house, and everybody's on vacation. So Harry's going to be there and I'll get a chance to talk with him. Mary called me the other morning and said that she and Harry were "together." I don't know whether they'd parted company or not, and didn't ask. It's none of my business, and I'm of the mind right now that none of this shit is any of my business. It's making me feel real bad, and I got the blues.

Mary meets me at the screen door. Harry's sitting at the table smoking cigarettes; Sean's watching the televisions. *Toy Story* is on one, and a seemingly educational kid show is on the other.

"Com'on in."

"Hi Sean!" I say jovially, but he doesn't look up.

I head for the table and sit down across from Harry. Mary says that Sean's been bleeding from his ear. We speculate on the cause of this, and Mary says that she's going to go clean it up, which will, by her intention or not, give me a chance to talk to Harry semi-privately.

They wonder whether it's his ear tubes coming loose. I tell them a story about my brother's recent trip to the Rockies. He was staying at 12,000 ft. and when he and my niece woke up in the morning, there was crusted blood in their ears.

Harry says that you'd think they'd grown in by now.

Mary finally goes to clean up the mess, and I say, "Harry, first off, I want to apologize for any stress I might have caused you."

He looks at me.

I said, "Harry, Mary told me that having me teaching Sean here was causing you stress."

I said, "I don't want to cause any trouble for you."

Harry looks out the north window in the kitchen, presumably toward Peoria. "It's just all these doctors don't know what the hell is going on. I mean, this neurologist has so many patients, and he doesn't know what's going on, and he might write down some note on the chart," he holds his hands and positions his head as if glancing with casual interest at a patient's chart, "and then he might read it and he might not, or he might have made a mistake, or maybe just not written anything down."

I said, "I want to know if it's alright if I come here and teach Sean."

"These doctors all say the same damn thing, I think they all read the same fuckin' books on autism, 'cause I keep hearing the same shit."

"They probably did, but I don't know if it even matters that much 'cause I don't know if Sean's got autism."

"Why can't they figure out what it is? First you hear one thing, then you hear another. That Juke is a clown. She's worthless. Sits down with my wife and kid and a half an hour later, he's autistic. You'd think since they have all these tests, they'd just give 'em, and figure out what was going on, and let us know. One says autism; one says it's hopeless, some kind of brain damage: I don't know what to think. They don't have to live with it; *we do*."

"We had kids in our school that were smart in ways but, well, like

George," Harry said looking at Mary who'd walked into the kitchen, washed her hands, and was sitting down on a third side of the table, "his dad owned a service station, and he knew the license plate number of everyone in town. Is that autism?"

"Well..."

"He had to go home and eat at noon with his dad because they thought he might have problems eating with us. Or something."

Mary and Harry talk about this guy and who he's related to, what he's doing now, finally whether it is, in fact, the same guy Mary is thinking about.

"In some ways," I say, "It really doesn't matter what's, uh, uh, doesn't matter about Sean and how I teach him."

Harry: "*What?*"

"Well, Sean's Sean, and I'm trying to work with him to get him talking. I try to play with him until he gets less sensitive when I touch him. Then I bounce him around, rub his back. Try it sometime, use pretty hard pressure while he's sitting on your lap, and he'll sit up straighter, and seems like he likes it.

"I try to roll him around, 'cause, well, it, it's what they call 'vestibular stimulation.' You know, you have your eardrum, then there's those little bones, then there's that thing that looks like a snail, the cochlea. It's got some sort of fluid in it, and little hairs; they're really nerve endings, and the sound goes through the fluid and vibrates those little hairs, and then they send signals up to the brain and if everything's working right, you hear sound. Sound, speech, language, it's all kind of related that way," I say, my voice echoing forth from a bottomless pit of ignorance.

"There's sand-like stuff in there too," I say with renewed authority, "and when you move your head to one side or the other, you know that you're not straight up and down any more 'cause that sand goes bouncing on those hairs, and your brain says 'off balance!'"

"So you can see, that balance, hearing, language, and speech are all hooked up together. That's why I like to dance with Sean." What could be more simple. "Actually," I tell them, "I'm not too sure about the details of all of that, but Sean seems to enjoy what I do with him. That's what I try to do, find things he likes to do, and then build, build, build. If he likes to jitterbug, then I try to get him to sing while he swings. It's what I'd do with any kid, really."

"The neurologist (Mary uses his name) said that LKS is a form of autism, is that true?"

"I didn't get that impression from what I read...but..."

Harry said that he didn't see why they couldn't just give him the medicine and see what it does. "But he's already taking that Depakote, and I know that stuff causes liver damage, what happens when he takes all the other drugs, and they, uh, they..."

"Interact," says Mary.

"Depakote's like phenobarbital," I say quickly, wishing to add that it's a barbiturate.

"That's all that doctor cares about is whether or not Sean's having seizures," says Harry, "he's got so many patients, just goes from one to another. Now they're talking about vitamins. B6, 'but you must take magnesium with the B6 or your body will not use it'," he says in a nurse's sing-song.

"Well he's going to give Sean the EEG to rule out LKS next week. I think he's thinking, 'I'll just give him the test and that'll shut up mom'."

"Did you ask him why he ruled it out, uh, outright, when you were in the hospital?"

"He said it's so rare..."

"Meantime we're payin' all these doctors to tell us the same shit or there's no hope: brain damage."

Mary: "Something about his medulla, brain stem."

"That's what I mean, they look at him, and see him acting like that, and say it's brain damage. How can they tell? Didn't they give a MRI? Can't they tell from that?"

"As far as I'm concerned, the first four years of Sean's life is gone; I mean look at him, all he can do is watch the TV. I wonder if he's gonna grow up and just be like this for the rest of his life and always need someone to take care of him. I mean he still *sleeps* with us. We had him in a crib once, and he fell out, and just," Harry makes a motion with his hand that looks like a brick tumbling off scaffolding, "just *fell* on the floor, on his head. I couldn't get to him fast enough; I thought he broke his damn neck."

"He learned how to use the video controls," Mary says.

"Seemed like he was doing OK, I mean he was always kind of slow, but then he just lost it," Harry tells us, "He was eating, starting to say a few words, then all a sudden, he just stopped."

"When was that?" I ask quickly.

"About 9 months ago." I don't look at Mary for confirmation.

"Usually, the onset of LKS is between 3 and 8 years old. That much would fit. But I wouldn't want you folks to hang all your hopes on LKS, it really is rare, something like .5 births in 100,000. Most neurologists will go though their whole career without seein' anybody with LKS. Whatever the uh, uh...well, Sean's going to need help."

"What is a neurologist anyway?" asks Harry. "Aren't they brain specialists?"

I say, "Brains and nerves."

"Why doesn't he know what's going on?"

"I don't know."

"I don't think they give a shit."

"I hate to keep bringing up secondhand comments to you, Harry, but Mary said that you thought the schools could take care of uh, whatever Sean's needs. I really, well, I really don't think it's going to be all that simple."

I point over to the school Sean attends and say, "For instance, Mary and I talked to Sean's teacher and speech therapist, and they said they had a rule at that school that kids can only get physical therapy if their, uh, if it's going to help them get around the school. If Sean's got trouble with his brain stem, physical therapy could help, but I'm sure he can get around the school just fine."

"And the kids love him," says Mary, "he just attracts them somehow. I don't know what it is, it's almost like he has some sort of glow about him. They just come around."

"They had what they called 'ungraded classes' at *that* school when I went there," Harry tells us. "Is he going to be in one of those?"

"Do they still have them?" I ask, and nobody seems to know.

"Those ungraded classes, when I was a kid, over at *that* school," he says looking out the west window, "I hate to even think about this now, but there was a kid there, Mike, he had arms about like this then," Harry's hands look like they're around a cantaloupe, "well, he used to follow me around, and now that I think about it, he probably wanted to be friends, maybe 'cause I was normal or something."

Harry is still looking out the window, towards *that* school. "One day, he came up behind me, and was babbling and yaking, and I slugged him in the stomach."

"You didn't! What'd you do that for?" asks Mary.

"He was bugging me, so I slugged him. He started crying like a little baby and ran back to his classroom. Then Mr. Cunningham, his teacher, came out and grabbed me by one arm and threw me up against the lockers." Harry turns back to us. "I hope *Mike* don't remember that; I see him down at the bars sometimes, and now he's got arms like this." Mike's arms are apparently a couple of inches larger in diameter than they were back in *that* school.

Harry asks me if they'll put Sean in an ungraded class in *that* school. I tell him we don't know what they have there. Harry says: "It'd be better if he was around the normal kids, 'cause if he's with those othern's he's just going to pick up on what they do; act like them and shit."

"It's not all *their* decision." Turning to Mary, I say, "you know those pink papers they gave you?" I turn back to Harry, "It's a legal document. If you don't like what it says, you have a right to due process in court, at a trial. That's what I mean about physical therapy; they just can't say they're only gonna give PT to someone for this or that reason. It's illegal. If the student needs it and the IEP team says he needs it, then the student gets it, whether the school likes it or not."

Mary asks if they can send him away to another school, like the one they sent so and so's kid down the street.

"If everybody thinks it's the right thing to do, and that includes you. Do you want him to go where so and so went?

"You talked to Drew's parents, right?" I continued. "They're just trying to get him in the regular kindergarten, and the school's putting up a big stink."

"Yeah, I heard you about got kicked out of that meeting," says Mary.

"Lost my temper," I said. "The principal said, 'there is no way that Drew is going into that kindergarten,' and I said, 'unless a judge makes you.' Then she got pissy and called me 'Mr. Linneman' and wanted to throw me out of the meeting, but I reminded her she'd be breaking the law, because, you see, parents have the right to have anyone they invite at those meetings, anybody, lawyers, doctors, taxi-cab drivers, it don't matter.

"The Special Ed teacher reminded me that Drew couldn't stack four blocks on top of each other, and she brought 'em along to *prove* it. I wouldn't of stacked 'em if she asked me either.

"Drew's dad's been haggling with them all summer over this, and you know what they did? They said he would be with the regular education kids half the time. You know when? Recess, lunch, PE, and music. I told Jay he ought to say, 'I'll trade you lunch and PE for math and reading.' He finally got a lawyer, thank god, guy I know just prevailed in two cases against that particular special education director. It makes 'em mad because then they have to provide the service on top of paying the parent's lawyer fees."

"We get a free lawyer at CAT," says Harry.

"Well, they can reimburse CAT then."

Mary asks me: "What about this secreton thing?"

I tell her that I don't really know anything about it, just that every once in a while, someone will come up with a "miracle cure for autism. Might be some drug, an herb, like DMG, vitamins like Harry was talking about, or some treatment like 'The Lovass Method,' or facilitated communication, or the TEACCH method. Some work better on some kids than others, but they don't work the same on all kids. Autism's a syndrome, and that means, at least with autism, that they can't point their finger at this or that, and say he's got autism because such and such isn't working right. Everybody gets all worked up; parents get false hopes, then the 'treatment' fades away, except for the kids it works on."

Sean comes into the kitchen and wants to sit in his mom's lap. He indicates this by stretching his arms up and grasping ineffectually at her clothing.

"You want to sit in my lap, Sean?"

"Eahhh." Or something.

"Com'on up, then," and she puts him on her lap.

I start to make some 'getting ready to go' kind of motions, like looking at the clock, saying, jeez, I didn't know it was 1:00 already, and asking when a good time to come back would be. We decided Tuesday, and Sean started reaching for me when I stood.

"He wants to play," said Mary.

"Well, I'd like to too, but I've got to get back." I grab Sean and hold him, rock him gently, and tell him that I'll be back on Tuesday and give him to his mother. My promise means nothing to him, and he is making pained sounds, not crying though. Sean lives in the present, or perhaps he doesn't understand me.

The ride home was mercilessly uneventful, and I didn't even have the good sense to turn on the radio.

Chapter Five

Jean-Marc Gaspard Itard and His Long Shadow

Despite Sean's lovable self—his uncanny ability to attract other children, for one—he had some distinguishing features that marked him as a character in the grand narrative of disability. The story is not one told through the eyes of idiots but scientists. Although the lens has changed over the years, the focus has always been on the scientific.

If one takes the work of Lynch and Woolgar (1988) to heart, science doesn't look like a plodding, implacable, immutable march to the ultimate truth anymore. When they turned the science of observation on scientists themselves, producing "fact" looked more like the pastiche of reducing observation to representation along with the very human enterprise of economics, politics, and the kind of baggage organizational sociologists probably study.

In this way, science is a story, and as such, has a beginning, a middle part, and various departures that serve as endings. If I (and to be at least semi-modest, most in the field of special education) had to mark the beginning of mental retardation's story, I would commence with the work of Jean-Marc Gaspard Itard.

Not unlike the little girl with the little curl, when Jean-Marc was good, he was very, very good but when he was bad, he was horrid. So pervasive is Itard's influence in the field of special education, Guess and Thompson (1993) remark that "many of the practices of special educators today (e.g., task-analysis, discrimination learning, errorless learning) are not new, but merely refinements of the work of earlier educators such as Itard" (392).[1]

---

1 "It was not until the middle of the eighteenth century that Britain and Europe turned to

Wild Children and Learned Men

As if society had the right to tear a child away from a free and innocent life, and send him to die of boredom in an institution, there to expiate the misfortune of having disappointed public curiosity (Itard 11).[2]

In seventeenth and eighteenth century Europe, there were celebrated cases of wild children captured from forests and fields among villages. They were of great significance to scholars of the time interested in observing human savages whose contact with the social world was limited. These children offered scientists the opportunity to demonstrate the truth of John Locke's notion that people are born unto the world like blank slates. Enlightened men felt that they, by *"...carefully collecting the history of so surprising a creature, would determine what he is and would deduce from what he lacks the hitherto uncalculated sum of knowledge and ideas which man owes to his education"* (Itard xxiii).[3]

A wild boy was taken in the woods near Aveyron, France, in September of 1799. He had been sneaking around in people's gardens, stealing potatoes, and begging for food. He ran away when men chased him. They knew he was around for a couple of years, and one time three sportsmen caught him while he was trying to climb a tree to get away from them.

Stories of the capture of L'Enfant Sauvage de l'Aveyron spread, and Minister of the Interior, Lucien Bonaparte (Napoleon's brother), not uninterested in the cause of science (and under not insignificant pressure from the recently established Société des Observateurs de l'Homme),[4] ordered that the boy be brought to Paris. In southern France the wild boy was held in an orphanage in Saint-Affrique

---

the education and training of their disabled populations. Onto the empty stage of special education stepped the pioneers—brilliant, innovative, often controversial and erratic philosophers, physicians, and pedagogues—who fashioned a new era in human history and paved the route that other educators would follow.... France was the crucial place; the period beginning about 1740" (Winzer 1993, 39).

[2] Please read *italicized* quotes in this chapter with a French accent.

[3] Itard wrote two memoirs of his encounter with the Wild Boy. They were written in 1801, and 1806, respectively. In my work, I have used a translation by George and Muriel Humphrey (1962) from a reprinted edition of Itard's work, entitled *Rapports et Mémoirs sur le Sauvage de L'Aveyron* which is out of print. For the sake of convenience, I will simply note citations of the Humphrey's work with Itard's name and the appropriate page.

[4] Later known as the Society of Anthropology (Lane 1977, 57).

for about a month and finally transferred to L'Ecole Centrale de Rodez, under the investigative eye of Father Bonnaterre, a local priest and naturalist. Although appeals from Paris continued without abate, the Commissioner of Rodez stalled, asserting that the province "needed time for local parents who had lost children to confirm that the wild boy was not their own," and, significantly, to give Father Bonnaterre enough time to complete his own studies (Lane 1977). Bonnaterre observed the wild boy for about six months at L'Ecole Centrale de Rodez.

Interestingly, Bonnaterre[5] thought he just *might* be observing a unique species of humanity. Linnaeus had published his *Systema naturae* in 1735 and catalogued wild children as *Homo ferus*.

But under urgent appeal from the Société des Observateurs de l'Homme, the Minister of the Interior ordered that the wild boy be immediately brought to Paris, and provided 740 francs for the week-long stagecoach trip.

Clair, the school's gardener, took care of the boy during the priest's observations at the school and during the inevitable coach ride to Paris. An old man with gray hair, Clair offered to be as a father to the wild boy should La Société prove incapable or lacking.

Bonnaterre wrote a scholarly account of the boy's behavior, and ends with these thoughts: "*Go forth, poor youth, on this unhappy earth, go forth and lose in your relations with men your primitiveness and simplicity! You lived in the bosom of ancient forests; you found your nourishment at the foot of oaks and beech trees; you quenched your thirst at crystal springs; content with your meager destiny, limited by your simple desires, satisfied with your way of life beyond which you knew nothing, this usufruct was your sole domain. Now you can have nothing except by the beneficence of man; you are at his mercy, without property, without power, and you exchange freedom for dependence. Thus are poor-born three fourths of the human race: nothing but bitterness was prepared for you in tearing you away from the protective dryads who watched over you*" (Bonnaterre, cited in Lane 1977, 48).[6]

---

5 Bonnaterre was no country bumpkin. He had written the section on zoology in the *Encyclopédie Méthodique*, "a successor to Diderot and d'Alembert's *Dictionnaire des sciences*" (Shattuck 1980). Bonnaterre fled Paris during the Reign of Terror and went into hiding under a warrant issued by the Committee of Public Safety. Bonnaterre wound up in Rodez and was appointed professor in 1796.

6 Note the rhetorical parallel between Bonnaterre's lamentation and Itard's.

The diagnosis of "wildness" or idiocy remains in question even to this day (Lane 1977; Shattuck 1980). Roger Shattuck makes a fairly strong case that the "Wild Boy of Aveyron" was actually a native of Lacaune in the Tarn district some seventy miles to the south of Aveyron. People around Lacaune knew about him and had captured him once or twice, exhibiting him in the village square to satisfy public curiosity. But folk around there knew his "story and never made very much of it" (Shattuck 1980, 19). An investigator named Guiraud, appointed by an Aveyron commissioner, submitted this report concerning the "wild boy," which I excerpt: "*During the day, he approached farms, walked familiarly, into the houses, and waited quietly and without fear to be given something to eat. The pity he aroused and the hospitable customs of the inhabitants of these mountains produced a kindly welcome. Everywhere, people offered him the things he preferred. Then he went away and hid in the most isolated spots. For a long time he prowled around the mountain of Roquecésière. He repeatedly visited one farm near that village, where he received particularly good treatment.... Slowly, he became familiar with the people and his intellectual faculties developed gradually*" (Shattuck 1980, 20).

One could imagine, or perhaps wish for cries of "*Liberté pour L'Enfant Sauvage de l'Aveyron! Dechainez L'Enfant!*" from the townsfolk of Lacaune. This is probably not the earliest instance of involuntary commitment for a person with disabilities in order to advance the cause of science, but science was very young in 1799.

The debate was followed in the papers, and while the postrevolutionary bureaucracy haggled over the boy's future, excited Parisians anxiously awaited the arrival of L'Enfant Sauvage de l'Aveyron. Upon his arrival they hoped to witness the awe inspired in the savage by the sophistication of their city.

When he got there, all he did was convulse or rock in his cage and try to hide from the curious citizens. He was dirty and didn't care what his food looked like; public interest in the wild boy waned. Professor Pinel[7] ("celebrated for his pioneering work in the scientific moral treatment of mental illness" [Foucault 1965/1988, 241-278]) diagnosed the boy as an incurable idiot fit only for the asylum of an institution. "*We know the...details of his life from the time he entered society—*" Pinel read in his

---

[7] "*It is within the walls of confinement that Pinel and nineteenth-century psychiatry would come upon madmen; it is there—let us remember—that they would leave them, not without boasting of having 'delivered' them*" (Foucault 1965/1988, 39).

diagnostic impressions before La Société: "...*his judgment always limited to the objects of his basic needs; his attention captured solely by the sight of food, or* by means of living independently, *a strongly acquired habit; the total absence of subsequent development of his intellectual faculties with regard to every other object. Do these not assert that the child ought to be categorized among the children suffering from idiocy and insanity, and there is no hope whatsoever of obtaining some measure of success through systematic and continued instruction?*" (cited in Lane 1977, 69, my emphasis).

His student thought otherwise. Jean-Marc Gaspard Itard, the father of special education (Montessori 1912), nodding to his professor's infinite wisdom in conceding the validity of his diagnosis to a band of uncertainty present in *any* scientific measurement, felt that the boy had a simple deficiency of contact with the world. This diagnosis augured well for his prognosis. And besides, Itard wrote, it should not be "...*forgot that society, in taking over this unfortunate youth, had contracted toward him binding obligations that must be fulfilled"* (Itard 5).

Itard developed an objective-based educational plan for the treatment of the wild boy's condition. It proceeded on the assumption that a deficiency in (social) worldly contact would result in a reduction of function in the sensibilities, such as hearing, sight, touch, and speech necessary to accommodate the development of the components of mental physiology that could only be nurtured by a gradual accumulation of the knowledge of society.

Sensibilities, men recognized, could be developed even in persons of primitive societies, owing, they supposed, to some kind of intimate contact with one another within their pathetic groups, so even "*[i]n the most vagrant and barbarous horde, as well as in the most civilized nation of Europe, man is only what he is made. Necessarily brought up by his own kind, he has acquired from them his habits and his needs; nor are his ideas any longer his own. He has enjoyed the fairest prerogative of his kind, the capacity of developing his understanding by the power of imitation and the influence of society"* (Itard xxi). However, the possibility of *refining* the sensibilities lay in the crucible of only the most advanced civilizations. Lack of development in the organ of touch, for instance, could result in a restriction of the hands to mechanical movement denying, before instruction, even the pleasure of running one's hands over pants of velvet. The wild boy suffered from these deprivations of sensation: "*His eyes were unsteady, expressionless, wandering vaguely from one object to* another, without resting on anybody; they were so little experienced in other ways and so little trained by the sense of touch, that he never distinguished an object in relief from one in a picture. His organ of hearing was equally insensible to the loudest noises and to the most touching music. His voice was reduced to a state of complete muteness and only a uniform guttural sound escaped him. His sense of smell was so uncultivated that he was equally indifferent to the odor of perfume and to the fetid exhalation of the dirt with which his bed was filled" (Itard 6).

You could take snuff and stick it up the wild boy's nose, and he wouldn't sneeze, such were his insensibilities. And despite his misery he couldn't cry: His secretion of tears was disconnected from his "... feelings of sadness, and in spite of innumerable annoyances, in spite of the bad treatment to which his new manner of life had exposed him during the first few months, I have never seen him weeping" (Itard 15).

Despite the addition of increasingly spicy foods to his diet, the boy did not develop his sensibilities even to the point of acquiring a taste for wine. Itard remarked that "[o]f all his senses, the ear appeared to be the least sensitive. It was found, nevertheless, that the sound of a cracking walnut or other favorite eatable never failed to make him turn around...One day I fired two pistol shots near him, the first appeared to rouse him a little, the second did not make him even turn his head" (Itard 15).

The wild boy was removed from the House of the Deaf and Dumb to the care of Itard. Mme. Guérin provided for the young savage's daily needs. She performed "this task with all the patience of a mother and the intelligence of an enlightened teacher" (Itard 12).

The wild boy would stare out of Mme. Guérin's windows over the lawn and garden, melancholy, endlessly swaying back and forth, looking longingly to the openness of the plains and fields. If a cloud moved to admit the sun or threaten a storm, he leapt delightedly about, as if he would jump out of the window to gain the freedom of the countryside. He waited for the most inclement weather and after it had driven others to more favorable environments, would visit the garden to hide under piles of trash or in odd corners. "During the night by the beautiful light of the moon, when the rays of that heavenly body penetrated into his room, he rarely failed to waken and place himself before the window. He stayed there, according to the report of his governess, for part of the night, standing motionless, his neck bent, his eyes fixed upon the moon-lit fields giving himself up to a sort of contemplative ecstasy, the silence and immobility of which were only interrupted at long intervals by deep *inspirations nearly always accompanied by a plaintive little sound"* (Itard 13).

In order to demonstrate his position that the wild boy suffered merely from a deficiency of civilization, Itard developed what the modern reader would recognize as an objective-based educational program:

1st Aim. *To interest him in social life by rendering it more pleasant than the one he was then leading, and above all like the life he had just left.*
2nd Aim. *To awaken his nervous sensibility by the most energetic stimulation, and occasionally by intense emotion.*
3rd Aim. *To extend the range of his ideas by giving him new needs and by increasing his social contacts.*
4th Aim. *To lead him to the use of speech by inducing the exercise of imitation through the imperious law of necessity.*
5th Aim. *To make him exercise the simplest mental operations upon the objects of his physical needs over a period of time afterwards inducing the application of these mental processes to the objects of instruction* (Itard 11).[8]

The teacher took great care not to be beguiled into false beliefs about his student's accomplishments. For instance, pursuing his 4th Aim, Itard began teaching the Sauvage some words. He started with *eau* (water) after his observation of the boy with his back to two people involved in a heated argument. A third walked into the room and uttered *"Oh!"* at which point, the Sauvage turned his head. In fact, the boy rarely failed to respond to the vowel *"O."* Itard, with illustrative instructional savoir-faire, christened the boy "Victor," (Veek-tow, French pronunciation) and began his instruction with the noun *eau,* and initiated a trend in education—assessing ability and preference in order to develop curriculum—that has become as transparent as it is dogmatic in the present.

Itard put a name to it, the "Imperious Law of Necessity," what we now recognize as operant conditioning.[9] He deprived the boy of water, and

---

8 Contemporary readers familiar with special education practice will no doubt be impressed by the similarity in phraseology and content of these goals. In fact, many critics have argued that the field's instructional methodology has not progressed much further than Itard. Indeed, the conflation between instructional methodology and educational outcomes, according to many authors, remains (see Trent 1994, for a review).

9 It is interesting to note that Itard's "Imperious Law of Necessity" presaged early behaviorists' (such as E. L. Thorndike and J. B. Watson) formulation of the Law of Effect by over a century. The Law of Effect "holds that other things being equal, those bonds that lead to a satisfying state of affairs are stamped in and those that lead to a dissatisfying or

"[w]hen his thirst was most intense, it was in vain that I held before him a glass of water, crying frequently "eau" "eau." Then I gave the glass to someone else, and who pronounced the same word beside him asking for it back in the same way. But the unfortunate creature..." was ultimately unable to pronounce the word, and Itard abandoned *eau*, "It would have been inhuman to do otherwise" (my emphasis, Itard 31).

The teacher "*changed the subject, without, however, changing the method. It was upon the word lait that I carried out my next experiments*" (Itard 31). After four days of trials, Itard succeeded in eliciting the word *lait* from Victor.

> It was the first time that an articulate sound left his mouth and I did not hear it without the most intense satisfaction.... . Nevertheless I made a reflection which in my eyes diminished the advantage of this first success. It was not until the moment when, despairing of success, I came to pour the milk into the cup which he gave me, that the word lait escaped him...If this word had been uttered before the thing which he desired had been granted, success was ours, the real use of speech was grasped by Victor, a point of communication established between him and me, and the most rapid progress would spring from this first triumph. Instead of all this, I had just obtained a mere expression, insignificant to him and useless to us, of the pleasure which he felt. Strictly speaking, it certainly was a vocal sign, the sign of possession. But this sign, I repeat, did not establish any relation between us (Itard 32).

Itard was not entirely unsuccessful in his attempt to educate the savage, although he never did learn to speak more than a couple of words like *lait* (the savage ventured daily into the Luxembourg Garden to the house of Citizen Lemeri for a drink) and *Oh, Dieu* the latter an expression he had learned from Mme. Guérin and used at moments of great joy. He learned how to say "*lli*," despite Itard's observation that the rolling *l* is a difficult, late developing vocalization in children. "*I am somewhat inclined to believe that in this painful linguistic labor there is a sort of feeling after the name of Julie, a young girl of about eleven or twelve who comes to spend Sundays with Mme. Guérin, her mother. Certain it is that on this particular day the exclamations lli, lli, became more frequent and, according to his governess, are even heard during the night, at times when there is reason to believe that he is sleeping soundly. The cause and value of this last fact cannot be exactly determined. It is*

---

annoying state of affairs are stamped out" (Chaplin 1985, 468).

necessary to postpone its classification and description until a more advanced puberty has allowed us to make more observations" (Itard 33). The wild boy's affections for Mme. Guérin were touching. Itard, who by necessity, had to restrict most of his interactions with the boy to those related to instruction, was somewhat less favored, because Itard recognized what he offered was of no immediate value.

It is interesting then, that Itard goes to great length to describe the boy's nonverbal communications, which were, in many cases, socially valuable functional communication skills. For example,

> *...what is more astonishing is the way in which he lends himself to these means of communication in that he had no need of any preliminary lesson, nor of any mutual agreement in order to make himself understood. I convinced myself of this one day by a most conclusive experiment. I chose among a number of others, an object for which there was no indicating sign, as I assured myself beforehand. ...Such for example, was the comb which was used upon him and which I wished to make him bring to me. When I appeared before him with my hair rough and bristling in all directions I should have been very much surprised if he had not understood me. He did indeed do so, and immediately I had in my hands what I wanted. ...He is scarcely less expressive in his way of showing his emotions, above all impatience and boredom. A number of people visiting him out of curiosity know how, with more natural frankness than politeness, he dismisses them when, fatigued by the length of their visits, he offers to each of them, without mistake, cane, gloves and hat, pushes them gently towards the door, which he closes impetuously. ...Many people see in these proceedings only the behavior of an animal. For my part I will confess I believe that I recognize in them the language of the human species, originally employed in the infancy of society before the work of ages had coördinated the system of speech and furnished civilized man with a prolific and sublime means of improvement which causes his thought to blossom even in the cradle, and which he uses all his life without appreciating what it is to him and what he would be without it if he found himself accidentally deprived of it, as in the case which presently occupies us* (Itard 37).

But Itard's interactions with the wild boy were not limited to instruction, intentional or otherwise. The boy particularly enjoyed these occasions. *"When I go to the house in the evening just after he has gone to bed, his first movement is to sit up for me to embrace him, then to draw me to him by seizing my arm and making me sit upon his bed, after which he usually takes my hand, carries it to his eyes, his forehead, the back of his head, and holds it with his upon these parts for a very long time. At other times he gets up with bursts of laughter and comes beside me to caress my knees in his own way which consists of feeling them, rubbing them firmly in all directions for some minutes, and then sometimes in laying his lips to them two or three times. People may say what they like, but I will confess that I lent myself without ceremony to all this childish play"* (Itard 25).

Itard wrote two memoirs of his project. The first, was an apparently premature celebration of his success in the education of the wild boy. The second was solicited from his Excellency, the Minister of the Interior, and we're fortunate because otherwise Itard just might have *"...enveloped in a profound silence and condemned to an eternal oblivion, certain labors of which the result shows the failure of the instructor, rather than the progress of the pupil"* (Itard 52).

It all seems to be a big plea to his Excellency by his manner, to continue his gracious interest in the savage. *"...all things recommend this extraordinary young man to the attention of scientists, to the solicitude of our administrators, and to the protection of the government"* (Itard 101).

In Itard's work with *L'Enfant Sauvage de l'Aveyron* we see several recurrent themes in the work of those concerned with others' disabilities. First, there is a separation between caregiving and instruction, from the standpoint of intervention, and on a personal level. Mme. Guérin was responsible for Victor's day-to-day care, leaving Itard free to conduct his "experiments." We know next to nothing about his governess's impressions of the boy. Second, Itard failed to see any avenue for linguistic achievement in Victor's utterances of *"lli, lli,"* which were assigned to childish affection for Mme. Guérin's daughter (it is odd though, that Itard in many cases 'followed Victor's lead' as in his attempts to instruct him in using the word *lait* [Victor *loved* milk] appropriately). Third, although he recognized their significance, Itard relegated Victor's nonverbal social competence (the comb was but one of many examples Itard related) to some pre- or subhuman status. Fourth, Itard eventually abandoned his efforts with Victor as a technical failure, emphasizing Trent's (1994) observation that there has always been a

> reliance on particularistic and technical ways of understanding and dealing with the problem. By "particularistic" I mean the tendency to analyze the problem of mental retardation into ever smaller pieces that can be more easily isolated and manipulated. Thus, a particular group of people like those labeled mentally retarded are removed from the general social and economic context; categories of learning deficiency or social friction are differentiated and refined; particular techniques are then devised for intervening at particular physical, behavioral, or cognitive points.... In the history of mental retardation, however, there has been an almost obsessive concern with the particularistic and technical. If we can wake

dormant senses from their lethargy, open the sutures of skulls to allow brains to expand, find the flawed chromosome, isolate and measure intelligence and social adaptation, refine educational technology or condition people to behave acceptably, perhaps then we can better care and control the thing—which ironically enough we have labeled a no-thing—that is "mindlessness" (274).

Itard's fellows at La Société des Observateurs de l'Homme had their own interpretations:

A reprehensible mother, a poverty-stricken family abandon their idiot or imbecile child; the imbecile escapes from his home and gets lost in the wood, not knowing how to find his way home; favorable circumstances protect him; he becomes fleet-footed to avoid danger; he climbs trees to escape the pursuit of some animal that threatens him; compelled by hunger, he takes nourishment from whatever comes to hand; he is easily frightened, because his intelligence is weak. This unhappy child is encountered by some hunters, brought to town, taken to the capital, placed in a vocational school, confided to the care of the most renowned instructors; the government, the city take an interest in his future and his education; scholars write books to prove that he is a savage, that he will become a Leibniz, a Buffon;...new essays are written; the issue is debated; the best methods, the most enlightened care are brought to bear for the education of the so-called savage; but from all these claims, from all these efforts, from all these assurances, from all these hopes, what is the result? (J. E. Esquirol, Itard's contemporary, and leading French alienist of the period [cited in Lane 1977, 163-164])

...this savage of Aveyron, a true idiot, filthy and disgusting, whom some people these days tormented by a mania for publication, would turn into a celebrity so they could become one too (Bory de Saint-Vincent, an influential naturalist of the day, cited in Lane, 1977, 171)

After addressing his 1806 request to his Excellency, Minister of the Interior for continued beneficence, Itard stopped writing about the boy. The plea was not unheeded, and the ministry allocated 150 francs yearly to Mme. Guérin toward her efforts to support the boy.

Civilized Men and Wild Children

In the end, Itard violated the contract, the *"binding obligations"* he had imagined Society (an emergent observant, surveillant "us") shouldered by capturing and attempting to educate his savage (Mannoni 1972). After a particularly frustrating pedagogical session, Itard laments: "'*Unhappy creature,' I cried as if he could hear me, and with real anguish of heart, 'since my labors are wasted and your efforts fruitless, take again the road to your forests and the taste for your primitive life. Or if your new needs make you dependent on a society in which you have no place, go, expiate your misfortune, die of misery and boredom at Bicêtre.... Had I not known the range of my pupil's intelligence so well, I could have believed that I had been fully understood, for scarcely had I finished speaking when I saw his chest heave noisily, his eyes shut, and with a stream of tears escape through his closed eyelids, with him the signs of bitter grief"* (Itard 73-74).

Ten years later, a naturalist named J. J. Virey, who had recently written *The Natural History of the Human Species*, with discussions of monkeys, Hottentots, Eskimos, Indians, and other 'savages,'" (Shattuck 1980, 27)[10] visited him and found him *"fearful, half-wild, and unable to learn to speak, despite all the efforts that were made"* (cited in Lane 1977, 167).

Thirty years later Victor died, presumably in the care of Mme. Guérin, in their cottage on the grounds of the House of the Deaf and Dumb.

Itard's student, Edouard Séguin, subsequently elaborated Itard's techniques making him a *cause célèbre* in the United States among the founders of the Association of Medical Officers of American Institutions for Idiotic and Feeble-Minded Persons, who upon his emigration to the United States (as Edward Seguin), elected him their first president. His visage graces the seal of the AAMR (American Association on Mental Retardation) to this day.

---

[10] Shattuck also informs us that the French word "sauvage" also referred to Tahitians.

Chapter Six
Emily

The situation in which we find ourselves at the beginning of our enquiry may be expected itself to point the way for us.

—Sigmund Freud,
Civilization and Its Discontents (1933/1962)

Emily and I are friends. We like to play together. She teaches me things. Now I know how to use the keyboard to call up color palettes when I'm working in my favorite graphics program on my computer. She taught me how to use the polygon tool, so now I can make spiky-looking things that are like fantastic diamonds or ice castles. Emily knows how to scoop up animals right from a book, and smoosh them real small so she can give them to me to put in my shirt pocket. A lion and a hippopotamus got into a fight in there, and my pocket was jumping all around. But they made friends, I said, and settled down.

Emily's mother contacted me after she'd talked with a mutual friend who said I was looking for research subjects. I wanted to work in the schools, to research the process of change that these institutions undergo when they work to unite students from special education classrooms with kids their age in kindergarten, first grade, junior high, or whatever. This process goes by different names, and I won't name it because no matter what I call it, the label will be outdated by the time I finish writing. I remember talking with a principal of an elementary school one time about the above process, and I think the currency of my terminology annoyed him. He said, "I call it mainstreaming; we *both* know what that means."

I think that Emily's mom just wanted me to be Emily's tutor, and if she had to put up with my efforts at school reform to get that, so be it. I didn't want to be anybody's tutor, but I thought I would; if I could get a chance to see what it looked like when a kid who would have been isolated in special education went to kindergarten in her own neighborhood.

But Emily and I are friends now, and I am really not too concerned about her school, as long as she gets good grades and a good teacher, and has fun on the playground, and likes her class, which is all a friend can hope for, I guess.

December 14, 1993

"Emily!" gets heard a lot in Room 6 at the Madison School Early Childhood Project. "Emily!" this and "Emily!" that, and Emily Emily Emily. Especially it gets heard by me who is totally focused on Emily and her interaction with others.

Emily has a hall pass, although no one else in her class seems to need one. She is closely monitored by staff members (Melva, Emily's teacher is out sick—maybe at a meeting) as to whether she remembers to hang it up on the wall just inside the door on a hook. Today she forgets and I'm sitting there next to Bonnie (a classroom assistant), who I'm talking to about something I don't remember. Bonnie makes earnest eye contact with Denise (Emily's personal classroom assistant) and a physical therapist. Bonnie shakes her head "no" with an exaggerated sad look on her face; Emily had not independently placed her hall pass on the hook when she stepped through the goddamn door. They conjecture about this and speculate over that—the conditions by which such a sad state of affairs had come into existence. A minus (-) will be recorded on Emily's data sheet.

Emily has to pull a wallet out of her fanny pack and open it up and look at pictures of all the things she's done today, like go to circle, go to this, do that. Now she's ready to go to gym except Denise unfolds a big blanket, and she puts a double-folded part of it on the bench outside the gym; the rest she lays on the floor by the east door. The other kids from Emily's class pass by them and go into the gym.

Then Denise and the physical therapist put down a mini-tram. "Emily!" had to put some pictures of activities she'd be performing on a Velcro board that was army green or puke green. She kept wanting to put this one picture on the board depicting some activity that "wasn't there" according to Denise. So then Denise bounced around with Emily, and Emily did one-footed jumps, and two-footed jumps, and big jumps, and little jumps, on the rug, and on the mini-tramp. Emily said, "Big Jumps!" when Denise said "Big Jumps!"

The physical therapist is talking with all this bouncing going on about Emily's progress and "doesn't she go horseback riding?" Emily's dad's a vet. The PT says that horseback riding is good for vocabulary development and vestibular stimulation.

I couldn't tell what was going on in the class, except that Denise had her covered most of the time. She sat at the table for a long time drawing words for Emily, and Emily would say "cat." I don't know whether she knows too many words like that, but Denise kept looking at me, smiling.

I ask Hope [a teacher's assistant and student teacher] about Emily. Hope says she's adorable "oh" "ah," and I'll really like her, and she has long brown hair and big blue eyes. I wanna know what's wrong with this kid, and how come I didn't see her in class sticking out like a sore thumb when I'd observed *so* carefully in that classroom at Madison. Three times. How brown is her hair, I ask, "like yours?" Hope tells me that it's darker, she thinks.

Hope says that Emily understood *everything* when they talked together in the bathroom, although someone else in there, probably her aide, said she didn't get a bit of it.

I still want to know what's wrong with her and how come she's autistic and have to ask: Does she rock? (NO) Does she have any repetitive behaviors? (NO) Does she hurt herself? (NO) Does she look at you when she talks? ("oh, maybe, she kind of looks around") Does she run or jump or do anything weird? (NO) I don't ask how well she can talk. Finally, I have to ask if there's anything at all wrong with her, and Hope tells me she's a "little dreamy."

December 29, 1993

For a while when I got home I was aggravated that I didn't save the kids' pictures to disk. Really, I should have saved a couple. Next time, maybe, we can do that, learn how to save, but I don't have any evidence of today's pictures.

They weren't really drawing anything anyway, except when they were writing their names, but they learned how to use most of the tools, and the stuff I made when I first got my computer was about the same, but I was very proud. I'd make little boxes filled with fish scales, little circles and big circles, or brick walls with ANARCHY written on them with white spray paint.

When I got to their house, Nicki ushered me and my computer into her office. She plugged in the monitor and the computer, and I turned them on. We went out into the living room, and Nicki said, "Do you remember Dan?" to Emily, who turns her eyes up at me for one or two seconds and moves them back to a plastic stand that holds a square of plastic; a bas-relief of a pretty white Dutch girl's head that you put paper over and rub a crayon sideways to make a picture. There's about five or six completed works of the same face scattered around on a plastic picnic table for kids sitting about three feet from a rather large television set. I turned around, and sunk into the chair where I was sitting last week was Mike. Nicki introduces me to "Michael," Emily's brother.

Somehow, I feel like we all of a sudden wind up in the office. I give Emily the disk that's got Kid Pix on it, and I tell her to stick it in. She put it in and gently pushed it until it got sucked up by the disk drive. Then I grabbed her hand and put it on the mouse so that two of her fingers were on the clicker. I keep my hand on hers and tell her to watch the arrow, and we kind of zero in on the disk icon. I say, "Click, Click" and then press her fingers and say "Click, Click!" while we click. The window opened up and I say "Click, Click," and Nicki yells (I think she really talks loudly to Emily) something like "click the mouse."

Emily does double-click the Kid Pix icon, and while it goes through its little start up routine, Nicki's asking me why wasn't the program on the hard disk, and I'm saying I can't copy it on to the drive because the floppy is messed up. She asks how much it cost, but before I could answer, she says "Forty dollars, I just got this one and the kids are done with it." She was showing me the box it came in that I can't even bear to look at (a computer program with educational pretensions), and I said I don't know how much Kid Pix costs; I stole it at work.

Emily is enthralled by Kid Pix and is moving the default tool, a big fat pencil, around the screen. I say "Do you want to draw?" and she nods "yes," and I say "Hold the clicker down" and push on her fingers just a little bit and drag ("Move the mouse") the mouse and a black line appears. Emily drops her jaw and says something and claps her hands and then grabs the mouse and draws a line pretty much by herself.

She makes big squiggles and little squiggles, and then I say "Do you want to blow it up so Mike can have a turn?" And she says "Ya." Nicki told me earlier, when I said I should have brought over two computers, that they needed to learn turn-taking around here; Mike has been really wanting to take one. Bad.

So I say "Click the eraser" and move her hand over to the eraser, and I say "We're going to blow it up!" and I say "Click!" and we move the mouse down to where the dynamite icon is, and I say "Click," and then we move up the firecracker tool to the middle of the screen, and I say

"Click," and Emily clicks it and the screen is destroyed in a nuclear holocaust. Now the screen is white and it's Mike's turn.

Emily backs away and leans against me with a look of awe or wonder or confusion or marvel or acquiescence or some combination on her face, and watches as I work with Mike. I am positioned as I was with Emily, on the right side of the computer, kneeling under a bookshelf that Nicki keeps on telling me that I'm going to hit my head on. She has her degrees hanging on the wall and when we first walked in, I was trying to look at them and she said, "Yep, those are my degrees; a lotta good they've done me." I can't even remember what universities she went to. Maybe Loyola.

I show Mike how to work the computer, using about the same method as I did with Emily. He catches on about as quickly as she, although I don't really think that he got the hang of lifting up the mouse and setting it down so that you don't wind up going off the edge of the table while you're trying to draw something. It's pretty funny to watch Mike because he does go right off the edge of the table but keeps the mouse in the air, level with the surface.

Michael blows up the screen, and it's Emily's turn. She moves the cursor to the lower left hand side of the screen and clicks and sends us back to the finder. Nicki asks "What's happening when she does that?" looking at the Kid Pix floppy icon. I say, "Don't worry about it for now," and act like I'm thoroughly engrossed in teaching her daughter how to write her name in pink, which I am. I give Emily fairly heavy assistance with the mouse, both in keeping clicker depressed and mouse movement as we make the part of the capital letter "E," and she writes the rest of her name, making little mistakes and fixing them. She writes 'Emily Jackson' with 'Emily' on top and 'Jackson' on the bottom, pretty much centered on the screen. She says, "Yay, Emily!" and claps when she's finished.

Nicki's explaining to Mike that they're going to get a computer as soon as she can go out and look at them (I smile at Mike, and tell him it takes grownups forever to get stuff like this and he nods at me knowingly) with her friend but that she has to get a "babysitter for two kids." Nicki is not directing any of this conversation to Emily. I think that I'd tried to say something about what might be happening in the future to Emily, and Nicki had stopped me, saying that "that's really beyond Emily's comprehension." Nicki tells me that they really need a college student to take care of Emily, at least, because one time they got a high school girl, and she just couldn't understand why Emily didn't act like a regular kid.

We play with Kid Pix, basically, for 2 1/2 hours, and Emily only leaves the room to watch the TV 4 or 5 times, and never for more than 3 or 4 minutes. I'm counting. Every time she leaves, I go with her, though.

She stands in front of the TV, and sways back and forth to the music on the TV, and twists her hips. One foot is out in front of the other, and she bends at the waist with her arms at her side.

There's a big cute cartoon bear on the TV falling down through the clouds, and I say "Look Emily, the bear's falling down," and a moment later I say "Which way is the bear falling, Emily?" She looks at me like I'm some sort of idiot, and I smile, and I say, "Just checking, Emily."

Things got a little tense later, because turns were getting unfairly divided and unevenly offered. Nicki and I are sort of talking around the subject of when I should come back next. She says Mike's in school till 4:00, conspiratorially hinting that if I wanted to just work with Emily, we could avoid Mike by scheduling time on Monday afternoon; Emily's not in school on Monday afternoons. I'm thinking about this and don't really know what to do and noncommittally say that I'd call later in the week.

Mike told me one time when his mom was out of the room that when he was sick over Christmas, he only got up to 102, but that "Emily had got up to 105." Mike looked at me like he'd got outdone again.

He was trying to get a turn off Emily, and she was standing there growing trees on the computer screen. She isn't responding as he pleads, asks nicely, asks not so nicely, demands, and finally asks me to give him a turn. She won't listen to kids, he says, only to grownups. "Hmmmm," I say, "What happens if you tap her on the shoulder, and ask nicely?" Nothing. I try it, and get the same result, but I don't raise up my voice above the level that I was talking to Mike in either. Mike and I start to talk about how we could go about securing a turn, when Nicki comes in and says loudly, "Emily, it's Michael's turn!" And pulls her away.

During one interchange, she was asking Mike who gave him the "geared up pills" or something to that effect. Speed. I think that he wasn't acting right or something, and Nicki was giving a narrative like you see grownups do sometimes—one that's allegedly directed at the child but whose real target is (are) the other grownup(s) in the room.

It goes something like, "You *don't* act like that when your father's around, do you, Mike?" Mike shakes his head up and down, agreeing, I suppose. Nicki then talks directly to me and says that it's amazing how differently they act when their father's around.

Emily is starting to get bent and hitting her brother not very hard, putting her hand over her mother's mouth, and doing a not bad job drawing. She's also saying "Shut up!" in a contextually appropriate manner and getting the desired effect. Nicki tells me this is a tough one because they're so used to using extinction (my term) when Emily "picks up something" (i.e., a word). Nicki doesn't know how to deal with this one. "Maybe we'll let Dan puzzle this out," she says to Mike. "You can't just not pay attention," she tells me. I say, "Well, it seems to be working for her," but I don't know if Nicki heard me.

Emily's still standing there in front of the computer, and we get her to blow up the screen, and since Nicki's starting to tell the kids it's time for me to go, I realize we're facing a dreaded "transition."

I ask Emily if she wants to learn how to shut down the computer, and we go to the file menu, and pull down to "Close" (that has a hand waving; "See, Emily, it's saying bye, bye!" I hear myself saying). Then we close the floppy disk window and drag the icon into the trash, and she gets it out and hands it to me. Then I show her where to press the switches that turn off the machine, and she does so. Nicki tells me that she does that with the VCR, has Emily turn it off, and Emily will at least do it, if not happily.

Emily goes out of the room and sits in the chair Mike was in when I came in. She's looking somewhat upset and angry. Nicki tells me that she's just doing that because she had a good time.

Nicki can't get Emily to say goodbye to me, but Mike does.

I take my computer out to the truck, and Nicki opens the door for me. I put in the computer and say I'll call later in the week. As I'm pulling out, she brings Emily to the clear glass screen door and physically prompts Emily to wave "Bye, Bye!" to me. Emily starts waving on her own. I wave back.

January 3, 1994

Before I went over, I made an objective-based lesson plan for somebody's benefit, mine, Emily's, or Nicki's, I don't know which. I put it in a nicely labeled folder but didn't get a chance to whip it out in front of Nicki. I did read it over a couple of times while Emily was working.

Lesson Plan

Goal: When we're done, Emily ought to know how to turn on the computer, open a SuperPaint file, save it to disk in her folder, and shut down the computer.

Objectives:

1)   Emily will turn on the computer by pressing the switch on the

monitor and pressing the switch on the computer.

2) Emily will wait for the desktop to appear without doing anything that is not really necessary to the StartUp action, such as moving the mouse around or typing. Well, she can, but just as long as she knows it's not going to speed things along or do anything.

3) Emily will create a folder that has her name on it and some sort of descriptor. This is a one-shot deal, and I don't know whether we should practice this, because really, it's not part of the goal, I don't think. Emily can type the name on the folder when she creates it. Emily should make this folder inside the "What, me worry" hard disk.

4) Emily will open up the SuperPaint folder and launch the application.

5) Emily will name and save a file to her folder, navigating through the "Save" dialogue box.

6) Emily will start to work on a document.

7) Emily will save her work a couple of times.

8) Emily will quit the application and save her work when it asks her if she wants to.

9) Emily will open up "What, me worry?" and find her folder.

10) Emily will open her folder.

11) Emily will open her document.

12) Emily will repeat 6, 7, and 8 above.

13) Emily will shut down the computer, closing all files and quitting applications, and choosing "Shut Down" from the special menu in the finder.

I got over there a couple of minutes late. Nicki opened the door before I had a chance to ring the bell. Emily came running down the stairs from the kitchen, saying "Pongo, puter, Pongo, puter!" I didn't understand what she was saying so I asked Nicki what Emily was telling me. Nicki said that Pongo was a character from *101 Dalmatians* and that Emily just calls people names that she hears in videos.

Nicki tries to get Emily to say my name a couple of times, and Emily just says it, imitating accent and intonation, like, "Dayen," or "Done." Myself, I liked Pongo.

I plugged in the computer, and I showed Emily where the buttons were behind the machine. I had to turn it around so she could reach it. She had a little trouble with the computer rocker switch but was OK with the monitor switch. Emily was quite impressed by the StartUp action, which involves a gray screen, then the "Happy Mac" icon that says there's a system file to start the computer, then a StartUp screen that I made from a scanned photo of my grandfather and "Uncle Fritz" at the home place a couple of miles out of Detmold, Germany. She pointed at the inits, one by one, as they loaded; first Virex, then QuickTime, and After Dark, DayStar, and Mac/PC.

I told Emily to double click on the "What, me worry?" hard disk icon, and I had to help her. I figured that the mouse was set for too fast of a double click and showed Emily how to open up the Control Panels. I made it so the mouse tracked "slow," and the double click was "slow." Emily saw the SndMaster icon, and said "sound." I showed her how to use it, and she was scrolling through the sounds and picking them out to play. You have to "select" or "highlight" a sound and then click it to make it play. Emily would make a selection and then raise her right index finger about six inches from the top of the clicker on the mouse and then stab it. Nicki said that they might have to buy me a new mouse. She turned to me and said, "She knows the word 'easy,' you can say that to her." I thought it was cute, and I didn't care if she broke the mouse, and really, I didn't think that she could.

Then we had to close a number of windows: the "Mouse Control," the "SndMaster," the "Control Panels." I showed her where the close box was on one window, and she closed the rest of them back to the finder and stared at the screen.

Then we had to open the hard drive called, "What, me worry?" The icon looks exactly like Alfred E. Neuman's head.

I told her to double click on it, and she did, and then I said that if she wanted to paint, she should double click on the SuperPaint folder, and then on the SuperPaint application icon. She did this and waited patiently while the program started up. Emily learned how to save. The program takes forever to save a document, and Emily did try to do some stuff with the mouse or keyboard (keybored?) while SuperPaint lumbered through its routine. Emily said "save," and then saved her document by pulling down from the file menu and selecting "Save."

After I showed her how, Emily used the selection tools to manipulate objects, distort them, re-color them, and so on. I just sat there and watched her.

Emily learned how to select objects and move them around. A selected object is surrounded by what the SuperPaint manual calls "marching ants." She'd hold out her hands like they were bird's wings, and wiggle her fingers while she watched the marching ants. Emily'd sing a little Christmas ditty and then move the selection where she wanted it after a verse or so.

There are a couple of different selection tools. There's a rectangle that makes rectangular (!) selections, a lasso that makes free form selections, a circle one, and a few others. When you make selections with the lasso, it's not easily predictable what the lasso is going to select (there's rules, I'm sure), at least in certain situations. Emily kept on experimenting with the lasso seeing what it would "take."

Emily discovered how to use the keyboard to make different palettes, like the color palettes or the tool palette "pop up." She remembered which keys controlled particular palettes; "H" for the texture palette, "C" for the color palette, and so on. She knew to keep the key down to choose tools or colors from the palettes. This is something I didn't know how to do.

The dreaded transition arrived; that is, it was time for me to go. I tried to get Emily to shut down the damn computer, and I think that she knew what "Shut Down" meant, because she wouldn't choose it. Only "Restart." So we had to watch the computer start up a couple of times, which is not one of my favorite activities. I finally get her to shut down. Nicki's right there, ready to just grab the little monster and jerk her out of her seat and be done with it, but I ask her to let me see what happens.

Emily goes out of the room and slumps onto the couch and grabs her blankey and sucks her thumb and looks at me. Nicki is making all kinds of apologies for Emily's behavior. I just look at Emily and say that she done good and that I'd had a good time. She just sits there on the couch, sucking her thumb and looking at me.

January 7, 1994

I called up Nicki in the morning and left a message on her machine that I was coming over. I reminded her that my "colleague" Hope was coming over. Probably this is the first time I ever called anyone "colleague" before. I said that if there was any problem with this, to please call me. She didn't.

We went over there, on time, maybe even a little early, and Nicki met us at the door, and Emily came running down the stairs, saying something unintelligible to me. I can't remember if Nicki translated or not. Nicki did say hello to Hope, and I stammer out some sort of introduction, which is totally unnecessary since Hope and Nicki are already talking about a teacher's room at the school where Hope works and Emily goes to school, how Hope had helped the kids celebrate Hanukkah, how Emily had danced the Horah and stirred the potato latke, and maybe some other things that I don't remember.

It's hard to be around Nicki and Emily together, because Nicki prompts Emily so much. Emily, though, seems like she's so interested in the computer that she doesn't give a hang about me or her mother for that matter. I will admit that I wish she liked me and thought that I was one of the cooler people in the world, but she doesn't and maybe never will. I don't know what she thinks about people in general.

I plug in the computer and monitor, and Nicki puts Emily in a booster chair, and I have to get her out of it immediately because I want her to know how to turn the computer and monitor on.

While the computer is ponderously laboring through its StartUp routine, Nicki's telling me that she'd gone down to the university to look at computers and that they'd picked out a "475." "Is, uh, that an IBM compatible?" I wondered. She said no, that it was "a Mac 160/—I don't know what." She said that they were going to get one and then get a CD-ROM to go with it, because the "lady" said you needed one to take advantage of the sound, and books, and educational programs that they were coming up with for kids. I start to explain that CD-ROM is just a kind of storage and allows you to "play" programs, but I'm interrupted because the machine has finally booted up and I had to go to work.

I get Emily to make a new folder and label it with her name and an "f" after it. "That stands for 'folder,' Emily," I say wisely. Emily drags her folder into another folder on "What, me worry?" and then we drag it out. I work with Emily to drag her painting from last time into the folder and then try to get her to double click so that she can get to her painting and open it. Emily does *not*, and did not for the rest of the day, get how to double click.

We have to go into the Control Panels, because I figure that Mouse Tracking and Double Click Speed are set too fast, so we do that. I finally, using firm assistance, "guide" her in double clicking, because I'm getting uptight with what I perceive as everyone else's expectation that she open up that Control Panel. I am virtually certain that she would have done it eventually with verbal goading.

Most of the work we've been doing in SuperPaint involves clicking, not double clicking, so I'm really not too surprised. I say "two clicks" and

Nicki says, "double click it, Emily, one, two." All of this is to no avail. With her one click, Emily highlights the document, and drags it around inside the "emily 1" window. She puts it in different positions, drags it around some more. I physically force her to open the file, and she says, "SuperPaint!" and all of us adults look at each other like the most intelligent, adorable thing in the whole wide world had just happened, which it had, in my opinion.

Emily then starts doing her thing with the program. She's drawing, and I have to remind her where some of the tools and palettes are hidden. She starts using the colors and selection tools and so forth. Hope and Nicki are impressed, and Nicki keeps on trying to get up and "go work," but I think she is either fascinated with what her daughter is doing or is worried that she'll do something weird, break the computer, or perhaps she stays to model good Emily management for me—probably a combination of at least a couple of these factors.

Hope asks, "Is this what you were trying to teach me, Dan?" I say that I was afraid so.

I have to force Emily to pull down some menus and other things, but she watches attentively and the fact that I had to "force" her to remember something doesn't deter her from using what I'd forced her to do. For instance, she was using the eraser, and I thought it would be a neat idea to erase a region of her painting and fill it with a color using the paint bucket. I did this with her one time.

Emily does not ever let go of the mouse. She may have squawked something like "no," or some other protest. She tried to smack me with her elbow, arching it at a 45 degree angle, ready to use it in defense, as if that was going to deter me.

Nicki starts telling us that Emily does *anything* that her teacher at school wants her to. She said that they'd joked about her going to kindergarten (next year) where they'd hang up a poster-sized picture of Emily's teacher, just so Emily would (know that big brother was watching) do what she was supposed to.

"Emily's not afraid of Dan," Nicki says. "What's she doing, Dan?" I said that she was trying to get me to leave her (the hell) alone. Nicki returns to the theme of Emily not getting away with anything with her teacher many times throughout the day.

Anyway, after I used physical prompting one time, Emily did this: Selected the eraser; erased part of her picture; selected the paint bucket; selected a color; filled the erased part with paint; and did it some more with different colors. Nicki asks me if I think that Emily knows what she is doing. I evade the question, saying that I know I've had a lot of trouble teaching, uh, uh...

Nicki fills in for me, "old people..."

"...the same things," I say completing my sentence.

Emily is singing some songs, and I'm not really paying attention, but Hope picks up that she's singing a song about the teeny weenie spider or something and starts singing along with Emily, in a quiet voice, letting Emily lead, and pronouncing the words clearly right after Emily initiated them. I think Emily started saying the words more precisely, so that I could understand them, but I don't know. I'm still trying not to say much, because I think it would just distract her.

Emily saves her document from time to time and gives me a shit-eating grin. Nicki asks me why she's doing that, and I say that for one thing, I can't help smiling back (wouldn't try to either) and for another, Emily "knows that I think it's a good habit to save often." Nicki asks me how much she understands, and I say something noncommittal. Nicki says that her husband Mark thinks Emily understands more language than what she lets on. This comment takes me a little off guard, because three years ago, there was a striking discrepancy between her and Mike's score in the "Conceptual Understanding" domain of that standardized test that the Autism Experts from Minnesota gave them. Emily's dad used to think she understood less than she showed.

Emily has remembered everything that she learned the other day. All of a sudden, she arches her hips and pushes back on the desk with both hands and says something that indicates to Nicki that she has to go to the bathroom. Nicki says, "GOOD!" and sweeps her out of the booster chair and up to the bathroom.

I feel the need to show off a little for Hope and start doing some fancier stuff with the program, and Emily runs back into the room, looks at the screen, starts to work, and then quits, and jumps into her mom's lap with her blankey, and sucks her thumb. Nicki thinks it's because she's tired, and asks "Why don't you want to work any more?" Emily just sits there in her lap looking at me. I suggest that it's because I wrecked her painting. Nicki does not accept this at all, even though I suggested it a couple of times. This is an awkward moment, as we all try to figure out what to do next.

I didn't have a lesson plan this time (and that *will* be the last time), but I had thought about introducing Emily to the pleasures of word processing with Microsoft Word; I started up the program, and Emily couldn't resist.

I asked Emily to save her document and she called it, "SDGGHJJJKKKKLLLGFIEW5RER5RE0DR5J" and saved it to the Word Folder. I wasn't about to teach Emily how to navigate through the "Save" dialog box at this point in time. She started typing, and I, of course, wanted her to use a larger font and forced (prompted) her to do this. Then I showed her how to select text and use drag and drop editing, which she did with ease, having learned this concept in SuperPaint. Then her mom got some cards out that had words like c a t, and b i r d written on them (for some reason, the letters are underlined) with nice pastel pictures drawn on them. When "bird" came up, Emily flapped her wings and said, "Fly," to me, and she looked a little questioning glance at me right in the eyes, for probably the first time that day, and I said, "Fly, I understand you."

We tried a couple of different things like changing font colors and sizes, but it seemed like what Emily really wanted to do was to type the name of the card, select a new card, delete the old name, and type the name of the new card. I, of course, tried to get her to hit return so that she'd have a list of all the card's names, but she didn't want to do that, and Nicki reminded us again that "She'll listen to her teacher." Nicki apologized to me for "stifling Emily's creativity" by breaking out the noun cards, and I said I thought everything was OK, that she was learning how to use the keyboard. Emily was using the ruler to set tabs and adjust the return, clicking here and there, not really knowing what she was doing. I had to make her widen the return, because the space she had it set at was too narrow for even the tiniest of words. Emily resists and tries to elbow me and grips the mouse, but when she sees what I'm doing, she slides it along by herself to about 5 1/2 inches.

Emily seemed to use this strategy for typing: Scan the keyboard using the left finger as a guide, or pointer, then look at the screen; position the finger in the general vicinity of the letter; look at the screen; look at the finger; look at the screen; make fine adjustments; look at the screen; zero in on the letter; look at the screen; hit the key while looking at the screen and smile when the letter appeared. Usually she'd hit the right letter, but if she didn't, she'd hit delete with her left hand. She was having trouble manipulating the cards in her lap because she was *not* going to let go of that mouse in her right hand for nothing. God only knows what I'd have done with it.

She'd save from time to time. Once she forgot, and the "auto save" box came up, and she clicked the OK button before anyone (except me) knew what happened. Nicki asked me, and I said that Emily just used the auto save.

It was close to 2:30, maybe a little after when we stopped. Except for a couple of minutes on Nicki's lap, she'd been using the computer since 1:00 with no sign of boredom or discomfort. I said to Emily that we'd have to quit after a couple of more cards, and she said, "No," and I said yes, and Nicki said yes and went and turned on the TV. Emily turned to go, and I asked her to quit the program and shut down the computer, and she did it, using the pull down menus. She had trouble with the switches behind the machine.

There was some show on the tube that had faces that were made up to look like human bodies, like Chevy Chase does, and they were making music. Emily danced. She swung her finger around in the air. She walked around the table (Nicki said that's how she danced). She placed one foot in front of the other and rocked in time to the music. She ran in time to the music. She wiggled in time to the music. We watched.

When we said goodbye, I think Nicki got her to say goodbye to me, but not Hope.

When we were driving back to town, Hope was wondering why Nicki kept on asking me whether Emily understood what was going on. Hope thought that she was used to having professionals tell Nicki what Emily understood, that if the Autism Experts were there, they'd be able to say what she did or did not understand, whether she'd conceptualized this or that. We laughed about this. I don't know what she understands, really. A precarious thing, understanding.

January 12, 1994

Well, I got back from Emily's a couple of hours ago. Her babysitter was there. She sat there and watched me "work" with Emily. I was there for 2 hours. Emily hung in there like a pro for the whole time, except once when she had to go to the bathroom.

I was not going to mess with the computer for nothing while she was gone. Emily came back and sat on the couch for about 30 seconds and then got up and went back to the computer, got into her chair, and said something very, very cute like, "There, that's better!" Her babysitter and I both laughed.

All day, as I was saying, the babysitter sat there and watched us. I was a little uncomfortable, because I ignored the babysitter most of the time and didn't even look at her, but I wasn't about to start up some kind of running commentary, conversation, or whatever; and the babysitter didn't ask any questions, so I just let it go and acted like I was absorbed in teaching Emily or whatever.

When I first got over there, I took my computer into the office, and the babysitter and Nicki came in for a second while Emily turned it on. I turned the computer around a little, and Emily was trying to reach around and hit the switches and look at the screen at the same time. Emily's small, and the effect was adorable as she tried to get her fingers on the switches and then move so she could watch the StartUp action, lose her position on the switches, and go back and forth like that.

As part of my lesson planning activities last night, I'd made a new icon for Emily's folder on my hard drive. It looks like a frazzled woman's head—except it's in color. Emily's still having trouble double clicking (I'd remembered to set the mouse first this time, though, so we didn't have to journey through the control panels). But she found her folder right away, pointing to her name with the arrow. We opened it up, and I had her open this data base file I'd made. It has a text field, a sound field, and a picture field. I'd made a little book; there's a yellow bird working on a computer, and if you double click on an icon of a speaker, it (my voice) says, "The yellow bird is working on the computer." The next record says, "The yellow bird says, 'Emily, Let's make some pictures!'" Then there's a computer that says "Let's paint!" And then, "It's your turn, Emily!"

The idea was to have Emily make pictures in SuperPaint and cut and paste them into the data base and make some sort of a book. I don't know why in the world I thought she'd be able to do this; you have to leave the data base (FileMaker), go into SuperPaint, draw a picture of the appropriate size (I did make an easel [a rectangle] that was the right size but it was largely ignored), select the painting, copy it, go back to FileMaker, click in the picture field, and paste the picture in there. And then click in the text field and type something clever and then double click the sound field and say something creative into the microphone (this involves clicking a "record" button in a dialog box, saying something, clicking the stop button, and then saving the sound), and then, of course, number the page. I don't know, what could be simpler? Emily did learn the basics of using FileMaker, such as clicking in fields to activate them, and moving from record to record. She also learned how to switch back and forth between SuperPaint and FileMaker, a simple task with System 7.

I gave up on this little activity and went back to working in SuperPaint, to make a long story short. We also played the "picture card" game in SuperPaint and Word. For a minute, I thought that Emily had "lost skills" typing because it seemed like she was slowing down, but what was really happening was that she was planning how to type two letters really quick, so if the card said "nest," she'd type "ne" with one finger really quick and then "s" and then "t." I made the brilliant suggestion that she type "st," and she started doing that with words four letters in length. She'd select these from her cards (i.e., skips over 3-letter word cards) and when she'd do it right (most of the time), she'd give me a high five. Sometimes she'd initiate the high five, and sometimes, she looked at me in the eyes and waited until I initiated.

Emily was letting go of the mouse to type. I was trying to get her to use the return key so that she could keep a list of words, but she does not want to do this. I was using child-directed learning. I tried to show Emily what I meant, and she erased it. I tried to force her, and she said, "You can't do that!" I said, "Yes I can." But it turned out that I couldn't.

Sometimes, Emily would play "typist." She would arch her fingers above the keyboard and alternate banging on the keyboard with the fingers on each of her hands. I noticed that when she'd get to the end of a line, she'd stop, and reposition the "I-beam" at the beginning of the new line. She didn't click the I-beam, though. I finally taught her the "concept" of word-wrapping by holding her finger on the "j" key until it wrapped around at the end of a line. She didn't use the I-beam after that.

Emily used her forearms, elbows, and really, her whole arm on the keyboard. Sometimes, she'd take her right hand and sweep her fingers over the keys and complete the movement with a flourish that ended with her hand aloft, excellently positioned for a high-five from me.

I talked real quiet to Emily. She'd look at me when I whispered her name.

She dropped the cards a couple of times, and I looked at her significantly until she said "help." She asked her babysitter for help once, and she helped her, but apparently the babysitter didn't know that we are supposed to fall into a dead faint when Emily "reaches out" to us in this way.

When it was time to go, I told Emily, "one more card" and she said, "OK." And then I helped her quit SuperPaint, and Shut Down the computer and turn off the switches. When she was done, she said, "See you Monday!" The babysitter and I laughed, and I gave Emily a pat on the back.

After I packed up and was heading for the door, the babysitter asked Emily if she wanted to say goodbye, but she was glued to the tube. When I was walking out the door, I heard a little voice say "See you!" and I said, "Ya, Emily, I'll see you Monday" (I have no idea where this Monday stuff came from). Emily was at the door. Then she said "Bye!" and waved while I made my way out the door.

January 14, 1994

There was a lot of commotion at the door, and I could hear Emily. The hard door was open, but the screen door was shut. Nicki opened it for me and the computer. I said "hi" to her and the kids. I kind of stood there trying to figure out what to do. My boots were probably "dirty."

Nicki told me it was OK, just walk on the carpet. I notice that she's got on Chinese slippers, and Emily has ballerina slippers, and Mike's got on stocking feet. Really, I wanted to take off my boots, but I was too uptight. So I clomped into the office with the computer, and Mike gets up in the booster seat. Nicki gives him some static about this and reminds him about what "they'd talked about."

He gets out of the chair, wondering out loud why it is that Emily "gets to do everything first." Don't worry, I think, someday you might be able to be on a sibling panel at our student teacher seminar at the university and tell them what it's like to have a sister who's autistic. While I was trying to figure out why I think sick thoughts like these, I hug him with my left arm from "my position" under the shelf, leaving my right arm and hand free to "prompt" Emily. Mike is standing right next to Emily's chair. Nicki's trying to get him to sit in the chair behind us (so he'll be "out of the way"), and I say that it's OK, he can stay with me. "They're pretty burnt out," she tells me, and "they might not last." Nicki's apparently setting me up for disappointment. She also warns me that Emily's going to be surly. I brace myself for the onslaught as Emily switches on the computer.

Nicki's telling me about Emily's "blooming" verbal skills and tells me that she doesn't know whether it's because of the computer or not. She looks at me like I'm supposed to say, "Yes, Nicki, learning SuperPaint, FileMaker, and Microsoft Word has been positively associated with enhanced verbal repertoires in autistic children."

"Where's Uncle Fritz?" I ask. Mike wonders who (the hell) "Uncle Fritz" is. I tell him he was my grandpa's uncle who lived in Germany, who now occupies the StartUp screen of my computer.

Emily counts the 'inits' loading, "1, 2, 3, 4," and then looks at me and claps when Thelonius Monk plays the opening theme as the computer starts up. Me and Emily think this is really cool. I'm still holding on to Mike. Nicki tells Mike that they'll have their own computer in a week, and that she'll get him a dinosaur program when it comes. Emily's trying to open "What, me worry?" and Mike's saying, "Mom, how's she know how to do that?"

Nicki reminds him that Emily's been working on this stuff for a while. I'm holding Mike across the stomach with one arm and with the other I reach out to help Emily double click the hard disk icon. We open the book I made in FileMaker first. She clicks on the sound icon, and I tell her to double click and she does it! She looks at Mike and smiles, and he's got to wonder where she learned how to do that out loud again. Emily plays the sound. Then she advances to the next record and double clicks on the sound again. Mike is not handling the computer talking about "let's paint," etceteras very well, and is squirming in my arms, pleading that we paint. I do something like pat Emily on the back, because I'm so tickled that she's started to double click, and she arches her neck and shoulders and waves her head back and forth like she's Stevie Wonder and reaches her hand up for a high-five.

Emily goes through each of the four pages of the book and then tries to find SuperPaint under menu bar icon, but the program isn't open. I help her find the application. Emily double clicks on the icon, and SuperPaint starts up, much to Mike's relief. Emily says "SuperPaint!" and then Mike says "SuperPaint, yay!"

Emily does a bunch of neat things with the program, and Mike is still marveling out loud how she knows how to do that. I know what people will say, Mike. She's "savant."

Nicki asked me if I wanted any food, and I said I sure did. She said that she could make me a meatloaf sandwich, and I kind of wonder whether to eat it or what. Then I figure that I'll be pestering these people for a while, hopefully, so I might as well tell the truth. "I'm a vegetarian." I make some lame joke about the carrying forth of the proud tradition of feeding teachers when they come by.

She's got some taco chips (Eagle brand) and salsa, she says, and that sounds wonderful to me because I haven't eaten all day. I tell her that would be great, and Emily says, "That's great!" She brings out the chips and a little bowl of salsa, that she tells me is "mild." I eat it anyway. Emily's grabbing for a chip, and Nicki tells her she doesn't like those chips. Emily eats around ten (I'm counting) of them throughout the session. That's a lot, since they're bigger than her hand. Nicki told me that she usually gets the smaller size at the store, but these big ones were on sale, and she got them for a dollar off.

Emily's working on the computer and eating chips, and Nicki's saying that she shouldn't be treating my computer like that, but I, for the umpteenth millionth time say that the thing is pretty hard to mess up and that I know this from experience.

The only problem was that I'd forgotten the mouse pad again. I could hear Emily mashing chip crumbs with the mouse. Nicki insists on getting uptight. I finally tell her point blank, "Don't worry, I know what I'm doing."

With Emily's help, I set the "Alarm Clock" under the apple menu for about 2 more minutes. It goes off (it sounds like an old-time wind-up alarm clock), and it's Mike's turn. Emily gives up the computer, inviting her brother to the seat. I hold Emily like I was holding Mike. I tell Mike he's got to make a new document and do a little graduated guidance with him, but he wants me to do more; he's not holding on to the mouse like his sister. He lets go of the mouse when I attempt to assist. I ask him to leave his hand there so I can "show" him what to do.

We make a new document and Emily says, "Save!" So we save. I tell Mike to just type his name there in the box. I point to the dialog box and Mike is baffled. What could be more simple? I hear Emily say, "Type!" and she points to the keys he should hit. I suffer some kind of ethical dilemma about whether I should let Mike find the keys or not without her, and then just let Emily show him, because he's slow.

Mike wants to use the eyedropper right off the bat. Why the eyedropper? I just don't get it. I tell him not to worry about it right now; we'd get to it later. Then he wants to use the eraser, but there's nothing there to erase. I show him how to use the paintbrush. And show him how to pick a color. "Pick a color," says Emily. "What color?" says Mike. I tell him to pick any color, and he picks some kind of olive drab, puke green color. Nicki says that they'd be good (her kids) in the Army, wouldn't they? Emily uses that green color too.

Nicki is pretending to do "paperwork" while I'm teaching her kids. She has some forms that look ominously familiar to me. She catches me looking and she says these are "the IFSP's,[1] I don't remember too much

---

[1] Individualized Family Service Plan.

about them, Dan. Maybe they just filled them out and I signed them; I don't remember."

I'd brought along some magic markers and some art paper because I wanted to make sure we had a fall-back position for the noncomputer kid. Nicki and I joked about how although I'd forgotten the mouse pad, I'd remembered the markers. I told her my act was together, if only barely. Nicki didn't like me using my "expensive" paper for the kids, even though I thought it would be a treat. She gets out some typing paper for the kids that she "buys by the ream."

Emily is using the markers to draw a picture of a yellow sun with a baby blue smiley face, and yellow rays, with a dark blue cloud and rain coming down on a house with a door and two windows. Nicki asks me what it is that Emily is drawing, and I say, "I believe that's a rain cloud." I know this because of the sound that Emily makes as the rain hits the roof. After a couple of turns, Nicki shows Emily how to make a chimney on the house. Nicki keeps telling the kids that they'd buy Dan another tablet and I try to tell her that I'd bought the paper for her kids. She is sitting on a chair looking down at Emily, who she says is lying on the floor nicely.

Nicki tells me that Emily has stopped saying "S-H-U-T U-P" (Nicki spells it for me), and replaced it with, "Hey, you can't do that." Which is much more appropriate, Nicki tells me.

I think that Emily was playing peek-a-boo with me. She would look in the TV in the office. She was looking at me, through the reflection, because when I'd look at the TV I could see her eyes. When I looked, she would look away and laugh. I didn't realize what we were doing when we were doing it. Nicki tells me that it's nice that she is looking at herself in the TV because Emily doesn't like to look at herself. Nicki notices that Emily's looking into the TV and says, "That's you, Emily."

Nicki brings me an apple and an orange. Emily says, "Apple." Nicki didn't want to get her one because of the mess it would make on the computer. I say that a little apple won't hurt things. Nicki goes to get an apple for Emily, who grabs mine and takes a bite. I say, "What do you say?" She says "Thank you."

The alarm goes off, and it's Mike's turn again. Emily yields. Mike is planning how he is going to paint so big with the computer that it's going to go off the screen. I ask him about this, and he makes big circles around the screen with his left index finger. I say, "Hey, do you want to use some pictures?" He says "Ya." I try to open the SuperPaint file that I made for Emily that has some clip art in it, but we're out of memory, because the kids have made such large files, and there's not enough to open another. Mike gets really impatient while we close down his sister's file. He says, "What are we doing? I want pictures." I tell him that he has to wait. I say that there's a lot of waiting when you work on the computer because it has to think. I say, "See the watch, that means it's thinking." We finally get the file open. I have packed the file with pictures, including some dinosaurs. He tells me he wants a picture of a Tyrannosaurus Rex with a Fender Stratocaster guitar.

I try to show and tell him how to copy and paste the picture into his file, but he removes his hand from the mouse every time I try to use a physical prompt and says things like, "You do it, dad, I mean, Dan." I help him get the picture into his file. I tell him he can pick a color and fill in the dinosaur. "What color, how do I do it?" He makes a couple of mistakes and is disappointed and gets a little frustrated. I know this because he says something like, "Aw, leave it like that."

"Pick a color!" says Emily.

We go on like this for a while, taking turns, eating, coloring, and having fun. I think Michael is a little burnt out after a couple of hours. He's relying on me to do the work with the program. I set the alarm for the last time, and Emily has to shut down the computer. She's a little fussy but complies.

Nicki asks her if she wants to watch TV. She tells me that Monday would be a good time to work with Emily, because CDL isn't in session that day. I say that's good for me. I say to Emily, "See you Monday!" but she is lost in the tube. I say my good-bye's to the speaking people and hit the road.

January 17, 1994

I wore my big boots that were easy to kick off at the front door. Emily has on her ballerina slippers, and she's standing in the office, looking at me, probably hoping that I'd turn around the computer so she could turn it on. Emily turns on the computer, and watches the StartUp action, looks at Nicki and points where the init icons will appear, and then counts them and claps for the Thelonius Monk StartUp sound. I *still* have trouble getting Emily to double click on the hard disk icon. Actually, she is just messing around, dragging it this way and that. I wasn't saying anything, or doing anything. Nicki asks me if I'm seeing what she'll do, and I say, "ya."

All of a sudden I hear, "Help!" Emily's shut the computer down and doesn't look too happy about it. "Can you restart it, Emily?" She doesn't say. I show her where the "Restart" button is on the shut down screen, and she starts it up, and starts calling for her mom, she counts the inits, claps for Monk, and points to the screen and says, "People!" I say "Ya, that's my Grandpa and his Uncle Fritz."

The AfterDark control panel icon had a shooting star, and Emily points to it and looks at me. I say, "Shooting star, Emily. It moves, doesn't it?"

We work on the computer for the rest of the afternoon and make some headway on the book activity.

At one point, Emily turns around in her chair and puts her slipper on my knee and looks at me. "Pick a color!" she says, and I pat her foot, rub her instep a little, and say, "Thank you, Emily."

Nicki's asking me a little bit about my research, "What do you do, write a diary?" I tell her that's about it. She said she wondered, because she's in "science, where you generate hypotheses, and do experiments." I tell her I don't know Emily well enough to generate a hypothesis, and that for now, I like working on the computer with her.

Emily learns how to use the microphone for her book. She records, and then listens to the sound, and starts to talk when she hears her recorded voice on the computer. She puts the microphone up to her ear, and says "Hello?"

Nicki tells me that Emily's taken a great deal of interest in the telephone, which is, "a mixed blessing, because she's really motivated to talk, but doesn't know what to say."

We work for a couple of hours, and I go. Nicki turns on the TV for Emily, who doesn't say goodbye.

January 18, 1994

I called up Nicki to make a meeting to try to begin to clarify my research project with her, since she seemed to be interested on Monday.

She tells me that she knows Emily best and that she'd be a good person to talk to. I agree, and mention that since she knows about the research process, I'd like to work with her, and maybe she could help me work on formulating some problems for investigation.

I ask if I could say "Hi" to Emily.

"Shoes," she says. Nicki told me Emily'd been wearing her high heels around that were too high, even for herself. I heard Emily coming to the phone, clomp, clomp, teeter, clomp.

"High heel shoes?" I ask.

Emily says, "Mommy's shoes."

"Are you wearing your mom's shoes?"

"Shoes."

We talk like this for a while.

I hear Nicki say it's her turn to talk and says to me that she doesn't want to take up any more of my time, and we say goodbye.

January 24, 1994

Emily was watching "Porky Pig" when I got there, and it looked like she'd just finished a bowl of cereal. I went in to say "Hi," but she was being shy, or something. Emily wasn't engrossed in the tube, but she didn't seem to know what to do about me. She wandered around, rocked in front of the tube, looked at me from time to time, and Nicki suggested that I just go in and turn on the computer. I was happy to, because it was a brand new LC 475.

I started to look at the Animal Program, one that Nicki had bought. Emily came in and climbed up on my lap. Nicki brought me some taco chips (small size, about the size of a silver dollar) and some salsa, an apple, and a bag of some kind of crackers.

Me and Emily started playing the Animal game. It shows you a picture of an animal, and you type in the name and the computer says whether you are right or not. The main menu asks you to select from categories like prehistoric animals, animals of the night, birds, insects, and so on. I disagree with how they labeled some of the animals. For instance, a sea gull is called "gull," but a duck is called "mallard."

There's an eagle, and Emily calls it an "eagle" but it's a "bald eagle." It looks nothing like a bald eagle, more like a condor. But over the course of the afternoon, Emily learns to call it a "bald eagle." She points at the word "bald" and then "eagle."

It's funny to hear (and see) her talk with her mouth full of taco chips. I can hardly understand her in the best of circumstances. She's trying to say "spider." Try that sometime, with your mouth full of taco chips. You will see what I mean. Nicki tells me Emily eats no chips except when I'm around.

She doesn't like Coke, Nicki tells me, but Emily pours it in my glass and says, "bubbles!" I stick my glass under her nose, and she says, "That smells good!"

The computer screen is dark, and we can see each other's faces on the glass. Emily clasps her hands over her head and cheers, "Yay, Emily!"

when we get a correct answer. We were having trouble discriminating between a seal and a walrus. I said, "Walrus." Emily looked into the screen and put her hands around my beard and made eye contact with me in our reflected faces. Still looking into the screen, she asks, "Man, how'd you do that?" I told her I did it with my brain. (Nicki said it was better for her to call me "Man" than "Nana"). A picture of a catfish came up and she said, "Catfish." I said, "Emily, how'd you do that?" She didn't know, or didn't say, so I said, "You did it with your brain, kiddo." She put her finger to her cheek and thought about that for a minute.

We played this game for about an hour. At first I was trying to get her to sound out words, and she was starting to get some of the consonants, like "t" and "b," but I kind of gave up, because I wanted to teach her how to type with two hands. I'd support her elbows, and she'd extend her index fingers, and we'd type. I know where the letters are on the keyboard, and I'd get her finger close to the right letter and she'd (in her parlance) "Push the button!" I could feel her working to hit the right letters, and we were getting pretty fast.

A new animal would come up. I'd keep my hands on my lap and ask Emily, "What in the world is that?" and she'd say, "A butterfly!" I'd say something like, "I hope you're right ...." Then, Emily'd pick up my hands from my lap so we could type the letters really fast.

Nicki is sitting at the other desk working on something. She said, "You guys are silly."

We'd type "butterfly." Then she'd have to hit return to see if we got the right answer. She'd zero in on the return key, hover around it, put her index finger to her lips, and I'd say, "You're scared, Emily; ha, ha, ha, Emily's scared!" Then she grabbed my index finger and made it hit the return key.

We played a different game that involved looking at the pictures of six animals, and then when you clicked, it hides the animals and asks you where the bald eagle is, or whatever. You could set up the program for two players. So it would ask, "Emily, where's the whale?" Or, "Dan, where's the tapir?" I think Emily learned my name. She'd say, "Dan, Help," or "Help, Dan," and stab my finger at the mouse. Sometimes she'd say, "Emily, where's the ...," when really it said "Dan," on the screen. I'd have to point at the place on the screen where my name was, and she'd say, "Dan."

But, she generally wouldn't let me have my turn, unless she was not certain whether her response was going to be correct, in which case, she'd grab my finger and make it elect the choice. My finger felt really big in her little hand. A few times, she'd grab my index fingers and make them type. Usually we got the first letter right.

At one point, I tried to make Emily use Microsoft Word, and when we launched the program, Nicki said, "How'd you *do* that?" I tried to show her, but Emily said, "You can't *do* that!" Emily didn't like working in Word in general, so we switched to SuperPaint.

Emily does some of the usual stuff and then selects the polygon tool. "Pick a color," she says, and presses the *c* "button" (I'll have to remember to tell her they're called "keys"; I didn't remember what the buttons were called at the time) to call up the color palette, and selects a pinkish color. Then she goes to work. As she experiments with the tool, I gradually begin to understand how the polygon tool works. I never had the patience to figure out the rules before. I just sit there and watch her, and by trial and error, she gets the hang of it. She made something that looked like a geode, but I called it an ice palace.

Nicki's trying to write over at the other desk, and she has a thesaurus. She says she just doesn't have any words. I wonder if she thinks that she should write by hand, and then type the material into the computer. I wonder if she knows that Microsoft Word has a thesaurus.

Emily and I keep on working in SuperPaint until about 3:00. Then we kind of disband. I show Nicki some basic stuff about Word and get ready to go. We forget to transition.

When I got home, I launched SuperPaint and played with the polygon tool.

January 31, 1994

When I got over to Emily's, I could hear excited commotion behind the door. I think Nicki was trying to get Emily to open the door for me, but Nicki wound up opening the big door, and I could see Emily standing behind the screen door with her finger in her mouth. Nicki says, "She was so excited when you drove up." Emily wanders around a little while I take off my boots.

Nicki goes to turn on the computer, and Emily follows us in there, and starts to get on the chair. There's a pillow with a blanket wrapped around it over against the wall, and Nicki points to it and says, "Emily sits on that, the blanket keeps it from sliding around so much." I ask Emily if she wants to sit on my lap; Nicki asks Emily if she wants to sit on my lap. Emily doesn't respond in a way that makes any sense to me.

I tell her I'd like to teach her how to write sentences today. Emily says: "Sentences!" So I pick her up and set her down in my lap, and she double clicks to open up the hard disk and starts talking about "Reader Rabbit" ("Reader Rabbit, Rabbit, Rabbit") and I say "Let's try to learn sentences and work in Word." I bet that sounded like more fun than a barrel of monkeys.

I prompt Emily to open the Word folder, and then the Word program. Emily has definitely "got" double clicking. Well, she's been using it, and I've tried to be objective about her use of it thus far, but she hasn't really been *that* consistent. But now she is. She's had practice on the new computer, I can tell. She clicks twice, and if that doesn't work, she clicks twice again.

Sometimes when I'm teaching people I get prideful and perhaps brag on them, and when they start not doing what they're supposed to (that is, what I've allegedly taught them), I get anxious. For instance, early on, I talked about Emily being able to hold onto the clicker and lift the mouse to reposition it so that she could move the cursor to a different spot on the screen without rolling off the mouse pad. Since then, every time she has to do this I start getting uptight that her initial progress in this area had led me to enthusiastically jump to erroneous conclusions. But today, she kept running into the keyboard one time, and then finally lifted the mouse up and smacked it back down on the other side of the mouse pad.

I can now report with confidence (and pride) that Emily can open files and folders by double-clicking. That means it's time to teach her how to select a file and open it with the "Open" option in the File menu.

Emily's got Word open, and I say, "Watch me!" I wanted her to learn about sentences in this manner: I'd type a sentence, and then Emily'd hit return and type the same sentence, using match to sample. I want to impress the little girl with my typing skills. I type out, "Snnu ;obrd om s noh ejoyr hpidr/" just as fast as I can.

"Uh oh!" says Emily. I look over her head and I see that my hands were off the "home row" or whatever by one button. Emily hits the delete key and wipes out my work.

"Let's try again," I say, *just* as cheerfully as I can. I type it out, this time right. "Now it's your turn."

"You turn," says Emily when she hits the "return" button.

I wait for a little tiny bit for Emily to make a correct response by hitting the "e" button, and when no response seemed to be forthcoming, I delivered the verbal prompt, "Emily, type your name," which worked.

Then I had to tell her each letter to type. I was all ready to do the physical support thing with her elbow, but she shook my hands off.

Emily's having a little trouble typing because she has some field notes that I wanted to give to Nicki clutched in her right hand, holding them against her chest. She pulls them out and looks at them from time to time, and says, "Ohhhh!, Emily!" and points to where her name is printed in a couple of different places. I try to take them away from her, but she keeps them with her all day. I am not mean when I try to take them away from her, I just suggest that she place them on the (fucking) desk (for Christ's sake) so that she can use two hands to type. Instead, she holds them with her left hand when she types with her right hand and vice versa.

I don't know why I don't try to take them away from her. They are a distraction, but I'm looking at her holding them, and thinking that they're about her. I say, "Look, Emily, I wrote about *you*." She can hold on to them forever if she wants.

Things get really complicated when Nicki brings out some food that she'd made for me. There were some bagels and cream cheese. She didn't spread any of the cream cheese on the bagels because she said everyone's different; they like different amounts of cream cheese on their bagels. Nicki said she'd make me a grilled cheese sandwich, and I really wanted one. I wanted one like a little boy wants one, so I said I'd love some bagels.

She brought me an apple, too, and Emily stole it. This really complicated her typing efforts. Apple in one hand, field notes in the other—hold the apple in the same hand as the field notes? No, that doesn't work. Put the field notes in the lap? No, they could fall off, or I might take them.

It's a Rome apple. Nicki always gets Rome apples (Nicki reads this and tells me that they're Gina apples, and that she doesn't always get them, just at this time of year). Nicki brings me out another apple for me and a plate, a paper plate with a snowy Christmas tree with a big star at the top and snowflakes in the air. The ink is royal blue. Emily picks up the plate and points to the tree, and says, "Christmas," to me with a moderate amount of significance. She turns her head toward me. I say, "plate," thinking that in the general scheme of things that she should put the apple on the plate for god's sake and put the plate on the desk. Apples go on plates; plates go on desks.

Emily says, "Christmas" and looks at me. I look at her big blue eyes and think about that stupid journal article about cute little autistic kids with their big beautiful eyes with long lashes; I get choked up just a little and look away from Emily. I look at the plate, point to a snowflake, and say, "Snowflake."

Emily says, "Snow."

We sit there, eating apples. Emily puts her arm around my neck. She tries to hug me but what with an apple, a paper Christmas plate, and some field notes....

"Reader Rabbit?" I suggest.

We go back to the finder and locate the "Reader Rabbit" folder, and Emily manages to steady her stuff long enough open the folder and the application. I'm not paying too much attention. The main menu comes up, and Emily selects a game that has twelve squares and behind each box is a picture of like a fishin' pole, a dot (an arrow points to the 'dot' on an 'i') and some other things. Nicki comes in and says, "It's interesting how they try to teach these concepts, isn't it? Sometimes, it just doesn't make too much sense, at least to me."

A little window comes up with a picture of a mouse and a hand clicking it, and Emily says, "Click the mouse!" Then you have to click on a box to reveal what lies behind it. If it's a fishin' pole, then you have to guess where the other fishing pole is. This game is child's play for Emily. So we play. She makes my finger make initial choices until she knows where everything is. Then she starts matching, making the selections herself. We fool around with this game for a while. When Emily gets a correct match, I say, "Superb!" and Emily says, "SuperPaint!"

Emily goes to the bathroom. I get off the chair, and I think I'll sit or kneel in front of the computer. I wanted to be where I could look at Emily. So I put the pillow up on the chair, and Emily climbs up on it when she gets back.

After a little bit, we switch to SuperPaint. I get Emily in the draw layer for the first time. I show her what handles are on draw objects. She puts the pointer on a handle and says, "Handle."

I show her how to select "Free Rotate" from the Transform menu, and how to turn an object around and around. She makes the object (a rounded corner rectangle) different colors and then turns it around and around like a pinwheel and then makes it a different color. And turns it around and around again. We distort things and stretch them.

Emily goes into the Apple menu and gets the Scrapbook. This is driving Nicki crazy, because we now have Word, SuperPaint, Reader Rabbit, and the Scrapbook all open.

"Close it!" says Nicki.

I say, "Use it!"

I show Emily how to copy one of her creations from SuperPaint into the Scrapbook. This takes a bit of doing, because Emily has to look at each and every picture in the Scrapbook, and I'd forgotten how it works (I don't use it). "There's another!" she says, as a picture of a pink party hat and some confetti appears in the Scrapbook window.

Nicki simply can't handle having all these applications open at one time and grabs the mouse from Emily and starts frantically closing windows. She gets it back to where just Reader Rabbit is open and says, "There, that's better."

All of the programs are still running, but Nicki doesn't know this. I'm a little surprised that there's still enough RAM to handle what's been going on, because they only have 8 K. In fact, we'd just got a message on the screen that told us that the computer was going to make us close the hard drive window (Nicki had somehow missed this one). I closed it. Nicki said, "That's the message my husband was getting! He said it was because we had too much stuff on the disk. How'd you fix it? There's not that much on the disk is there? Are we really running out of room?" I quail under this barrage and just tell her they aren't going to run out of room for a long time. I guess Mark was on his kid's case for making too many files. "Nicki," I say, "just do what the computer tells you to do and you'll be OK," and I keep focused on Emily.

Emily's slouched back in the chair, and Nicki's leaning over it with her arms crossed over the top, rocking Emily back and forth. Emily is languorously making choices in the Reader Rabbit game, not really paying attention to what's going on. Nicki gives her some grief—teases her—about this, but Emily's just playing, and we both know it.

"Emily, let's work in Word."

"OK."

I show her where the Word folder is again, and she launches the program. She plays "little typist." I snatch the mouse and jack up the font size to 24 pt. While Emily's playing typist, I see that every once in a while she types, 'cat.' I decide to use this against her.

I say, "Type 'Emily cat!'" What could be more fun!

She types 'emily cat.' I have to tell her to make a space. Eventually, Emily will understand the importance of spaces, and maybe she does now, but I don't know. I say "Hit 'return.'" She says, "You turn!" and taps the return key. I notice that she either whacks a button or puts her finger on it and slowly depresses the key until it makes a letter on the screen. "Delete" is one that she whacks.

Then I tell her, "Type 'Dan Cat.'" I tell her the letters, "d-a-n <space!> c-a-t." The space is very important to me. Emily hits the buttons, searching with whatever finger happens to be free of field notes, plates, apples, or whatnot. Emily has been eating that apple for about an hour.

We go through this process and wind up with a list that looks like this:

EMILY CAT
DAN CAT
KITTY CAT
MICHAEL CAT
MOM CAT
DAD CAT

I stick my finger at each of the words, and Emily says them to me. She says "Keee cat" for kitty cat and "Mommy Cat" for Mom cat, and "Daddy cat" for dad Cat. "Mike Cat" for Michael Cat.

At one point, I stopped sticking my finger at the words, and Emily picked it up and jabbed it at the screen. Then she started saying the words again. I don't know what to think about her reading Mom as "Mommy," so I let it go.

I'm at a serious loss here. I can't think of any more words. Then I use a trick that I've learned: "Use your eyes, Dan." Mom used to tell me that and probably still would. I'm supposed to look out of my eyes to see things that I can't find.

So I looked out my eyes and saw that Emily was sitting in a chair, and we wrote, "CHAIR CAT." Then I noticed we were in a house, and we wrote, "HOUSE CAT." I was on a roll. I said, "COMPUTER CAT," and "KEYBOARD CAT."

Nicki comes in while my finger is pointing to CHAIR and prompts Emily: "What are you sitting on? CHHHH, CHHHHH," and then whispers 'chair' to Emily.

Emily says, "Chair cat."

Nicki asks, "How'd you get Emily to *do* that?" She was talking about using the return key to make a list of sentences.

"I don't know," I said, "Maybe just luck." I didn't want to elaborate on how I'd been ineptly trying to get her to do this since we first started on the Mac.

She loses interest in the game and uses the application menu (I think I helped her) to go back to Reader Rabbit. It's about 3:00, so I get ready to go. Nicki tells me that Emily comes home now and tries to tell her things about school, like, "House." And then she gets out a picture of a house she worked on.

February 7, 1994

I meet Emily and Nicki at the door of the Children's Research Center. We go to the stairs, and Emily points to her ears, and Nicki tells me that she'd got her ears tested here about a month ago and probably thought it was going to happen again. We go down the stairs, and Emily holds on to the banister with one hand and my hand with the other. She kind of floats. We get to my office and play with the computer for a while. Nicki brought me a cold caffeine-free Coke, an apple, and some crackers. Emily and I share everything except the Coke, even though Nicki is telling her that she isn't hungry.

We go up to the Xerox machine to do some copying. Janis is up there and I start to figure out what to do, while Janis takes firm control and introduces herself to Nicki, who says she's "Emily's mom"; "Nicki Jackson," I interject. I point to Emily and say, "Janis, this is Emily; Emily, this is Janis." Janis gets down on one knee and looks at Emily, and says, "Hello, Emily," and smiles. Emily doesn't know what to do about Janis, but she points at me and says, "That's Dan!" and starts jumping around like she was in some kind of Michael Jackson video, laughing her fool head off. "I know," Janis says, "he's a funny guy isn't he?" We watch Emily and laugh with her, and Janis leaves after a while.

That was the first time Emily said my name without anything from anybody. I was in awe, because I think she psyched that situation out so nicely.

I get her a stool to stand on so she can press the buttons on the Xerox machine, and when she hits the green one, she leaps into the air and I support her under her arms and let her down gently. Emily runs around to the back of the machine, bends at her waist, sticks her arms out like a fledgling chick, and wiggles her fingers until the copy comes out.

She says, "Ohhhhhhh!" when a copy comes out and puts it in a pile. Emily helps me cut out a pie chart with the paper cutter. I call it a finger chopper. Nicki laughs, but me and Emily make sure the cutter bar is all the way down when we're done.

I lay the pie chart on a piece of blank paper and tape the top down. I give Emily a piece of tape and she tapes down the bottom. We open up the paper cartridge in the Xerox machine and put in an overhead transparency. Emily gets up on the stool and presses the button. And leaps with abandon into the air. I catch her again and she runs around back.

We cut out a bar graph, and I lay it down on another piece of paper, and this time, Emily just takes the tape from the dispenser and tapes the graph to the paper. We open up the cartridge, and put in an overhead. Emily flies up onto the stool, and presses the button, floats to the floor and slides around back, gracefully receiving the overhead with two hands like she was the queen. She places it in a pile with the other overhead, and signals for me to lift the lid of the machine. Emily takes the original and puts it with the other one.

We gather up all the papers and overheads, and Emily doesn't want me to take some of my stuff and starts crying. Nicki and I try to help her out by making a Xerox of her hands, but Emily pulls them away because she doesn't want that light bar to go under them, and Nicki puts her hand there. This ploy is totally ineffective, because Emily knows which overheads and handouts are the important ones. Kind of reminds me of playing with my dogs. If you are playing stick or ball with my dogs and try to distract one with another stick or ball, they always know which one is *the* stick or ball, whether you know it or not.

We head back down to my office, and Emily just throws a fit. Some woman from across the hall comes in to say hi to Nicki. Emily is trying to hit her mom, and is crying so bad it looks like her face has been out in the rain. We can't do anything. We try, I tell Nicki I'll just give her the copies, but alas, Emily "has to learn."

Nicki and Emily go, and I head out with them. Nicki's apologizing left and right, saying that I shouldn't be upset and so forth, and I remind her for the four billionth time that Emily's behavior is not going to bother me.

Later that day, I see Nicki and Emily and Mike at the special education office. They are getting a videotape I was supposed to get for them this AM. When I see them, I remember what's supposed to have gone down. Nicki says that she was afraid that she'd see me there, and I would be guilt tripped, which I was. I say "Hi" to the kids, and Nicki tells me, "See, she's calm now, she calmed down right after we left the office." Surprise! Mike says, "The office?" I say, "Ya, we went to the office." He looks sad, and I say, "Do you want to come to the office sometime?" He says yes.

I look at Emily and she says, "Hi, Dan!"

Mike has some kind of dinosaur in his hand.

February 14, 1994

When I get to Emily's white house, the big door is open. I knock or ring or something, and Emily comes to the door, touches the handle, and moves away. I open up the door, and Nicki says hi, and turns to Emily who is in the corner. Nicki tells me that she was trying to get Emily to open the door for me.

Emily's over in the corner of the living room, and she glances up at me. Nicki says, "You're not going to be shy, are you?" From the corner, Emily looks at her mother and at me quickly and says, "Movie!" Nicki says yes, there's a movie on, and Emily runs to the TV. And sidles over toward me, and Nicki asks her, "What do you want to do with Dan?"

"PUTER!" comes the response.

I ask Emily if she'll help me print.

"Print!"

So Emily settles down in the chair, and I tell Nicki that I've finally come up with an informed consent form, and maybe we could print it. I turn on the computer and touch the monitor button, and we talk about something, I can't remember what. Emily gets a little restless, and points to the monitor on/off switch, and says "screen." "Dan turned it on," Nicki tells her. But it's dark, and I check and I hadn't turned it on. I'm a little disappointed that Emily didn't turn it on herself.

I start to give Emily the disk that has the informed consent document on it. Nicki takes it from me and inserts it into the drive. My finger points to the disk icon, and I say "Open." Emily double clicks it, and there's a few documents in there, including one called "consent emily." I look at the titles and am relieved that I didn't have any on them with smartass sarcastic double entendre names. Just regular old names. I say, "Find Emily," and Emily points the mouse to each of the icons and finds "consent emily," and opens it.

I ask her to print it. She goes under the File menu and highlights Print; she looks at me like she's trying to get permission. I say "Print it, kiddo!" Nicki has to tell her it's OK. "It's OK, Emily, print it." I get the feeling that there may have been incidents.

Nicki told me once how this kiddy book program printed out 40 pages and that was kind of appalling. Emily lets loose of the mouse button and hops out of the chair. Nicki says, "It's not that exciting, Emily." But it is. Emily flexes at her waist, does her bird wing thing, and watches the paper come out. There's two pages; I just wanted it on one. I guess the little printer does different things to documents than a laser printer, so I reset the top and bottom margins.

Nicki says, "It's just amazing to watch someone who knows what they're doing. Mark worked on that for hours." And I tell her someday, she'll get to where it's second nature.

I check the page break and ask Emily to print it again, and she's a little hesitant again. And gets pretty excited again when the StyleWriter prints. And does her cute little repetitive behavior.

Nicki is asking me whether I think kids should learn to use a mousepad. She said that at Emily's school, the "lady" wasn't teaching the kids how to use the mousepad, and they were just running that mouse all over the place. I can't remember whether I passed judgment on this practice. I think I said that I thought it was a good idea, but I didn't say how hard I know it is for people to learn the skill. Personally, I think the lady was taking the easy way out.

I tell Nicki I was thinking about teaching Emily how to play Spectre (I felt like I had to ask and was worried about it because one time Nicki said that she'd better not let Emily see Spectre because she'd get overstimulated by it), and she said that Mark plays it with her. I'd stayed up half of the night last night playing the game, exasperating as it was, trying to figure out how me and Emily could play it. I thought that I could manipulate our battleship through cyberspace, and she could blast tanks. I sat on the chair, and she got on my lap.

I did start with manipulating our battleship, and Emily knew how to blast tanks. You use the space bar to blast away and the keypad to move the battleship through cyberspace. She got a little bored with this, I think, even though she was happy to blow up tanks. I'd say, "Thank you, Emily," and she'd say "Thank *you*, Dan."

But, she didn't like me maneuvering the tank. I know this because she put her right arm under my right arm and lifted it off the keypad. I sighed, and knew that I was going to have to teach her how to use the keypad.

I did it like this. I selected a slow but sturdy battleship for us. I supported her elbow and positioned her hand over the keyboard. When the game started up, I just told her, hit 8 (go forward), hit 2 (go backward), and so on. I used different views of cyberspace, so that she could see what she was doing. I let her experiment, to see what would happen. She'd see a tank coming at us, and she'd say, "Uh oh!"

She'd run into something, and I'd say, hit 4 (go left). Emily starts to get the hang of it.

Nicki came in and said, "She figured that out?"

I said, "Ya, pretty much." I didn't say that the little rat would have it no other way. The little rat calls our battleship a "car." I try to show her how to use the "radar screen."

We play for a while and I discover that the arrow keys do the same things as the keypad, and I try to get Emily to work with the arrow keys, because I know it would be easier for her, but this is just too much. She gets frustrated. She wants to use the keypad; then she wants to use the arrows. We get destroyed over and over by the red tanks. I want her to try the arrows. Nicki suggests we do something else ("You see, she got overstimulated"), like Reader Rabbit. We find it and open the program, and we're going to do the memory game again, it looks like.

Emily launches Reader Rabbit, and some information box comes up and tells us that the volume may be set too low. I tell Emily to go to the Control Panels, and then help her select Sound. It's all the way up, so we go back to Reader Rabbit, and apparently, everything's OK. Nicki asks if this is normal for a computer to act like that, and I say that Reader Rabbit doesn't follow standard Mac interface so it's hard to tell.

So we play, and Emily always wants my finger to press the mouse button if she's unsure. I needle her about this. I say, "Em-ilyee's scayr-ed, na, na, nana, na!" Nicki looks at me. Emily grabs my arm to make it hit the mouse button, and my arm and finger just go limp!

Emily takes her left hand off the keyboard and makes it push down her right finger on the mouse. When Nicki and I regain our composure, I say, "See, Emily's facilitating her own typing, isn't that nice?"

After a while, we go to work in SuperPaint.

While Emily's working in SuperPaint, Nicki strokes her hair, and says, "I'd like to do something with your hair, but you won't let me will you, Emily?" No response.

Then, I want to print the picture of the House of the Deaf and Dumb. Nicki want to know what that's all about. I tell her about Itard. She laughs, and says that's an appropriate name for the Father of Special Education. "EEtard, like REEtard."

I want one of the pictures, but Emily won't let me have one. "She learned that at the Xerox machine," Nicki tells me.

Emily takes her pictures of the House of the Deaf and Dumb and goes and sits on the overstuffed chair in the living room.

I bid farewell.

February 21, 1994

I called up Nicki at about 1:00, and she told me their computer was still getting repairs. So I go home, and get mine, and take it over. Emily's standing in the door, and she opens it for me! I practically drop the computer and hug her. Jill (who was a student teacher in Emily's classroom) is sitting in the living room talking with Nicki, talking about a shopping trip. They don't notice the remarkable success, the wonderful achievement that Emily had made. Well, I guess she did only get the door open enough for me to stick my boot in, but I still thought it was cool. We all trundle in to the office, and Nicki warns me that the VCR might start recording, because she was taping *Godzilla* for Mike.

Thus forewarned, I asked if she could take a few of the things off the desk so I could set down the computer. I plugged it in and turned it sideways so that Emily could turn it on, and her finger touched the rocker switch, but I had to physically prompt her to turn it on. Then, she had to get around front to watch the StartUp action.

Jill said, "Yours looks different than ours. How'd you get those pictures?" referring to the clever icons that I'd crafted.

"Dan knows how to do everything," Nicki told her.

I'm watching Emily, and I say that I'll show them how a little later.

Emily is standing in front of the computer and double-clicks on the Spectre icon. I hoist Emily on to my lap, and we start playing. Emily does not want me controlling our battleship. So I let her guide the machine around cyberspace while we get blasted to hell by the robots. I'm trying to prompt her by saying "press 8," "press 6," and so on. We play for a while.

"Mark moves the ship around, and the kids blast away. They were really proud the other day because they got to level 17 or something," Nicki tells us.

Emily gets very excited while we're playing and raises her hands up with her elbows pointed down and wiggles her fingers with her palms forward. Nicki tells me nonchalantly that they're trying to get Emily to stop that at school, by telling her "No," and putting her hands to the waist. The rationale is that when she gets to kindergarten, the kids will think she's weird.

I'm thinking that her teacher must not have enough to do. I say something like, "Well Nicki, you've had to deal with stuff like this before, what do you think?"

She tells me that the Autism Experts say to "just let it go."

I breathe an inward sigh of relief. This is probably the first sensible thing I've heard from the Autism Experts, and I start to think that maybe they're not so bad after all, and I feel a little solidarity with them.

Jill says, "I wiggle my fingers all of the time—just ask my husband—even when I'm ironing." We laugh.

Emily says, "Help!" She's crashed into something and doesn't know whether to press 4 or 6 or 8 or 2 or what. She keeps on pressing 5, which does nothing at all.

Nicki says, "That's another thing; how do you get out of that game if you want to, but you're not finished."

"Simple," I say, and press Command-Q, and we're out of that game. Emily looks at me, and Nicki says, "How'd you do that?"

"I pressed 'Command-Q.' That's how to quit virtually everything."

Wanting to impress Jill, I say, "Emily, do you want to take a look at your book?" I don't know if she said "yes," but I help her maneuver into her folder and we open up the book. Emily shows us how it works, and Jill asks me if that's ClarisWorks or something, and I say that its a Claris program named "FileMaker." Emily goes through the book and gets to the end and I suggest SuperPaint.

Emily's working in SuperPaint, and the discussion concerning whether or not they ought to be modifying Emily's "self-stimulatory" behavior at school resumes. I say something like, "Well, if you're really worried about it, bring it up at the IEP meeting, and if they don't do what you want, you can take them to due process." I smile sweetly.

Emily's making a nice painting. She says "Book!" I about shit, and say, "Yes! we'll put it in your book." I help her choose the selection tool and we select an area of her painting. Then I say "Cut!" and get her to the Edit menu, and she pulls down to Cut, and cuts the selection out of the picture. Then I help her get FileMaker going by selecting it from the application menu. I slyly press Command-N to get a new record and grab Emily's mouse hand to click in the picture field and then say "Paste!," and she goes to the Edit menu and selects Paste, and her picture is pasted in the field.

Then, Emily plays "little typist" in the text box, and I suggest that we make a sound. I get up and plop Emily down on the chair and get the microphone. After I plug it in, I help Emily double-click the sound field, and I hit the record button. I say "Talk, Emily!" She's been making a bunch of bubbly looking things but just eats chips into the microphone. It really sounds like it when we play it back.

Emily keeps eating potato chips like a pig, and Nicki apologizes to us and reminds us frequently that she actually does feed Emily from time to time. In the text field of the book, we write, "emily's eating potato chips."

Emily goes off to the bathroom, and we hear some yelling and screaming. Jill asks me if I think Emily's being funny (she does seem a little subdued today—Nicki mentioned that Emily was a little disappointed when Jill walked in the door first instead of me) because she's here, and I say I really don't know.

Emily comes back, and I ask her if she wants to work on sentences. She says, "Sentences!?" so we open up Word. She plays little typist for a while, and Nicki asks if I think it would be instructionally appropriate to introduce the word cards at this juncture, and after careful consideration, I judge this intervention to be warranted.

While Nicki's getting the word cards, I show Emily how to change to color of the text on the screen with the Character dialog box from the Format menu. This is great fun. Then, more to impress the assembled grownups than anything else, I show Emily how to change the text highlight color, using the color Control Panel. I can just tell Emily to get Control Panels and she does. Emily chooses a gaudy purpley-pink that looks like the color of a Popsicle.

Emily takes the word cards and puts them on her lap. She selects one and leans it against the monitor and types it out. She hits return and makes a list but stops at the bottom of the page. I wonder if she thinks the words will go away if they are not all on the screen.

We try the pinball program I'd brought over. It takes a while for Emily to learn that she can keep the ball alive with the flippers. She wants to wiggle her fingers and look at the ball and doesn't seem a bit concerned when she gets drained. Then I hold one of her fingers on the "z" key that controls the left flipper. She keeps her right hand in the air, wiggling like a bunch of squirming worms. She's getting the hang of the right flipper, but she keeps wanting to put both her arms up in the air. I tell her "hands on the keyboard!," and she puts her left hand on the "z" key. I keep trying to push her right hand onto the "/" key to control the left flipper. I tell her to keep her hands on the keyboard.

We go through a couple of games like this, and finally, Emily learns to use the "/" key. It's not easy for her; she wants to put her hands up and fly away because the pinballs are so pretty. She does and I tell her to "put your hands on the keyboard" and she does. Quickly. She doesn't look at me or anything; she just puts her hands back down. She moves her face up close to the screen, and I can see her face and eyes tracking the ball. It is amazing. She flips that ball up to the top of the machine, left, right, right, right, left.

She knows how to start new games from the File menu, of course.

Jill has to go back to school and says goodbye. She and Nicki finalize some plans about shopping.

"Well," I say to Nicki, "that's one way to get Emily to quit wiggling her fingers."

March 7, 1994

I call up Nicki in the morning, and she says that the baby-sitter's coming over so that she can get out to do some errands. Nicki tells me that she's taking her computer to be worked on again tomorrow, that they're going to replace "the board." She wonders if I think that will fix it, and I don't know.

Hope comes with me, and we can see Emily at the screen door when we drive up. She's standing there smiling. Hope says she'll take the computer so that I can greet Emily. I go up to the door, and Emily runs around in little circles in the living room. Nicki opens up the door, looks at Hope, and says, "It's 1994, I guess." I suppose this means that Hope is acting as the beast of burden.

Emily runs up to us and says something I don't understand. Hope says the computer is getting heavy and goes into the office to set it down. Michael's in there at the computer, and he says that he's going to show me how to play "Lemmings." Nicki plugs in my computer. Hope settles down with Michael for a round of Lemmings, and the damn cat sits her lap. That's good, in a way, because I stepped on its tail a couple of times whilst we were getting settled, but it's bad because Hope is allergic to cats and will suffer.

The babysitter is there so that Nicki can do some errands while we play.

I grab Emily and stand her up on the desk so she can turn on the computer and help her bend around. "There she is!" referring to the rocker switch. She doesn't hit the switch that turns on the monitor. I help her down and she gets in the booster seat. I'm anxious to work on sentences, because that's what I'd been thinking about that day, among other things. I thought we could write sentences that read, "Emily is..." and fill in the blanks.

I'd wanted to make a long list:

Emily is cat;
Emily is strong;
Emily is funny;

and so on. So she could scroll up and down the list and see that the list wasn't going to disappear. But I hadn't done this. Instead, I opened up a document called "Holly," which is a story Hope and I had been writing about another little girl. We scrolled up and down through the story, and when we got back to the top, Emily typed, "emily." Real quick, I said, "is, space, 'i,' 's.'" Emily typed it and then she put her index finger on 'c' and we both knew she was going to type 'cat,' so I said, "cat." We typed a number of phrases, like 'emily is strong,' Emily is this and that.... She hit return after each phrase. This activity was messing up our "Holly" story, and I was a little concerned, but I figured that we could close it and not save any changes.

Emily stopped typing and scrolled down through the document and wiped out a couple of sentences by moving the insertion point to the end of the sentence and clicking and using the 'delete' key. She saved her changes before I knew what she was doing. Well, actually I saw what she was doing, and in a snap, I decided to let her do it, just because I didn't want to yell, "STOP!" or grab her hand or something. I had a hard copy at home, and Hope has one too, so I let it go. Maybe I groaned.

"There, that's better!" Emily said.

I think I kind of steered Emily into SuperPaint because I wanted to see how she'd do with the book today. I was pretty excited about how she was working with it last week. So we made a picture in SuperPaint, and cut it, and then opened up her book in FileMaker, and pasted it in there. I asked if she wanted to make a sound, and she said, "Yes." I got the microphone, and Emily double clicked in the sound field to open up the "record" dialog box. She said some things into the microphone. We made a couple of records like this, in the sense of new records, or pages for the data base book. One interesting thing was that for one of the records, when we were using the microphone, she started saying, "1, 2, 3, 4, 5, 6, 7, 8, 9?" She thought up saying numbers all by herself. We worked on the book for about half an hour and then played pinball. Emily was pretty good at this but still cheers when the ball escapes her flippers. Emily gets up to go to the bathroom. Mike comes over to my computer and wants to show me something in SuperPaint. He does and I show him how to cut pictures into the book. I notice he drops his hand to his lap when I offer hand-over-hand assistance. I worry that my hands are cold, but I explain to him that I'd like for him to keep his hand on the mouse so he can see what we're trying to do.

Emily comes back from the bathroom and gets on the other computer. I tease Emily for being fickle. I say, "Emily's got a new one, na, na, na, nana, na!" Emily swings her shoulders back and forth in the chair and smiles but doesn't look at me.

Michael is about to make a sound into the microphone, and following up on my teasing of Emily, he says, "Dan is throw-up, Dan is throw-up!" This elicits a fairly rapid response from Nicki, who does not want Michael to lapse into "toilet talk." I ask Nicki if "throw-up" is toilet talk, and she says, "No, but he knows what I'm talking about. If he starts using it, just remember he learned it from his dad." I laugh, and think about how Nicki's told me that she lapses into what I imagine is toilet talk when she uses the computer sometimes. She seems pretty concerned that Hope and I not think that her kids swear or at least that it's not her fault.

I'm watching Emily out of the corner of my eye and trying to pay as close to undivided attention to Michael as I could. I can hear Emily saying, "Cut!," and I'm dying to know what she's doing over there. Michael and I start playing pinball, which he says is easy. This initial impression of his does not last long, and he wants to play Kid Pix. I get the disk.

Hope, who's allergic, is really starting to suffer from the cat. I figure we'd better go and tell Nicki so, who apologizes profusely and says "that old cat doesn't need to be in here." I shut down my machine and we beat a hasty retreat. I ask Emily to get the door for us, and she does! She opens it up wide and says, "Bye, Bye, Dan, Bye." And we say goodbye to her to. A mind boggling performance. I've never seen Emily act like this before. She's yelling "Bye!" and a bunch of other things to us that I can't understand all the time we were walking out to the car. She's yelling to us when we get in the car. She's yelling to us when we drive down the street. I honk, and we wave.

March 9, 1994

I go over to try to fix Nicki's computer. I take out the Apple IIe processor, and Emily helps me with a screwdriver. I notice that Nicki is quick to put the tools away when we're finished.

I remove some of the inits that have to do with the processor and some of the applications that go along with it. Emily's in the other room with her babysitter relaxing. I work and work without results, and after an hour I finally figure something is wacky with the screen saver.

Emily comes in with an animal book. She scoops up a bird's nest and smooshes it up in her hands like a snowball and holds it out to me. I stick it in my pocket. She gets me a hippopotamus, and gives it to me. She scoops up a lion. They start fighting in my pocket, but they made friends, I said, and my pocket calmed down.

She scoops up a crocodile, but doesn't get the mouth I notice. I say, "Hey, I want the mouth, too!" Emily says, "NONONONONO!" I say, "YESYESYESYES!"

I tell Emily that I'm going to stick my finger in the crocodile's mouth, and my finger starts sliding into its jaws. Emily says, "NONONONONO!" and grabs my finger away.

March 14, 1994

I drove up just as Mark was leaving. He and Nicki hugged, and Emily waved bye-bye. I pulled up next to Mark's truck, and he signaled that I could stay there, but I backed out and parked on the street anyway.

Emily backs into her mom's legs and then runs to the front of the house and touches the front door and says, "Uh-Oh!" and then dashes into a corner and hides her eyes. Nicki comes around and Emily joins her and we walk in the door. Emily runs into the office and plops herself in the chair in front of the computer.

Emily wants to play this game called "Busy Town" or something like that on the CD-ROM, and so we do. It's a little bit boring, but I put up with it, trying to imagine what it's like to be a kid playing it. There's a fire station, a soda shop, the beach and wind, and some other places, actually a lot of places that a kid can go. You use the mouse to go to a place in the town and then click, and you go inside. If you go to the beach, the cursor turns into a whirl-wind, and you can blow the hats off people's heads, make a kite fly, fill the sails on a boat and blow a cloud in front of the sun. The screen dims when the cloud covers the sun. Emily says, "It's raining," and she raises her hands and wiggles her fingers while she lowers her arms and I can see that it is indeed raining.

Nicki brings us out some crackers and cheese, and I devour the stuff, because I'm starving. I feel like I haven't eaten in days. I like crackers and cheese. It makes me feel like I'm at a party.

We find ourselves at the soda shop, and customers keep coming in and wanting cake or broccoli and a glass of milk. The mouse makes this little cat-like creature scurry about getting the order ready for the customers. Emily doesn't spill any of the drinks, but Nicki tells me that Mike spills the drinks all the time just so he can see what happens.

Nicki brings me out some more food. I've about had it with this kid's perspective stuff, and somehow, I get Emily to quit the game.

"There!" she says.

Phew, I think, mentally wiping my brow.

"Let's write some sentences!" I exclaim enthusiastically.

"OK," says Emily, and I help her get Word open. My clever plan for the day is to make cat sentences and put voice annotations in them. But the microphone doesn't work. It says there isn't a voice annotation file in the System Folder.

We write some sentences, and somehow, I get Emily to use different words after her first word; today the first word is Emily. We write, "emily horse," "emily zebra," "emily big." I have to think up all of these words. Just any word will not do. "Emily frog," for instance, does not go over. Next time, I'll try some verbs.

I've been helping Emily type with two hands by supporting her at the elbows, and directing her fingers toward the right keys. When I stop moving her arm, she looks down and gently presses the key and uses "delete" if she makes a mistake.

After a while, we quit Word, and I get Emily to work on her book. We open up the book, and then open up the HyperCard file called Art Bits. I show her how to navigate through the stack. She picks out an apple, and we select it, and get "Copy Picture" from the Edit menu. "Coffee!" says Emily. "Cah pee!" I say. "Coffee!" says Emily. Semantics aside, we get the job done. I know she knows how to cut pictures but not copy. I'd taught her how to cut first so that she could see the picture disappear from the screen, figuring that might make a little more sense in the grand scheme of things. If you copy something, it's still there. If you cut it, it goes somewhere, and it seems like if something goes somewhere, you can put it back somewhere else.

And in this case, we open SuperPaint, and paste it into an Untitled document. Emily is happy to see it there, and I suggest that she color it. At this point, I still think the pumpkin is an apple, but Emily reminds me that it's a pumpkin.

"OK, smarty, what color's a pumpkin?" Emily selects a very nice shade of orange from the color pallet, and I show her how to get the paint bucket to dump orange paint all over the pumpkin. Then we select the pumpkin with the square selection tool, and "Coffee!" "Cah pee!" I say.

We open FileMaker from the Application menu, and I show Emily how to make a new record. "New Record!" I say with gusto. "New!" says Emily. We click in the picture field to activate it, and then I say "Paste!" and Emily pastes the picture into her book. She activates the text field, and we type "pumpkin" into the text field. The sound field is not working so we can't say anything into the microphone.

"Let's make another," I say.

"OK, Dan." She says my name!

I say, "Get HyperCard from the Application Menu." She knows where the Application Menu is, but I have to point my finger to guide her to the HyperCard application. Emily navigates through the stack and finds a picture of a Stegosaurus. We select it with the square selection tool, and she selects "Copy Picture" from the Edit menu. "Copy!" she says. And I am delighted.

I help her open SuperPaint and she pastes the picture into the document with the orange pumpkin. I show her how to move the Stegosaurus with the arrow. "What color is the Stegosaurus?" I ask. Emily used the paint bucket to make it yellow. Then she makes its fins purple. We have to use the magnifying glass to do this, and a couple of times she makes a mistake, and I show her how to select Undo from the edit menu. We have to use the magnifying glass because if you don't get the right place with the paint bucket, the whole screen, or the whole animal, or whatever, will turn the color of the paint that you're using. I show Emily how to use the space bar to make the "grabber" hand active so that you can scroll around in an enlarged picture. Emily pastes her picture in her book.

We print the record. Emily says, "Here it comes!"

Nicki says, "See, a complete sentence!" It is a wonderful complete sentence. Nicki helps Emily punch some holes in the print so that she can put it in a book that she's making of her computer drawings.

We make a penguin, and a man on a bicycle riding away from a baby that's floating down through the air. The man has rainbow colored pants on, and his face is flesh colored, and the bike has red tires. Emily uses the "grabber" hand, the magnifying glass, and the "Undo" option from the Edit menu without too much help from me.

Emily clicks in the text field underneath the man on the bike, and we type, "the man on the bike is riding away from his baby fast!" Nicki says that she's gonna put us away for child abuse. Emily is singing some song about "Happy, Happy, Joy, Joy, Joy." I thought we ought to write that in there, so we type "Happy," and then I figure I'll show her how to copy text, and we highlight "Happy," and Emily starts to resist. I sort of force her to copy it and then move the cursor and paste the new "Happy" next to the old one. Emily starts crying and selects "Undo Paste" from the Edit menu.

"Look," says Nicki, "real tears." Emily was sprawled back across my chest, sobbing, telling me, "No, No, No!"

I tell Emily that I was really sorry that I was just trying to show her something new. She leans up to the computer and grabs the mouse and selects "Redo Paste" from the Edit menu, and "Happy," reappears. "There!" says Emily.

Then we type "Joy Joy Joy."

I ask Emily if it's time for me to leave. We've been working for about two and a half hours. "Yes!" Emily says and runs for the door and swings it open. She opens the screen door. I'm trying to keep up. She starts yelling "Bye, Dan!, Bye, Dan!" And I'm saying "Bye, Emily, Bye, Nicki thanks for having me over!"

Nicki says not everyone gets such a grand adieu. Emily says "Goodbye!" to me all the way out to the truck and then goes back into the house and looks at me through the curtain.

March 21, 1994

I get over to Emily's at about 1:30. She tries to open the door, but Nicki beats her to it. Emily runs and jumps on the couch and puts a pillow over her head and kicks her feet and laughs. I bury her with cushions. She leaps out of the couch and runs to the computer and starts saying "Animals," and I recognize that I'm in for a session of Animals.

Nicki brings in some cheese and crackers.

I play Animals with Emily. She plays a different game, one that you have to identify an animal based on descriptions like, "I live in the water," "I can get trained," and so on. We don't do so good at this game because Emily moves through the hints so quickly. Another new game has as its object picking out the animal that doesn't fit with the others, like if there's a walrus and a bunch of dinosaurs. Emily's just leaning against my chest and not really paying too much attention.

We try to write some sentences in Microsoft Word. The idea was to write a sentence and then have Emily say it into the microphone, which is working today. We write, "emily lives in a big white house," and she can't really say it. I ask Emily, "What do you want to write?" She looks frantically around and says, "Baby ducks!" OK. We write baby ducks, and I look around the room and notice that she was looking at a picture of some geese with little goslings that was hanging on the wall. I'm trying to type "babby ducks," and Emily keeps telling me "NO!" and I'm saying "What do you mean?" And finally I get the idea that I'm spelling it wrong. Baby, that is.

I suggest we work in her book.

We open up HyperCard first. She looks at a number of the pictures. Actually, all of them, and none seems to be satisfactory this afternoon. The other day, I'd brought over some clip-art files I have, and we opened up SuperPaint, and Emily found a picture of a Japanese celebration of some sort, a lot of men holding up a shrine that had a bunch of stuff on it. We started coloring the people and the little parts of the shrine. We were using the magnifying glass, and when we'd make a mistake, Emily'd say "Oh, oh!" and select Undo from the Edit menu. I had my hand over hers on the mouse, and I was actually doing a lot of the work and making a lot of the decisions. I took my hand off, so I could eat or gesticulate while I was talking with Nicki, and Emily said, "Hand! Dan, hand help!" Nicki translated for me, "She wants your help."

After we get everything colored in to Emily's satisfaction, we selected the picture and copied it into the clipboard, and I said to open her book. She shook her hand away from mine and went to the hard disk icon and opened up her folder and opened up her book and pasted the picture in the book. We wrote some text in it, and then Emily spoke into the microphone and said something about a party.

We went on like this for some time, a couple of hours. It was kind of quiet, we spoke softly to one another. I had to remind her to use her brain a couple of times. "Brain!" she said. This prompt usually was enough to get her to remember to do a step that it looked to me like she was going to forget, like to copy a picture once we selected it.

Emily had to print each new page we made and after she'd printed it, she'd go out in the living room and call, "Mahhhmmmy" in a kind of sing-song voice, and Nicki would come in and punch holes in the print so Emily could put it in her book.

We worked until around 3:30, and I asked if it was time for me to leave, and Emily said yes, and got the door for me, and said, "Bye, Dan!" and kept saying it all the time I was walking to my truck.

March 28, 1994

Emily is knocking on the inside of the screen door, smiling at me, and waving to me when I drive up. She makes a pretty good attempt at getting the door open but just can't quite do it, so I let myself in. Nicki comes down the stairs and greets me appropriately, and says that her mom had called and asked what Emily wanted for her birthday, and Nicki said that Emily might like a new computer program. Nicki got one from MacWarehouse, but she wanted us to test it out to see if I thought it was any good.

This grown-up stuff is about all Emily can take, and she is grabbing on to Nicki's knee, moving her pointed finger toward the office.

"Let's test it out," I suggest.

Emily has a picture in her hand that Nicki wanted her to show me from school. It had some cut-out things from magazines pasted on it.

The program is kind of dumb. Some kids are playing soccer. Minh, a new girl on the block, wants to play, and the friendly children invite her into the game. They explain that you can use your feet, your knees, your head, and your hips to hit the ball, but not your hands! And make sure that ball doesn't hit you in the face. It goes through about 15 screens to tell us all of this and there's a little animation, and the words are printed across the top of the screen when a woman's voice reads them.

This program is supposed to help you learn to read. One module asks you questions, like, "With what part of your body are you not allowed to hit the ball?" I tell Nicki I can hardly understand that sentence.

Nicki asks Emily what she thinks about the program, and Emily goes under the File menu and selects "Quit."

"That answers that," says Nicki.

"I guess so," I say.

I notice that Emily has let the picture she had from school slide off her lap.

"Let's write some sentences!" I suggest lightheartedly.

Nicki goes off into the kitchen and gets me a caffeine-free coke, some taco chips and salsa, and some grapes. Emily and I tear into the taco chips. Emily turns to me and goes to kiss my cheek, gets close to my beard, and says, "Hair?" and squishes through the whiskers and gives me one anyway.

"Thank you, Emily" I say, "how about a grape?" I get a grape and give it to her.

Nicki tells me that they like hugs and kisses around her house but that not just anybody gets them.

We open up Word, and get out a big font, and Emily uses the Character dialog box to change the color to yellow. We write: emily lives in a big white house. I make her type a period. I'm supporting her at her elbows so that we can type pretty fast. I make her hand go way up in the air and stab down on that period and bounce her hand back up into the air. Because I figure that it's never too early to learn the pleasure of getting a sentence *wrote*. "Period!" I say, "that's it!" We type a couple more sentences like that, and then Emily prints out the text and goes to get Nicki to help her put the pictures in her book.

We type some more sentences, one I remember was, "dan lives in an apartment." I let go of Emily's arms and we eat for a second, and she raises her arms like a maestro as the orchestra rises and holds them there until I grab her elbows again. Things are going so well, I think, that we ought to type some sentences about what Emily likes to do. This will get her thinking, I think.

As kind of a warm up, I say, "Who are you?" and tell her to say, "I am Emily."

"Who are Emily?" she says.

"No," I say, "you are Emily."

"You are Emily," says Emily.

"Who are you?" I say, "and then *you* say, 'I am Emily.'"

"Who are who?"

I give up. Mainly because I'm laughing so hard. I know I shouldn't be, because autism experts call this pronominal reversal or something, and somebody, probably my mother, said that I shouldn't laugh at other people's disabilities, even though I'm cracking up thinking about it now. She'll get it though.

I give Emily a big hug, and we start typing again. I want her to type, "emily likes to...." But I just cant get her to type 'to'. She keeps wiping it out with the delete key. Finally, she tries to type '2' and I stop her.

I say, "To, t-o, to."

Emily puts a 'w' on the end of 'to.'

I give up and say, "OK, Emily likes two," and I think for a minute, and say, "Emily likes two things:" I tell her to hit return, and we type 1. Then I ask, "What do you like?"

Emily looks around the room, and says, "Baby ducks."

So we type "Baby ducks."

"What else do you like?" I ask.

She says, "Anteaters!"

So we type, "2. Anteaters."
It looks like this:
emily likes two things:
1. baby ducks.
2. anteaters.
Then we do it with me. It looks like this:
dan likes two things:
1. taco chips.
2. grapes.
We print this out, and Emily gets Nicki to fasten them in her book.

We work on the database book for a while, and it's time for me to leave. Or I ask, "Emily, is it time for me to leave?," and she hops out of my lap and runs to the door and opens it for me and says, "Goodbye, Dan!" and so does Nicki.

April 4, 1994

Hope and I went over to Emily's. Emily's watching for us out the door, and I think she opened it for us. She hurried into the office and turned on the monitor but needed a little help with the rocker switch at the rear of the computer.

They'd got a new program called "Stickybear's Reading Room," and Emily wanted to show it to us. This is actually a pretty good program, I think. One of the activities you can do is choose a noun, then choose a verb and a preposition, and then pick an object. So you can say, "Stickybear jumps over the moon." And then you click an icon that looks like a TV, and the sentence appears, and a little cartoon shows Stickybear jumping over the moon.

Another game makes you choose the right word from a list. So, you might get a sentence that says, "Stickybear jumps over the _____." And you have to pick from a list of words like bucket, Sara, giraffe, or tent. The right word has a picture, like a ball, or a giraffe rolling or dancing around.

Apparently there is some controversy over whether Emily can really read this or whether she is picking up on some other cue. Mark thinks one way and Nicki thinks another.

Anyway, we play this game. I'm asking Emily to say the words and using my finger to point to them. When the sentence comes up, Emily says, "You turn, Dan," and grabs my finger to point to the words. I notice she's having trouble with *the*.

I say, "Emily, look at me." She does. She makes eye contact and doesn't look away. I say, "The." She says something that sounds like "*the.*" "Look at my mouth; go like this when you say it." I put my tongue at the tip of my front teeth. Emily sticks her tongue out at me. "Say *the,* Emily." And she says *the.* We work like this for a while, and I think she gets the hang of saying the.

Emily puts her arm around me and leans into my body and says, "Hand!" I squeeze her with my hand, and she holds on to me.

We were playing the fill-in-the-blank game, and I asked Emily to slow down a little and say the words. Nicki tells me that she usually tells Emily to "read" the words but that telling her to say the words might be a better idea. I think that saying *read* is a better idea, since that's what Emily's doing. Nicki and I go back and forth about this while Emily plays.

There's a picture of Emily and Mike up on the bookshelf. Nicki tells Hope that she doesn't look disabled in *that* picture, and that she's sending it to all of her relatives. Then Nicki realizes that she's talking right over Emily's head and apologizes for calling her disabled in front of her face. Then Nicki says, "Don't write that in your diary, Dan, that I called my daughter disabled."

"I will," I tell her.

"You can have one of the pictures," she says.

I say that bribery won't work, but I'd really like one.

I have to go to the bathroom, and I ask Emily if it's OK, and she says "No." She points to the place on the floor where I've been sitting.

"Dan has to go potty," Nicki says.

"No."

I go anyway. While I'm in there, I think I could test whether Emily was really reading those words or not by writing them in Word.

I get back and hoist Emily on to my lap and say that we're going to open up Word. Emily doesn't want to, but I do. She is protecting her mouse hand by putting her right hand over her left. We grapple with the mouse, and Nicki's making some smart crack about how "I always let the child take the lead...."

"Who's the child?" I snap.

We get Word open, and I write some words that are in the Stickybear program, and sure enough, Emily can read them. She can't get *in* for some reason. I point my finger at *in* on the screen and squeeze her stomach in an effort to force the answer from deep inside her. She says, "Don't sock!" and gets pretty mad at me. I say I'm sorry and all and hope that the grown-ups didn't notice.

I write some sentences. I ask Emily for words. She has trouble thinking up words. She says "Elephant." So I write "Elephant likes Emily." Then I point to the words, and she reads "Elephant likes Emily."

"What else?" I say.

"Anteater."

"OK," and I write "Anteater likes Emily."

My finger points at the words and Emily says them. Then she repeats them and excitedly says, "Anteater *likes* Emily!" And I know that Emily realizes that I wrote that the anteater likes her, and I think she's pretty happy about it.

We go back and work in Stickybear for a while.

Then we work on another animal program. Maybe it's a zoo. I can't remember. But you can go to a forest, the Arctic, a desert, the ocean, a rain forest.

There's a game to this program, somehow, but Emily skips over the lengthy text that might give us a clue as to what it's all about. Nicki almost acts like this is an indication of Emily's laziness or unwillingness to read.

We wind up in a forest and find a porcupine. Emily says, "Porcupine" and opens her arms to sky. "Porcupine!" and I open my arms to the sky. Emily grabs Hope's arm, and soon we are all porcupining away. We discovered a number of other animals. You can click on a pair of binoculars and see a close-up picture of the animal you've found. Emily calls the binoculars a "camera."

It's getting toward 3:30, and I tell Emily that we've got to go, and she looks a little disappointed. I ask her to get the door for us and she does.

April 18, 1994

Nicki answers the door. She tells me that Jill's coming over.

Emily's wanting me to go in the office. She has a CD, but I can't read the name of it, and I ask her if that's the game she wants to play, and she says, "Yes!"

Nicki comes in the office, and I ask her about Emily's "progress." Whether she's noted any changes since I started working with her. At least that time period.

She says that Emily really has changed. For one thing, Emily's more accepting of her father and goes to him when she wants something, and it's not always "on mom." She talks more, and Nicki can hear her trying to formulate sentences when Emily talks "nonsense."

I don't want to play the game that Emily has, whatever it is, but it's fun enough just being here with her. She takes the cushion off the chair, and I get the idea I'm supposed to sit there and provide a lap. It turns out we're going to play "Just Grandma and Me." I pay careful attention at the beginning, so I can find out the name of the androgynous youth. Its name is "Little Critter." We play the game for a while. Emily gets up and meets Jill at the door. She doesn't really say "Hi," but she doesn't really not say "Hi," either. I think that she kind of spins around a little.

Emily and I go through the game. Really it's not a game but an interactive story. She reads some of the passages. She mispronounces some of the words, and I say, "Emily, look at me." She looks at me. She looks at me directly, and with a little question in her eyes, and maybe a little violation, almost, like "Why did you make me do this?" and "I'll go along with you" all wrapped up together. That's what it feels like when Emily looks at you.

Little critter makes a sand castle, and there's a flag, a red flag that's flying in the wind. The ocean pours over the fortification, and all that's left are some heaps of sand that look like piles of ice cream. The flag is still sticking up, and it's not wet enough that it can't fly limply in the breeze. Emily points at it and says something that sounds like "forest!" I don't understand, I tell her. "Emily, look at me," I say, "can you tell me what you're saying?" She turns to the screen and points, saying that word I don't understand. She says it again, and I still don't get it. "Emily, look at me. Melt," I say. Emily looks at my mouth and puts her lips together; "mmmmmm" she says. "Melt," I say, and she says, "mmmelll" and I say "mmmelll-teh" and Emily says "Melt."

I sing to her:

And so castles made of sand;
melts into the sea,
eventually.

Somehow, I never thought I'd be singing a Jimi Hendrix song to a little autistic girl like it was some kind of goddamn lullaby. I tell Emily that "melt into the sea would be better grammar," but she's clicking on the shell that has a hermit crab who comes out snapping, and Emily throws her arms around my neck and buries her face in my shoulder in abject terror. I hold her tight. We go through this a couple of times. It feels good to protect Emily.

Emily gets to a part of the story where everyone is kind of languid (at least the grown-ups) on the beach. Kids are playing. Clouds turn into dolphins or cows or teddy bears when you click on them. A harp plays as the clouds change their shape, and I make like I'm playing a harp, and Emily imitates me.

Emily gets to the end of the book, and Little Critter asks us if we want to look at again, and it turns out that we do, but we don't use the interactive mode this time, and the story is read to us.

After it's over with, I get Emily to go back to the finder, and she opens up that animal game that has a zoo with exhibits to visit. I'm thinking that we can take some more snapshots of the screens and paste the animals into Emily's book and make some sentences and have Emily use the microphone to record herself reading the sentences.

Emily doesn't like it, but she lets me have a turn now and then, and I take snapshots of the screen from the finder by pressing command-shift-3. I bag the dolphins and a couple of anteaters and a porcupine.

My plan works, and I get Emily to open up SuperPaint and her book. She opens up the snapshot of the anteater, and we copy it into her book. I ask her if she wants to write about the anteater, and she does. We write,

anteater likes emily

print the picture

dan

This effort is not entirely Emily's, but a collaboration on her and my part. I have to keep on thinking up sentences until she hears one she thinks we should write. We click on the sound field, and Emily reads what we've written into the microphone after a few false starts. When Emily reads the sentences into the microphone, I get so excited I hug her to death and tell her she's the smartest little thing that I've ever seen and bounce her on my knee. She turns to me and looks at me and says, "Print."

So we print the picture. And Emily takes it into the dining room, and Jill asks Emily if she could read it to her, and Emily reads it. Emily comes back, and I put the printed picture in her book.

After a while, Emily starts playing "Lemmings" and I go, but she gets the door for me.

April 25, 1994

Today I got over to Emily's and rang the doorbell. She came and answered it and opened up the door. She rattled around the handle a little bit before she opened it.

I realized why it is that I'm focusing so much on Emily's door-opening behavior. L'Enfant Sauvage, according to Pine's 1803 report in Lane (1977), had trouble unlocking a door when he was in a room full of people (that he wanted to get out of) despite the fact that "*he remembers very well that the key must be turned in the lock in a certain direction in order to open the door, but, during the several months I have been observing him, he has not managed to memorize this slight movement of the key in the lock and, put off by the enormous difficulty of the enterprise, he will lead someone to the door to help get him out* (60)."

Emily and Nicki are working on a sticker book at the plastic picnic table. You have to put stickers in places, like the biggest ball and the smallest ball, and the medium ball. Some things are a little ambiguous, like there's a series that has a bike, a car, a truck. What's biggest? The little tiny picture of the truck or the huge bicycle? You tell me.

We're playing, the three of us, and of course, Nicki and I are in teacher mode, so we're asking Emily what word is what. We come across "climb," and I say, "Emily, read that word."

She sounds it out, "Cllll, immmmeb" and then says "Climb!" There's a ladder there, but I was still pretty impressed.

Nicki goes, "Ta da, da, da; ta da, da, da," imitating the "Twilight Zone" theme.

I say, "Where'd she learn to do that? In school?" I was a little miffed that someone had taught my little darling something.

Nicki said, "I think you taught her how, Dan."

"I did?"

"Ya."

"When?"

"I don't know, I always hear you guys sounding out words in there."

I can't for the life of me remember sounding out words with Emily. Nicki tells me that she's pretty sure about it, because her teacher sent home a note today that said they were going to start working with Emily on letters, and they got out some ABC's, and she just started naming words that began with each letter. She looks for the note but can't find it. I just kind of scratch my head.

I can't remember what Emily's doing while all this is going on. I look on the table and there's a picture of her with a pony tail sticking out to one side and her tongue hanging out of her mouth. "Lovely," I say. Nicki tells me that "She let them put her hair in a pony tail." I immediately want to see if I can get Emily's hair into a pony tail, and I grab her hair and say "pony tail!"

"Pony tail!" says Emily. I don't bother her, just pat her on the back because she's so cute.

We finish up the picture book and go in to work on the computer. Nicki asks if Emily would like the cushion or sit in "Dan's lap."

"Dan's lap," says Emily.

Emily really doesn't seem like she's into the computer today. We fool around copying pictures and making messes out of them in SuperPaint. When Emily types today, she sees how little pressure she can use to 'click' the keys. Her hand bounces away from the keyboard when the key goes down.

Emily looks at me and says, "Get tape?" and slides off my lap and goes into the other room. I wander out there with her. She goes up to Nicki and says, "Tape, tape, tape."

"Don't you want to use the computer with Dan any more?"

Nicki tells me she probably wants to watch "Sesame Street." This is a new thing, I'm told: Up until a week ago, Emily would not watch "Sesame Street." Because of the monsters. They scared her. But then they watched a show on PBS about the Muppet guy that died and showed how he made the Muppets, and then Emily wasn't scared.

We watch "Sesame Street." Today's show is brought to us by W and T.

I'm still in teacher mode and am asking Emily all sorts of stupid questions like, "What's that spell?"

Emily sticks her hand in my beard and turns my head back toward the screen. I make some dumb comments about a tarantula, and Emily shoves my face at the TV. I sit quietly and watch with Emily. She starts talking, telling me in halting, start-stop, incomplete sentences about the show. I sit quietly.

"Count!" she says.

"Yes, Count," I say. I figure we're going to count. But no, the Count Dracula puppet is on TV, all of a sudden.

"Name!" Emily says.

"Dracula?"

"No, Name!"

"Vampire?"

"No! Esssss!"

"S?"

The Count visits the Countess, who is lying in bed. I am quiet.

We watch the show for about 40 minutes or so. I just pay attention to "Sesame Street." Nicki comes in once or twice. She says Emily hasn't been eating very well, but between the two of us, we've gone through four bowls of popcorn by now.

Emily goes and gets some wind-up toys. Nicki tells me that the speech therapist uses them with Emily. My job is to wind up the toy. Cars roll around; ducks waddle; alligators wag their tails and Emily talks about them.

"Look! Rabbit."

I stay quiet, and I wind up toys.

After a while, I tell Emily that I have to go, and she says, "OK," kind of dejected, and Nicki giggles.

"Can you get the door for me, Emily?" I ask.

"Sure."

Emily opens the door and says, "Bye, Dan!" and waves.

I get in my car and drive home.

May 9, 1994

I don't know what I'm going to do with her today. But I just walked up to the door and rang the bell, and Emily ran up to the door, smiling but not looking at me. She was looking at the computer room and saying "Uh, pu, ter; Granma-da's house, anickanicka, Granma-da's house?"

I said hello to Emily and to Nicki, who was sitting in that chair in the living room. I asked her how she was. She said OK.

Emily is in the office, tugging at the cover of the computer and my heart. Nicki's had the cover for a couple of weeks, maybe a month. I have the same kind.

I turn on the rocker switch at the back of the computer, and Emily grabs the CD with "Just Grandma and Me" on it, and I hear the computer booting up and flip on the CD drive and hope it gets going in time to mount. Nicki comes in and turns on the monitor for us. Emily sticks in the CD, and a window opens, and she double clicks on the icon.

Emily is talking to me, "See?" she says as she points to the arrows on the screen, "see?" She clicks on the button that says you can "play the game" instead of the button that reads you the story.

The first screen comes up, and Emily is still showing me the arrows, and saying something to me that I don't understand at first; it's a long sentence. Then she says, "Book open." I say, "Ya, the open book, I get it." The first screen looks like a open book, and that's where you tell the program whether you want to play or get read to. Then Emily clicks on the backward button and shows me the book again.

We go through the book. There's about 12 or 13 pages. It seems like the program has changed. New things pop out when you click them. Like the mailbox. I thought when you clicked it, the lid dropped open and you saw some white eyes with black pupils in there, but this time when Emily clicks it, the lid drops open and water spills out, and there's a fish in the water. Things like this keep happening.

It used to be that when you clicked on the little teddy bear who is fishing at the beach on screen 4 or 5, he would pull in a big freighter, whose bow takes up most of the right hand fifth of the screen and made a big fog horn sound. Now Emily clicks on this little teddy bear, and he pulls in a boot (not boat), that Emily calls a shoe, and a fish pops its head out of the opening at the top of the boot and jumps back into the water.

I can't figure out what's going on. Emily is really into talking today, excited; and I feel really strange and I don't know why. "Whata boutadis?" she asks me, clicking on a cloud. It turns into a casserole or something, and Emily says, "Lovely, delicious...ice cream, ummmm!"

"Dan," this is the first time she said my name today; She didn't say it all day, and I've been here about an hour, "Whata boutadis?" and she clicks on another cloud that turns into a castle, and we hear music like we were knights around King Arthur's table. Another cloud becomes a tug boat, and it goes, "Tooooooooot," letting out a little puff of smoke as it fades back into the clouds. Emily points to the cloud that turns into ice cream, and says, "Dan, whata boutadis?" and I say, "Lovely, delicious ice cream," and we both say "ummmmmmmm!"

"Lovely, Dan," she says and claps her hands, "lovely!"

Emily points to the tug boat cloud, and says, "Dan, whata boutadis?"

I say, "Tug boat, Emily."

"Lovely, Dan," she says and claps her hands, "lovely!"

She points to the castle cloud and says, "Dan, whata boutadis?"

I say "Castle, Emily, castle."

"Lovely, Dan," she says and claps her hands, "lovely!"

Emily points to the tug boat cloud, and says, "Dan, whata boutadis?"

I say, "Tug boat, Emily."

She clicks and the cloud becomes a tug boat.

"Lovely, Dan," she says and claps her hands, "lovely!"

She points to the castle cloud and says, "Dan, whata boutadis?"

I say "Castle, Emily, castle."

She clicks, and the cloud becomes a castle.

"Lovely, Dan," she says and claps her hands, "lovely!"

Emily points to the tug boat cloud, and says, "Dan, whata boutadis?"

I say, "Tug boat, Emily."

She clicks and the cloud becomes a tug boat.

"Lovely, Dan," she says and claps her hands, "lovely!"

Emily points to the ice cream cloud, and says, "Dan, whata boutadis?"

I say, "lovely, delicious ice cream, ummmmm, Emily."

She clicks and the cloud becomes ice cream.

"Lovely, Dan," she says and claps her hands, "lovely!"

She points to the castle cloud and says, "Dan, whata boutadis?"

I say "Castle, Emily, castle."

She clicks, and the cloud becomes a castle.

"Lovely, Dan," she says and claps her hands, "lovely!

Emily points to the tug boat cloud, and says, "Dan, whata boutadis?"

I say, "Tug boat, Emily."

She clicks and the cloud becomes a tug boat.

"Lovely, Dan," she says and claps her hands, "lovely!"

After a while, Emily looks up at the book shelves and says something. She goes out of the room, "Maahhhmee," she intones sweetly.

Nicki says, "Do you have to go to the bathroom?"

"Book."

They're back to the office now, and Nicki says to me with a shrug, "Sometimes she wants one and sometimes she doesn't." To Emily: "Which one do you want?"

Emily says something I don't understand, and finally, they figure out that she wants "F."

I hear them in the bathroom, Nicki's telling her that she shouldn't worry, that I wasn't going anywhere. I remember that I have the new version of Spectre in my pocket and decide to seize the opportunity to get out of Just Grandma and Me. I've been dying to see how Spectre runs on computer with a 68040 processor.

Down on the floor there's a couple of books about autism. I think about my review of the literature or lack of it. Oh, I pick up the books and look at them. There's a folder underneath them, and I look in the folder, and there's a bunch of journal articles, some from the *Journal of Autism* and the *Journal of Applied Behavior Analysis*. Nicki's been studying; I ought to.

Emily comes back to the office with F. She opens it up. It's a circa

1964 version. Nicki must have got it when she was a kid, like I did. My grandma bought one for me and Kurt. Kurt, who used to read them in his bed when he was four or five. I was 10 when we got them.

Faber, I read. Fair. Emily's turning the pages. Families. Lots of families. I wonder to myself about how the portraits of "Families" have changed over the years in *World Book*. There's a family of Neanderthals.

I ask Emily if we can load Spectre on her computer and hand her Disk 1. She quits Just Grandma and Me and sticks Disk 1 in the drive. Emily opens the icon and clicks on the installer. She uses the default settings and copies the game on the hard drive. I just sit there and watch her reading or paging through the encyclopedia and using the mouse to command the computer, switching disks when it wants her to. I don't know if she knows what she's doing or whether Macs are just user-friendly. She points to the dialog box and mutters something about the progress bar, and how it's moving from the left to the right. She points back and forth between where it is now and where it will be in a minute. We sit.

After Emily's done I want to play Spectre, and I make her open up the program, and she has to copy my serial number into a dialog box. Idly, I try to get her to read the numbers and letters and copy them, but she doesn't so I just read them out to her, and when we're done, I say, "Hit return."

"You turn," she says.

Spectre is really nice on their computer. It doesn't really work too well on mine. Emily's not too interested in it. "Let's go outside," I suggest.

Nicki's been on the phone in the other room for about 20 minutes. I only hear her voice once in a while. Emily leads me to the back door, and we go outside. She sits in the dark shade under the eves on a chair with her book and indicates with her hand that I ought to sit down on this little table. I do, but I really want to play in the sand box. Emily gets a wire brush from the gas grill and starts brushing the glass window that lets you see inside the thing. She brushes the legs. She comes back and sits down with the book. I tell her that I want to go to the sand box.

The sun is blazing, and the air is clear. The farmers haven't planted the field behind her house, and it looks wet and like weeds might turn it into a mess at any minute. It'll be a couple of days before they can get back in, maybe even more because it has low spots, and places that look like water's been running in it. And it's supposed to rain on Wednesday.

"Story about O."

"Huh?"

"Once upon a time there was an 'O', and over, and over, and over. The end. Dan, tell me a story about 'O'."

"Once upon a time," I begin, "there was an 'O', and over, and over, and over. The end. Emily, tell me a story about 'A'."

"Once upon a time, there was an Anteater, and over, and over, and over, and they lived happily ever after. The end."

"Emily, tell me a story about...'B'."

"Once upon a time there was a bird. The trees. The chair," she said looking at the chair and the trees, "and over and over. And they lived happily ever after. The end. Dan, tell me a story about..." Emily looks around for a letter. She sees her house, maybe, and says, "'H'?"

"Once upon a time, there was a Horse, and his name was Henry. And he was happy, and over, and over, and over, and they lived happily ever after."

"The end," Emily added.

Nicki had walked out in the middle of my story, and I felt kind of dumb. "Emily," I say, winking viciously at Nicki, "tell me a story about 'E'?"

Emily looks up at me and squints in the sun. She smiles sweetly, composing herself, and says, "Once upon a time, there was an Eagle!"

Nicki and I laugh, Ha, Ha, Ha.

Emily laughs too, and looks up at the blue sky, and says opening her arms to it: "The sky, the clouds..." Emily lowers her gaze and looks at a spruce tree and continues, "The tree, and the bird." A bird lands on the tree. "And they lived happily ever after. The end."

"Very nice story," says Nicki, and she claps, and Emily claps, and I join in.

"Dan, tell me a story about 'G'."

"Once upon a time," I say, "there was a giraffe. And her name was ..." I giggle because I can't think of a 'G' name. "Gertrude?" and Nicki laughs. "And the Giraffe named Gertrude was green and ate..."

"Grapes!" Emily tells me.

"That's right! Grapes!" How could I not have known? "And over and over and over. And they lived happily ever after. The end."

"Mom, tell me a story about 'S'."

"Once upon a time there was a snake...and his name was Sam and he lived in the sand...and they lived happily ever after, the end."

"Emily..." I pause trying to think of a letter. Nicki laughs at me while I recite the alphabet, "Tell me a story about 'J'." I snarl at her triumphantly.

"Once upon a time," Emily begins, pausing, and I grin over at Nicki. Emily looks up and squints, and says, "Once upon a time there was a Jet." Emily laughs, and says, "Anicka nickanicka nickca, and the sun and the roof, anickanicka nicka nicka, and the clouds and the sky. And they lived happily ever after. The end."

We trade stories like this for a while.

Then Emily runs out into the yard toward the fence, and Nicki tells me that she going to look at the bird nesting in the boxes. There's three of them.

Emily runs in the house. Nicki wonders what she's up to. Emily comes out with a flashlight and runs back to the bird houses. "Michael started that," says Nicki.

Emily's sticking the flashlight in the hole of the bird house. I go over to her. I don't run. Nicki's watching. I kneel down and look in.

Emily's talking excitedly, but I can't understand her.

"Emily," I say, "tell me about 'B'."

She says, "Bird...babies. Bird babies."

"Yes, bird babies."

We look at the other bird houses.

Nicki walks over and says to Emily that she thinks I might even "have to go home now."

I say, "Ya, Emily, I gotta go."

"OK," says Emily.

We walk over to the back door, and Emily extends her hand to me and leads me through the house. She opens the door and lets me out. Nicki and Emily come out, and I start rubbing some mud off my truck, and Nicki tells me not to do that because I'll get dirty. "What are you trying to do? See how thick it is?"

Emily gets into my truck. She's standing up on the seat. She's bouncing around in there. Nicki grabs Emily out of the truck, and Emily looks a little confused. She sticks her thumb in her chest and says "Emily."

Four Years Later

A year or two after I started working on my masters degree in 1990, they started building the rest stop, just this side of Farmers City. In a sense, it was like O. Henry's story of the last leaf. As I completed my courses, began my doctoral studies, and took the 1.5 hour (one way) commute, I came to believe that should they finish before I, all would be lost. As they graded the land, began the road-building, dug in drainage, I studied and wrote. Just as I came to see their enterprise as complete, some new project would begin; a playground, dog-walking zone, picnic tables, drainage ponds, you name it. I clung hopefully to the be-leaf that our target dates would coincide.

But they won, and when I stopped there for a quick nap (the trip for me has a soporific effect) on the way to see a former student in Urbana, the place was done. They were washing the bathrooms.

Emily met me at the door, and her long hair, lighter than what I'd remembered, was up in a pretty braid, and she had gold nail polish that smelled of bananas. She gave me a socially appropriate side hug. The last time I'd seen the young girl, she was going into kindergarten; she could speak very little of her mind. The night before, she'd asked me, "When are you going to visit *me* again, Dan?" Emily carries the formal diagnosis of autism.

Nicki, her mother, doesn't remember exactly when she could start taking Emily to stores without her throwing a fit. She told me it was when she started to understand money and that she could only buy what she could afford. Most of the time I ever spent with Emily was with her on my lap learning everything I knew about Macintosh computers, which is quite a bit.

Mike, Emily's brother, and their dad, Mark, were out "scouting." Mark has a friend who runs some cows on an unstraightened creek, and Mike finds all manner of wildlife, rocks, other debris, and generally intrigue on these trips.

My tape recorder is on as I ask Nicki and Emily if it is alright to preserve these moments, and it is.

Dan	Now it's going to record everything we say.
Emily	Hey, this is a cool recorder. What kind is this?
Dan	It's a Marantz; it's the kind that reporters use, radio reporters.
Emily	Ohhh...
Dan	It doesn't look like it has a microphone to it, but see the VU meter going up every time you talk? Talk, talk, talk, see? Now you say something to it.
Emily	Hiiii! (laughs and so do I). Well, how's your day?
Dan	Well, it was pretty good...I got pretty sleepy coming over here.
Emily	You got tired, didn't you?
Dan	Yeah, I don't know what it is, something about this drive to Champaign...and so...
Emily	And so?
Dan	I had pull over near Farmers City to take about a 10-minute nap.
Emily	Ohhhuh!

Dan   I think I had to drive this drive too many times.

Nicki and I talk about my old black truck and my new red truck, how the old one leaked oil, so I had to park it in the street, how I could pull my new one in the driveway if I wanted (but I didn't).

Dan   Are you being shy because that tape recorder's on?
Emily Um mm (negates).
Nicki She plays with her friends on a tape recorder.
Emily Um hmm (affirms).
Dan   Oh! What kinds of things do you do with it?
Emily Sometimes we do funny things on it.
Dan   Like burp?
Emily Noooo! We usually tell the news, what we're doing now.
Dan   Um hmm.
Emily Sometimes we do pretend, like the weather!
Dan   Well, tell me, what's the weather like today?
Emily Well, it's sort of like shiny, sunny, that's what I mean. And sort of like kind of cloudy too.
Dan   If you were the weather person, what kind of day would you tell everyone that it is?
Emily It's a good day! A good day to go outside.
Dan   And why is that?
Emily Because it's so sunny and nice, and it's just a nice day to go outside and play, do all that stuff, and look for critters. Um hmm. Time to go scouting.
Dan   Time to go scouting? Does Mike come back with critters.

Nicki tells us that last week Mike and Mark came back with a little snapping turtle. They took it back today. Nicki asks Emily to tell me what they have in the sandbox out back.

Emily We have some snapping turtle eggs hidden in the sand.
Dan   Where'd you find them?
Emily Well, one of mom's workers told her that, oh, that they had a big snapping turtle in their pond, not like our pond [a subdivision pond], but a different pond, like a regular pond, and the snapping turtle laid eggs. So now we have, like, 20 snapping turtle eggs in our sandbox.
Dan   20?????
Nicki 20.
Emily (laughs)
Dan   Oh my god. What are you going to do when they start hatching?
Nicki Where are we going to let them go?
Emily Homer Lake, probably.
Dan   Homer Lake?
Emily That'd be a nice place for them.
Nicki Unless you want to bring them to your place!

Dan	No.
Emily	Why, do you live near a pond?
Dan	No. Not really.
Emily	Good, you don't want to get *bitten* by a *snapping* turtle.
Dan	My dad used to tell me that if you got bitten by a snapping turtle, it wouldn't let you go until sundown.
Emily	That's just like Joe, he always tells stories. Even dad.
Dan	Um hmm. I think my dad's a lot like Joe.
Emily	Why? Because when Mike was four, he said that if you salted a bird, you could catch him.
Nicki	Salted what?
Emily	Salted his tail!
Nicki	What did Mike find out?
Emily	That it wasn't...even true. He just went like this (she gets out of her chair and waves a pretend salt shaker about and giggles). He went like this, eeeeee, just salted everything, and not even the bird's tail. I think you are right. Your dad is just like Joe, absolutely, just like Joe.
Dan	(laughs) Who is Joe?
Emily	My grandfather.
Dan	When are you going to go see Joe?
Emily	In about four days (today is Sunday), but three days really.
Dan	Why three days?
Nicki	She's just looking ahead.
Dan	You're just scratching today off, huh?
Emily	She told me that last night. And dad sent me a letter this morning. My brother *created* me a mailbox!

Emily goes upstairs and gets the mailbox that Mike made. Nicki tells me that Emily is getting ready to go into fourth grade. Family members are supposed to send her letters nightly to communicate important matters such as when vacations are to commence.

Dan	Your mom told me you have some computer games you want to show me.
Emily	Yes I do. Museum Madness.
Nicki	Tell him who gave it to you, loaned it to you.
Emily	The neighbors, the new neighbors across the street. Look at the window...No, look *through* the window, see the dirt pile?
Nicki	That's a good marker, I guess.
Emily	That's the one.

It turns out that these people are expecting a baby and that they are in special education, Ph.D. students, and Nicki asks me if I know them. I don't. It's just been too long. "I know the secretaries," I say. Ellyn left, Nicki informs me. Well, I guess I don't know them either.

The neighbors moved here "about a year ago" according to Emily. Nicki confirms this.

Nicki	What's another one you like? Think of the ones you and Emily play.
Emily	Ooooooh I know one. Well there's...there's the Babysitter's Club on computer.
Nicki	Mmmhmmm. That might not be as much fun for Dan, don't you think?
Emily	Mmmm no. It's a girl's computer game, that's why!!!!
Nicki	(laughs) Well, you never know, he might be interested in seeing it.
Emily	Well, he might be interested in seeing Museum Madness more than the Babysitter's Club.
Nicki	Anything else that you play on there? How about Spectre?
Emily	Mmmm yeah. Spectre VR and Spectre. Now we have two of them.
Nicki	Do you play with Spectre by yourself or just help Mike?
Emily	I usually help Mike shoot.
Nicki	She shoots.
Emily	And I know where to target shoot at. Mike thinks that I'm really good at target shooting. Like, I mean like, where to go I can usually point where to shoot because he usually doesn't know where to shoot. (laugh)
Dan	Because he's too busy steering?
Nicki	It took him a while to get that steering figured out...
Emily	...right, and he has a problem, he has a problem with this stuff. That poor child. With his, with his fing...with his four fingers he steers and then how do you shoot with your thumb? That's the problem with Mike.
Nicki	Well we'll show...I mean...
Dan	(over Nicki) What about, what about the other hand, the other...
Emily	Yeah, I mean he really needs help.
Dan	Oh, OK.
Emily	He really does! He always, he always says can you shoot for me? And I say "Suuure!" and then it's not very hard to shoot. And usually he sometimes moves into things. When, when he's always like...then he lets go of the thumb and it turns out to be kaboooom. Not every time but sometimes.

We have a short discussion about whether Spectre games can be saved, how to play them over AppleTalk networks, how the games need to have different serial numbers so you can do this, and so on. Nicki reminds Emily that I don't have much time to be playing computer games because I need to write.

Emily	Oh well,
Dan	That's alright.
Nicki	Yeah, Dan doesn't need to be playing all the time. He needs to get his work done.
Emily	Yeah, that's good. (Laughs) That's good anyway! Cause he always needs to learn.

All	(Giggle)
Dan	I'm ready to retire.
Emily	I think you're about ready to go to sleep, right?
Dan	What?
Emily	I think you're about ready to go to sl...
Dan	(over Emily) No I'm, I'm, I'm wide awake now.
Emily	Good.
Dan	Believe me.
Emily	(*sing song voice*) I do think you're wide awake now too.

The discussion turns to their pathetically outdated computer and how it can't run the new games. Four years ago, when they bought it, I'd recommended getting this particular model, "You see," I said, "down the road, do you want to have a $1,400 outdated computer or a $4,000 outdated computer.

Dan	You look like a Mike clone almost!
Emily	WHO?
Dan	You do!
Emily	Nooooo I don't! (laughs)
Dan	Yeah, you do a little bit.
Emily	That's because we're twins!
Nicki	You are?
Emily	Yeaaaah, when there's a different kind of person.
Dan	(Laugh)
Emily	When they have if they have a different egg except that they are a different person...when they're a different...
Nicki	That's OK, don't be nervous. I know what you're talking about. We talked about identical twins and nonidentical twins.
Dan	Mmmhmmm.
Emily	I know.
Nicki	And that they have to be born at the same time, but you and Mike are how much apart?
Emily	One year apart but...
Nicki	One year and three months, right, so you couldn't be twins. Because you weren't born at the same time, right?
Emily	Riiight, so...
Nicki	You can look a lot alike, but you're not twins.
Emily	I know! We're sort of like twins except we're one year apart.
Nicki	Sort of...
Emily	They always say, "Wow, you just look like my brother!"
Nicki	(Laugh) Sort of like twins. But not really.
Dan	Fortunately, your brother is kind of cute. And so, so...
Nicki	(laugh)
Emily	Oh, Mike's a boy, he's handsome then.

Dan	Well, whatever. I think you're allowed to say boys are cute up until a certain point.
Nicki	Yeah.
Dan	You know when they get to be 13 or 14, it starts to bother them.
Emily	Uh oh. You better not say that, Dan.
Nicki	Oh, Mike won't care, Mike's only 10.
Dan	Yeah, so you got another year to say he's cute and then...

Emily and I sit down and play Museum Madness. A boy has to wander around the cellar of a museum trying to get up to the first floor. You have to wander around. To me it is not fun. I don't like computer games to begin with, as we shall see. Somehow it reminds me of math failures, and such. The thing that stands out, though, is that Emily remembers the sequence of pictures that allows her to open the combination lock that guards the basement. She does this very quickly—a person must remember an American flag, a tree, and about five other icons to get in. Emily has no problem with this.

Our little boy, the one who is exploring the museum, has to wander endless halls in the basement looking for keys.

Dan	Where are you taking me!
Emily	(laughing) I, I don't know-ho-ho-ho!
Dan	You're going get me dizzy, Emily!
Emily	(laughing) I don't know where I am!
Dan	Take me somewhere; you *are* making me dizzy!
Emily	(laughing) Sometimes I know where I am, and sometimes I don't know where I am. I don't know why I'm making you so dizzy! Ohhhh! Thank you! I wanted that (she finds her way into a room).
Dan	(grumbling) Thank heavens.

Somehow we get the boy upstairs, and then we have to reconstruct a map, and finally she remembers how to do it.

Emily	Finally we put the map together. (sighs), Yeah, yeah, But where are we going to go?
Dan	I dunno.
Emily	What does he say—(quoting text) "Use the map to sel..." Oh I know, I know what to do, and then you choose...Not this one, not this one, not this one...Robots!
Dan	Robots?
Emily	Perfect!
Dan	What's so good about robots?
Emily	Because I always wanted to be a robotics.
Dan	Oh you want to be *in* robotics?

Mike, who has recently arrived back from his scouting expedition is helping us at this point. He reminds Emily that she's only wanted to be in robotics for a day or two.

Dan   Were you born yesterday?

Emily   I always wanted to be a robotics person. The kind of robotics person that wants to make toys and stuff. What does it [the game] say? *"Throughout history, humans have dreamed of having machines to perform tasks for them. These machines have often taken human-like form. Any machine that performs in a human-like manner is a robot."* Robot? *"Robots are not intelligent in the same way humans are, although they can perform complex tasks and do elaborate...*

Dan   Elaborate [long a, verb, to express in great detail].

Emily   Elaborate [short a, adjective, detailed].

Dan   Oh! Elaborate, you were right!

Emily   Elaborate!!!

Dan   Elaborate!!!!

Emily   ...calculations. They cannot think. Today computers control the actions of robots." Hmmmmm!!!

Dan   OK.

Emily   Oh, I know what he does! Can we go on? Yeah man, we can go on. Hold on, just a second...go back, I want to see something. Oh good. Good, there's something.

Dan   You can make one?

Emily   No you can't. We have to put all the pieces together, I know...(whispers). There we go! Oh, finally, something happened.

Dan   Put a cap on that boy!

Emily   Mmmmmm...Is that right?

Dan   How should I know...It looks right!

Emily   Oh no...yep, it is right.

Dan   Fits.

Emily   Perfectly.

Dan   You can kind of see its shadow.

Emily   UH huh, Something is...that means something is wrong here. Let me see something. Just a second, boy...(whispers) just a second.

Dan   (whispers) OK.

At each exhibit, we have to assemble a robot. Then, an evil dynamism (poststructuralist?) deconstructs the robots and reassembles them into an evil robot who (that?) shoots harmless sparks at us but is nonetheless infuriating because it has destroyed our masterpieces! Our objective at this point is to somehow distract this monstrosity, hit its off button, and get the parts back to the original museum exhibitions.

We fool around with this for an ungodly amount of time. Finally we give up in frustration. I suggest that we name the game "Emily's Failure" and save it.

"That's cool! That's funny!" says Emily

Emily types. And laughs. "How 'bout this—'Emily and Dan's Failer.'"

"Emily and Dan's Failer?" I moan.

"Correct!" says Emily.

Nicki brings us in a menu from a nearby Chinese restaurant. The menu is huge, and I order the Hunan vegetables.

I exclaim with enthusiasm, "Want to see my dissertation? Say yes, children!"

"Yes!"

"I would lovvvve to see your dissertation, Dan!"

"It's on the web."

"I didn't know you had a web site."

I have to explain that part of it might not be working because the server at Illinois State University is down. I knew it would probably be down this weekend but thought I'd try.

"I think it is down," says Emily, "but he's guessing, not me."

I point at my home page's address and the concoction loads.

Emily asks: "Um, uh, this program is cool, but I'm just going to ask you this one question."

"Which is?"

Gesturing toward the screen, "*What* is this about? It's like..."

"Why does everybody ask me that question? It's about people with different disabilities," I say uncomfortably.

"And what does this"—she gestures toward the screen again—"have to do with *that*?"

I proudly show the kids this little animated GIF I drew.

"You made notes?"

"Yeah."

"But it writes a line, then erases a line..."

"Yup. That's about the way it goes."

I show them the page where I've coded a riff from Bob Marley's *Rat Race*, and Emily says: "Hey! This sounds like party music! Where is that music? At your house?"

I decide after many, many questions, to show them how to make a web page.

"It's simple," I say.

"Yeah," says Emily, "once you know a whole bunch of computer things."

"Do you have uh, uh, uh, uh..."

"Dan, what do you *need?*" asks Nicki.

"SimpleText?"

I start laboring through the HTML coding necessary to make Emily a simple web page. We say what Emily wants to be, a robotics engineer, a vet 'like her dad,' or a 'Waiter.'

"Do you know French?"

"Nooo."

"There's a word for this, the French say *Serveux*..."

"Yeah! That's what I want!"

Emily and Mike wonder whether the page is on the web now and whether everyone will see it, and I tell them, no, that it's on their computer.

"Where's yours?" "Where's mine?" "How do you do it?" "How do you put pictures on it?"

Nicki takes off to get the food.

Emily writes that her brother fights with her. I tell her not to forget the *fair pair*.[2] What's that? "If you do something mean, you have to do something nice" or something like that. Some people say you have to say three nice things if you say something mean (a relic of my administrative training). Emily writes how her brother is an artist, lets her play Spectre with him, and that Mike makes her laugh.

We are getting very excited as the web page takes shape. So excited, in fact, that Emily jumps into my lap and holds on to both sides of my head.

"I'll make sure your head doesn't pop off, you see, I *had* to do that, so your thoughts don't explode. It's getting old you know."

"You mean implode from the vacuum," I mumble.

Emily finds my necklace of broken African trade beads. "Are you a cool dude?" she asks. "Because of your necklace."

"I like to think so."

We work for a long time straightening out the coding and adding pictures to Emily's page. "You kids must be getting very bored with me," I

---

[2] This is a term applied behavior analysts use to reinforce the concept that if you extinguish one behavior, you should teach another to replace the function the extinguished behavior once served.

declare.

"No," says Mike, "we're children who *understand*."

The food *est arrivé* and it was delicious.

Chapter Seven

Definitions, Re-Definitions, and (No More) Definitions

Emily was diagnosed with autism, as were the other children about whom I've written. Along with that diagnosis comes an 80 percent chance the child will have some level of mental retardation (Turnbull, Turnbull, Shank and Leal 1999, 411). It's inevitable that the focus of the children's interpretive communities will converge on the "mental retardation question." Questions such as "Why isn't our child (or "this student") learning to talk?" or "Why can't our child (or "your child") behave?" will be asked. The important activity of resolving the mental retardation question will form a basis on which to build a case for the mindedness of the child.

For instance, if the child has autism but no mental retardation, it is likely that his or her interpretive community will consider "mind" as present but hidden. If mental retardation is detected, then "mind" will become contested territory.

The specter of mental retardation creates an altered set of expectations. At the same instant that people act as if some aspect of mindedness is obscured or obliterated by the condition, they will grant mindedness in the subtle ways I described in Chapter Two. I will now turn to some of the definitional aspects of mental retardation.

But first, I would like to review a scientific investigation, in a manner of speaking, from "the other side of the looking glass." The purpose is to provide a straightforward example of how the diagnosis of mental retardation interacts with the notion of mindedness. Social construction of reality (and diagnoses such as mental retardation), for Melvin Pollner and Lynn McDonald-Wikler (1985), implies that social fabrication is possible, as the title of their paper implies. "The Social Construction of Unreality: A

Case Study of a Family's Attribution of Competence to a Severely Retarded Child," will serve my purpose as the timeworn warp and woof of mental retardation throughout which humanity is woven.[1]

Pollner and McDonald-Wikler document a family diagnosed with *folie á famille*, a psychiatric condition similar to *folie á deux*, in which two people participate in the same delusion. In this case, a family had beguiled itself into the unshakable belief that their severely retarded daughter was normal, that she only acted retarded when she was out in public. You can imagine that for the family, this was a point of considerable irritation and perplexity.

They had been to numerous local clinics where their daughter had been diagnosed as severely retarded. "This was rejected by the parents and instead was regarded by them as an indicator of [their daughter] Mary's capabilities—she had fooled the clinicians" (243). Eventually the family found themselves at a national disability clinic where staffers told them the same thing (that is, their daughter had [*once again fooled the staffers into believing she had, hee, hee, hee!*] severe retardation).

Standardized tests showed that with the exception of Mary, all family members showed normal to above normal intelligence. Personality tests (the Minnesota Multi-Phasic Personality Inventory) revealed no psychosis; regardless, clinical judgment (itself polemic, as we will see below) must have prevailed, and the entire family was diagnosed as delusional. "A highly refined testing procedure revealed that the mother was disposed to delusions under stress. She was seen as the locus of the family delusion..." (Pollner and McDonald-Wikler 243, my emphasis). Thus, the initial diagnosis of *folie á famille* was amended to *folie á famille, imposée* (an initial reader of this manuscript insisted that I check to make certain that this was not the April Fool's edition of *Family Process*. It was published in June of 1985).

Not knowing French, I'll take *imposée* to mean imposed, and in this case, by the mother. Mothers, specifically, and parents of children with disabilities in general, share an oppressive burden of blame in disability literature for their children's condition (see Bettelheim 1967, for a discussion of "parentectomy," that is, the removal of parents [and subsequent institutionalization of their children], for the remediation of

---

1 The "warp and woof" are the fibers that run crosswise and lengthwise in a loom upon which spun wool is woven.

disabilities such as autism). Not incongruously, in "The Social Construction of Unreality..." the authors credit the parents with fallacious, delusional attributions, and construction of false competencies within their severely retarded child.

Pollner and McDonald-Wikler, using all of the tools of phenomenologically oriented researchers positioned in a social constructionist framework, were guided by the following question: "How does the family do it? What sorts of skills, practices, and strategies are utilized to create and then 'discover' Mary's competence?" (1985, 244). The researchers' data consisted of the findings of the "extensive clinical evaluation (242)" at the clinic. These data included videotapes of family interactions with Mary at the clinic upon which the authors' build their arguments.[2]

Pollner and McDonald-Wikler uncovered these practices that the family used to construct the reality of their daughter's incompetence.

The Social Construction of Unreality

Framing.[3] The family prestructured the environment in such a way as to enhance the competence of Mary's performances. For example, a game of ball served as a framework for developing a vocabulary of participation. For instance, Mary could "catch the ball," "drop the ball," "play well (or not very well)," and so on. In one sequence the authors describe "... the mother [as having] twice requested...'Give Mommy the ball'; when Mary simply continued to stand while holding the ball, the mother said, 'You don't want to give me the ball,' thereby narratively transforming obliviousness into a willful reluctance to give the ball" (Pollner and McDonald-Wikler 1985, 245).

Postscripting. This practice involved closely observing Mary's activities for possible cues as to what she might do next and then making a request for her to accomplish the act. In the words of the authors, the family was "commanding the already done" (Pollner and McDonald-Wikler 1985, 245). In one example, for instance, Mary began to climb into a chair, and

---

[2] In the text, the authors build tables in which "what is said" is juxtaposed against "what really happened." But it is actually an interesting way to present the data. David Goode, as we will see, uses a similar technique.

[3] Gubrium and Holstein (1995) cite this work in their position paper concerning postmodernism and individual agency. The citation refers not to the content of Pollner and McDonald-Wikler's work but their rare empirical use of Goffman's (1974) conceptualization of Frame Analysis.

the mother requested that Mary have a seat.

Puppeteering. This family practice was, according to Pollner and McDonald-Wikler, one of the most convincing displays of the family's artfulness in their social construction of unreality. It took *extensive* analysis of the videotapes to uncover the command-driven accomplishment of tasks that were actually covert physical manipulation of Mary's body accompanied by verbal requests and comment. On one occasion, while playing with blocks, the mother asked that Mary place a particular block in the center of a circle of blocks. Mary collapsed to the floor with a block in her hand. Her mother, while helping her to stand, pointed to the center of the circle with one hand, and with her other, pushed the block-holding hand to the center of the circle of blocks. "Mary's movements," then, "were often artifacts of the family's physical engineering of her body" (Pollner and McDonald-Wikler 1985, 246).

Semantic Crediting. Here, Mary would respond to nonverbal, "behavioral" (247) cues that were paired with a verbal message. In one example, a knock on the door drew Mary's attention, and her mother asked if someone wanted to get in the door. Mother pointed to the door, and Mary walked to the door and attempted to open it and did so with mother's assistance. "The inference that one would make about Mary's mental acuity would vary dramatically according to which stimulus one considered to be the crucial one: the verbal request or the accompanying cues. The familial claim, of course, was that she understood the words spoken to her and that her competence far exceeded the level of responsiveness involved in merely reaching for an outstretched hand or turning to a loud noise" (Pollner and McDonald-Wikler 1985, 248).[4]

Putting Words in Mary's Mouth. Mary's family insisted that her utterances were perfectly understandable. Family members accomplished this by repeating what Mary said, interpreting her "interactionally capricious and unintelligible" (Pollner and McDonald-Wikler 1985, 248) vocalizations in a contextually appropriate manner. On one occasion, Mary was wearing a new robe, and Father asked if she'd like to see it in the mirror. Mary was "gurgling" (Pollner and McDonald-Wikler 1985, 249), and Father said that she didn't like the robe. Mother asked, "You don't like the robe? It fits you" (Pollner and McDonald-Wikler 1985, 249).

---

4 Itard (1801) mentions that the L'Enfant L'Aveyron turned to sounds that were meaningful to him, such as a walnut cracking.

Mary "gurgles," and Mother asked what Mary had said to her father. Mary again said "Mmmmmmmm, gurgle" (Pollner and McDonald-Wikler 1985, 249), and Father said, "She thinks it's too cheap!" (Pollner and McDonald-Wikler 1985, 249). "In 'repeating,' or heavily implying the meaning of Mary's utterance by their response, family members were in fact creating and broadcasting the meaning. If we are not mistaken, such work allowed the family to avoid embarrassing disagreements, to perpetuate the fiction that Mary was speaking intelligently, and to develop a shared version of precisely what Mary said" (Pollner and McDonald-Wikler 1985, 249).

Explaining the "Bright" Direction. When Mary's family did notice errors in Mary's behavior they were likely to interpret the errors not as "recognizably inadequate (Pollner and McDonald-Wikler 1985, 249), but as further evidence of her competence. "Thus, for example, instances in which Mary's behavior seemed to defy interpretation as a directly responsive action were treated as the product of Mary's proclivity toward 'teasing' and 'pretending.'...The net effect of such explanatory and descriptive practices was to inhibit the growth of what could have been an enormous catalogue of incompetence.... Indeed insofar as 'faking' or 'cheating' are higher level activities requiring sophisticated reflections and interpersonal manipulations, there is a sense in which ostensible failures ultimately served to enhance Mary's image among family members" (Pollner and McDonald-Wikler 1985, 250).

And what, I ask, is wrong with that?

Mental Retardation

The professional organization in the United States most responsible for defining mental retardation is the American Association on Mental Retardation (AAMR). Its origins date back to 1876, when six men, all superintendents of institutions for feeble-minded people, joined together to form the Association of Medical Officers of American Institutions for Idiotic and Feeble-Minded Persons. James Trent (1994) reports that the formation of the group was, in part, an attempt to dodge the arrogance of the lunatic-alienist's organization, The Association of Medical Officers of American Institutions for the Insane (presently the American Psychological Society), "who insisted that only lunatic-asylum superintendents could enjoy membership" (67).

The Association of Medical Officers begat the Association for the Study of the Feeble-Minded in 1906; 1933 brought another change in name, The American Association on Mental Deficiency (AAMD) (Scheerenberger 1983). Through the 1940s the term mental deficiency would come to replace, at least in the scientific literature, the organization's original terminology, that is, *idiot, imbecile, feeble-minded,* and *moron* (Scheerenberger 1983).

In 1959, the AAMD proposed and adopted the term "mental retardation" with the accompanying definition: "Mental retardation refers to subaverage general intellectual functioning which originates in the developmental period and is associated with impairment in adaptive behavior" (Scheerenberger 1983, 218).

The "developmental period" lasted until the approximate age of sixteen years. The new definition included five levels of mental retardation: borderline, mild, moderate, severe, and profound.[5] Although this definition reflects concurrent deficits in intelligence quotient (IQ) *and* adaptive behavior, valid assessment tools to measure adaptive behavior were largely unavailable to practitioners at that time (Scheerenberger 1983) and, as we shall see, in the present day as well.

The problem of just what constitutes subaverage general intellectual functioning has plagued the AAMD (renamed The American Association on Mental Retardation in 1987) for the past half century. The 1959 definition marked "subaverage" performance on intelligence tests as one standard deviation below that of the population mean of a person's age peers (Blatt 1977/1994). In 1973, "subaverage" became "significantly subaverage" and was redefined to include only people who scored two or more standard deviations below the mean. Burton Blatt, questioning the statistical machinations, chided that "With the figurative, and possibly literal, stroke of Herbert Grossman's [chair of the Association's Terminology and Classification Committee] pen, a committee sitting around a conference table reduced enormously the potential incidence of mental retardation, never having to see or dose or deal with a client, only having to say that, hereinafter, mental retardation is such and such, rather than this or that" (Blatt 1977/1994, 71).

Grossman's committee again refined the definition of mental

---

5 Mental retardation is a developmental disability, meaning that the condition is defined as arising during the "the developmental period" (childhood, essentially). This distinction is necessary to differentiate the disability's sequelae from those caused by, for example, traumatic brain injury, that can manifest at later stages of life (whether or not humans are continually developing organisms does not appear to be at question here).

retardation in 1983 (Hickson, Blackman, and Reis 1995) as follows: "Mental retardation refers to significantly subaverage general intellectual functioning existing concurrently with deficits in adaptive behavior, and manifested during the developmental period" (42).

"Significantly subaverage" remained two standard deviations below the mean of an individually administered IQ test. The "developmental period" came to an end at age 18. The category "Borderline Mental Retardation" was unceremoniously tossed in the recycling bin of discarded terminology.

In 1992, Luckasson et al. introduced *Mental Retardation: Definition, Classification, and Systems of Support* (the 1992 system). The new definition was heralded by the publishers, the AAMR, as well as others, as a paradigm shift not only from previous diagnostic codes, but "part of the rhythm of change that has spanned the years from the 1950s to the 1990s" (Luckasson and Spitalnik 1994, 82). The major motifs in this rhythm of change included: (1) a situationalist rethinking of mental retardation in terms of a functional interaction between persons and environments rather than an absolute trait (to the extent that such could be measured, given the stochastic nature of assessment methodology) of a particular person or category of persons; (2) the interaction of mental retardation itself with environments including transcending modes of thought whereby a person with mental retardation is transformed from "...a burden, to being a person with challenges" (Luckasson and Spitalnik 1994, 84), from an object of fear, an eternal child subject to coercion and control, to a recognition of fully empowered membership in the human community; and (3) pragmatic changes in the service delivery system, including real jobs, real schools, real teaching, real competence, real acceptance, real healthcare, real homes, and real affirmation of family.

Nevertheless, the 1992 AAMR definition reads: "Mental retardation refers to substantial limitations in present functioning. It is characterized by significantly subaverage intellectual functioning, existing concurrently with related limitations in two or more of the following applicable adaptive skill areas: communication, self-care, home living, social skills, community use, self-direction, health and safety, functional academics, leisure, and work. Mental retardation manifests before age 18" (Luckasson et al. 1992, 5).

The definition includes four assumptions for its appropriate application:

1. Valid assessment considers cultural and linguistic diversity as well as

differences in communication and behavioral factors;

2. The existence of limitations in adaptive skills occurs within the context of community environments typical of the individual's age peers and is indexed to the person's individualized needs for supports;

3. Specific adaptive limitations often coexist with strengths in other adaptive skills or other personal capabilities; and

4. With appropriate supports over a sustained period, the life functioning of the person with mental retardation will generally improve (Luckasson et al. 1992, 1).

The upper boundary of mental retardation remained outside two standard deviations below the mean of an individually administered IQ test (IQ = 70-75).[6] The 1992 system disposed of the four categories of mild, moderate, severe, and profound mental retardation, leaving a single category (i.e., mental retardation).

The classification of mental retardation within the 1992 system is "multidimensional" in that it measures functioning across four dimensions in a three-step process. The diagnosis of mental retardation is established in *Step 1* by the detection of an IQ score below 70-75, concurrent limitations in at least two or more adaptive skill areas, and the functional limitations having manifested themselves before the age of 18.

Diagnostic *Step 2* involves an analysis of the person across four dimensions of: (a) intellectual functioning and adaptive skills, (b) psychological and emotional considerations, (c) physical health and etiology, and (c) environmental considerations. The idea that the dimension of environmental considerations is included (for instance where a person lives, has fun, goes to school, or works) "allows for a more holistic view of the person and his or her life and the latitude to imagine what the person's optimal environment would be" (Luckasson and Spitalnik 1994, 87).

The level and types of support a person needs in each dimension are determined in *Step 3*. Supports levels include: (a) intermittent, (b) limited, (c) extensive, and (d) pervasive.

Thus, the 1992 system was not only a systematic diagnosis and classification of individuals but became a recommendation for intervention. "This use also moves the diagnostic process away from the labeling of individuals (e.g., 'a person with severe retardation') to the description of a person and his or her needed supports (e.g., 'a person with mental retardation with extensive support needs in the areas of

---

[6] Standard Error of Measurement is always present in norm-referenced assessment such as the IQ test.

communication and limited support needs in the area of community use')" (Schalock et al. 1994, 183).

The formulators of the 1992 system not only envisioned intensities of supports (intermittent, limited, etc.) but proposed and delineated categories of support resources, and support functions whose application would lead to these desired outcomes: "1) Enhanc[ing] adaptive skills level/functional capabilities; 2) Maximiz[ing] habilitation goals related to health, physical, psychological, or functional wellness; and 3) Foster[ing] environmental characteristics of community presence, choice, competence, respect, [and] community participation" (Schalock et al., 1994, 185).

The extensive detail of the 1992 system was intended to contrast sharply with previous definitions of mental retardation (and idiocy, imbecility, feeble-mindedness, mental deficiency, and moron-ism, for that matter) in its virtually prescriptive nature (contrast the 1992 definition to that of 1983—at least the guidelines for its appropriate application—for instance), and the explicit reliance on professional and clinical judgment for application.

As noted above, the lack of reliable and valid tools for assessment of adaptive behavior has been a persistent problem and recurrent theme in making the diagnosis of mental retardation since the earliest days of its scientific identification (Scheerenberger 1983; Schalock et al. 1994; Luckasson, et al. 1992; Luckasson and Spitalnik 1994). Schalock et al. (1994) point to the fact that "[C]hief among [the] issues [of assessment of mental retardation in the 1992 system] are the challenges involved in refining current assessment practices and embarking on major efforts to develop new instruments and procedures that are responsive to the changing zeitgeist" (187).[7]

---

[7] "People write the history of experiments on those born blind, on wolf-children or under hypnosis. But who will write the more general, more fluid, but also more determinant history of the 'examination'—its rituals, its methods, its characters and their roles, its play of questions and answers, its systems of marking and classification? For in this slender technique are to be found a whole domain of knowledge, a whole type of power. One often speaks of the ideology that the human 'sciences' bring with them in either discreet or prolix manner. But does their very technology, this tiny operational schema that has become so widespread (from psychiatry to pedagogy, from the diagnosis of diseases to the hiring of labour), this familiar method of the examination, implement, within a single mechanism, power relations that make it possible to extract and constitute knowledge." (Foucault 1977/1979, 185).

As a result, and in the interregnum, clinical judgment remained as pervasive in the 1992 system as it always had been. Schalock et al. (1994) state that clinical judgment was in fact, a "key factor." The authors maintain that "[t]he 1992 System advocates for using professional/clinical judgment to make decisions and employing an interdisciplinary team process to integrate and blend the multidimensional assessment and needed supports information. The team process not only requires certified personnel (e.g., psychologists determining IQ level) but also the use of clinical judgment involved in developing the Individual Education/Habilitation Plan" (Schalock et al. 1994, 187).

The authors remind us that the increased focus on clinical judgment does not differ from current practice in that the American Psychological Association (arrogant bastards though they may be) has always advised clinical judgment in the administration of norm-referenced adaptive behavior scales. Further, clinical observation remained a critical factor in ferreting out those instances where people have had limited access to the kinds of *support resources* (personal, other people, technology, services [Luckasson et al. 1992, 102]) and the *support functions* (teaching, befriending, financial planning, employee assistance, behavioral support, in-home living assistance, community and school access and use, and health assistance [Luckasson et al. 1992, 102]) they need. In fact, Schalock et al. (1994) conclude that with the addition of these needed supports (presumably after their identification and delineation using the 1992 system), some proportion of people with mental retardation "may no longer exhibit limitations in adaptive skills consistent with the definition of mental retardation."

The persistent optimism of the 1992 system was hard to miss. But "disability treatment professions (e.g., special education, psychology, and rehabilitation)," wrote Douglas Biklen (1988) in an article entitled "The Myth of Clinical Judgement," "operate on a model of individual assessment, diagnosis, and placement. That is, in order to determine the best strategy for educating, rehabilitating, or otherwise serving people with disabilities, professionals must first consider individual needs and the findings of research about the best approaches for meeting such needs." Biklen pondered the range of support options actually available to the professional/clinician: "[W]hat options are available to them? Are the best practices typically among their possible choices? In other words, how does the professional environment frame the professional's work? Do professionals truly have the freedom to exercise professional judgment, or are the professionals and consumers alike merely functionaries and pawns in a world of narrowly restricted, love-it-or-leave-it 'choices'?" (1988, 137).

Thus, highlighting the social, political, and economic forces underlying "clinical judgment" Biklen argued that "clinical judgment is drastically limited by the influence of non-clinical factors...[and]...may even be mere window dressing for practices that in fact contradict clinical judgment" (137). Doing so, he underscored Trent's (1995) contention that a simple redefinition of mental retardation would not alter the attitudes that define the place of these members of society. "Only on rare occasions," Trent writes, "did [The Association of Medical Officers of American Institutions for Idiotic and Feeble-Minded Persons] wonder out loud whether mental retardation could be cured. And when they did, they usually assumed that the road to a cure was through treatment. Few would have guessed that it could come through redefinition as well" (20).

Trent (1995) asserted that the "AAMR's *Mental Retardation: Definition, Classification, and Systems of Support* had a postmodern ring to it" (21). The situational, support-oriented nature of the definition suggested to Trent, that although through all of its history, the "AAMR has maintained that lack of intelligence is the essential basis for mental retardation...words such as relative and conditional appear and reappear, suggesting that mental retardation, like other medical and social conditions in the 1990's has fallen beneath the sledgehammer of deconstruction" (21). [8]

Although deconstructing mental retardation, or at least certain aspects of "it," is the purpose of this book, I would like to suggest that the 1992

---

[8] The definition of "mental retardation" is, in Trent's opinion, "deconstructed" by the 1992 system in the sense that its language quietly questions the "immutability (or even reality) of intelligence" (Trent 1995, 21), and by the implication that "definitional cures" become possible (by way of environmental modifications, reconfigured, or previously unavailable personal supports, etc.). In some crucial ways, these departures from "business as usual" undermine and subvert the assumptions of historical meanings of mental retardation.

system does something more familiar than that. It merely refocuses, extends, expands, and intensifies the gaze[9] which constitutes the disciplinary matrix of the science of mental retardation.

---

[9] I use the term "gaze" in the Foucauldian sense. Sheridan (1980/1990), in describing the meaning and significance of Foucault's term states that: "Suddenly doctors were able to see and to describe what for centuries had lain beneath the level of the visible and the expressible. It was not so much that doctors suddenly opened their eyes; rather that the old codes of knowledge had determined what was seen. For doctors to see what [they] were trained to see those codes had to be transgressed and transformed. What occurred was not a return, beneath the level of language to a pure, untrammeled gaze, but a simultaneous change in seeing and saying. What made that change possible was a complex of events that included...a new definition of the social status of the patient, a new relationship between public assistance and medical experience, between health and knowledge. ...This was achieved by a convergence of the requirements of a political ideology and those of a medical technology" (39-40). The parallels—seeing, saying, and political ideology in medicine and mental retardation—are, I hope, obvious.

Chapter Eight
Woody

Field Notes, June 27, 1994

The reader had a little room off a store that sold magic crystals, incense, books about Native American chiefs, shamans, and so forth. Her son was in the store when I asked who could read my tarot cards. I felt somewhat the fool asking such a question because Cassadaga, Florida, has the highest per-capita population of psychics and mediums and such of anywhere in the United States of America. Everywhere you look there's a retreat for this, healing for that, and a reading for the other. Her son ran down a hill to get *my* reader.

Why it is so hilly here, in this part of Florida, I don't know, but the town is perched on a hillside, overlooking a salt pond. The drive from the highway is along an all-so-familiar absolutely straight North-South road, shaded by a canopy of not-so-familiar slash pines and pin oaks hung with Spanish moss, the understory a tangle of palmettos.

Sandra let me in the room when she got there and put out a sign that said she was open. There was a wooden chair where I figured I was supposed to sit. She sat on the other side in a beat-up upholstered chair. There were some big crystals on a rabbit hide on the table. I kept rubbing my little finger through the rabbit fur while she told me about me; I poked at the crystals with my index finger while she talked and carefully examined the indentation the crystal made on the end of my finger.

Sandra seemed like she was 50, but later I found out that she was 60. There was crap like old torn-up *Good Housekeeping* magazines, bags of trash, and trash not in bags piled up around on the floor, and in drifts up against the walls. She fished around in a bookshelf and found some Tarot Cards. It is not the Rider deck.

"I collect them," she said shuffling the cards about seven or eight times. Then I cut them. She dealt an array, frowned, and then laid out some more.

I blurted out that I work with a little autistic kid, and she sighed wearily, "You're a healer."

She said, "Yours is a spiritual journey, you know. You feel a lot, but bottle it up inside, maybe something that happened to you earlier, I don't know. Like they said, 'Shut up, we don't want to hear about it' and you learned to just keep quiet." She makes a swatting gesture, and I see me swatted into a corner with the other garbage.

"We don't touch much anymore, but you shouldn't be afraid to touch because you're a healer. You know doctors, they heal, but sometimes it's the nurses and other people around the sick person that makes the difference. They touch. Don't be *afraid* to touch the children you work with.

"Over here, you saw me laying out her cards, then I stopped, but I needed more. I see a lot of notes, notes all over the place. Do you write?"

"Yes."

"Are you in graduate school?"

"Yes."

"Getting your Ph.D. or something?"

"Yes."

"Don't stop writing those notes. They're important. I see a book, sometime, maybe not right away, but sometime."

"Everything is hard for you. That's not really bad or anything, just a lot of pain. But always remember that you are on a spiritual journey, that's your way."

"These notes, I know you read a lot and it's theory and book learning, but the notes are something else. Make sure you write down what you see; what *you* see, not what the theory and all see. Because you might see something different. You *will*, I think."

"You try very hard to make people happy, very hard. But the bottom line is that you will do what you know you need to.

"Do you have any questions?"

"No."

"Every passage will be hard for you. You see all these cards with dark passages? That's what they mean to me."

She told me that I get messed up by details, like money, and what time it is, but that it's just because I'm looking at something else.

She asked me how I felt, and I said *fine* and went back out on the street in the glaring sun, got in the car and drove to the edge of town, where I watched a man digging clams in the saw grass. A couple of herons stood at the edge of the still water and snapped an occasional minnow.

Conversation with Greg Miller, July 1, 1998

I talked with Greg Miller on the first of July, 1998. He has a sister with some kind of developmental disabilities. He's been around "mentally retarded people" all his life, he tells me.

"I started out in the special education program there but faded out—that's where I heard about the Center, at Illinois State University—the teacher there knew a lot about writing programs, but she didn't ever see any kids. I guess that's the way it is nowadays, I have a sister in Colorado, and all she does is write programs, never sees the kids but writes a lot of programs. I wasn't real interested in working with that aspect of kids, I realized."

"I know how you feel, I'll tell you, I'd much rather work with kids than say, uh, uh ..."

"Administrators?" Greg chuckled.

We laughed. Hee, hee, hee!

"It was weird when I came to work at [Group Home A]. It's funny but when I started working at [Group Home B] (another Center-operated children's home), it was weird then too. I'd never been around disabled people who were verbal. Five out of the eight kids were verbal."

In the background, on the tape, I hear Abe. He's diagnosed with autism. He's saying, "Wah, wha, wha, wha, wha, wha, wha, wha, wha, wha, wha, wha, wha, wha, wha, wha, wha, wha, wha, wha, wha, wha, wha, wha, wha."

"I started working here last April, and at least only two of the boys here were verbal. It wasn't as, I don't know, fun, I mean not fun, but different, 'cause the boys here aren't as *social*. Like Abe, Woody, Manny, they could go a whole day without any contact, and it wouldn't bother 'em. They like it that way, at least it seems like it, sometimes."

"How can you tell?"

"'Cause they run out of the room when you walk in and stay to themselves, or if you try to get close to them, they react negatively, like move away from you. You can tell when they're happy or unhappy after being around them for a while. The kids at [Group Home B] were more affectionate, and I was just used to them being there for you."

"Do you ever do stuff to make 'em more social, or do they even care about it, or what do you think?"

"Everybody was surprised about how much Woody liked me, 'cause I was used to the kids at [Group Home B]. I'm not afraid of getting hurt, cause I'm used to that too. So I'd nuzzle up to him, any kind of affectionate pats or anything. I've had more success in that department with Woody than with Abe or Manny."

"Cause he's more reachy-outy? Or what?"

"Sometimes, or maybe he feels that I'm not afraid of him, or something, he comes up and touches-face with me and hugs me more than some of the other staff."

"How do the other staff react to Woody?"

"I think that some of them are afraid of him because he's bitten people, like some of the subs, they're just more aware of his existence in the room—they're afraid. They're less tolerant of his hyperactivity so they don't mind if he sits in his old room for a couple of hours or goes outside—he's fine, as long as he's not in pain or hurt. They'll just leave him be because they don't want to risk being bit or having everything loud."

"What do you do that's different than that?"

"I think I just pay more attention to him and talk to him. Some people, because the kids aren't verbal, they don't talk to them, as much as they talk about them? Like Woody understands 80 percent of what you're saying."[1]

"How can you *tell* that?" My voice sounds clipped, military, somehow.

"Well, like put on your seatbelt, Woody, or..."

"Do you think it extends further than taking instructions? I guess it's easier to tell if he's taking instructions, now that I think about it."

Greg: "Right,..."

"Uh, like if people are talking about him, I wonder if he understands, like, saying something like 'I wish Woody would go outside,' I guess I

---

[1] Vilfredo Pareto in 1897 formulated what is now known as the 80/20 principle, or simply, the Pareto Principle. He noticed that 20 percent of our carpets get 80 percent of the wear and tear. He generalized this to economics: 20 percent of the customer base accounts for 80 percent of revenues. Social scientists have appropriated the Pareto principle in a variety of ways. For instance, in a social service agency, 20 percent of one's clientele causes 80 percent of the troubles. Greg noted that Woody and Ian understood 80 percent of what was going on around them. This leads me to believe that perhaps there would be some merit in research directed toward the "discovery" of a Pareto principle of mindedness.

don't know what people say about him?"

"Well, really, it's not using his name, but I'll tell him, 'we're going to go swimming,' he understands that."

"Do you treat him like he understands you?"

"Ohhh yeah."

I tell Greg about how Woody and I talked at Bloomington High School, and I asked him if he did that here. He said he'd like to, but he has to work with subs all the time, even though he's Woody nominal 1:1 support staff. He tells me that Woody loves his freedom, but 'they' made a schedule for him. Greg allows that he probably needs the schedule but loves his freedom, and that's a conflict for him. The schedule would be nice, but Greg can't keep to it because he's working with subs all the time and will be for the next month. He has to train them. The other problem is that 'they' haven't purchased another car, so they have to split the Center vehicle between both houses, and, "That's a pain."

"I just take him out in my car. And that's kind of tricky. I had my radio on, but it was on above a certain decibel and Woody got upset and tried to bite me; there was a lot of traffic, and we had to pull off on a side road. I have to have him in the front seat, 'cause he can take off his seatbelt. If he's in the back, he could reach up and grab my hair or get me around the neck. If we had a van, I could get him back further or in a bucket seat; he'd at least be further away from me."

"Woody lets you touch him, and there's none of that avoidance you see with other people?"

"Because he knows I'm not going to let him bite me. I'm not going to be intimidated. For some reason he trusts me."

"Do you think he feels safer around you?"

"Probably, and I talk to him. Not like two year olds. I talk to them all like regular people, and that's probably why they like me as much as or the way they do."

Dan: "And so..., I start all of my questions with '...and so,' don't worry, I'll edit it out later to make myself sound better. I don't have my questions with me, forgot 'em. My thesis, or hypothesis, what I'm writing about, whatever, is that people's minds exist only to the degree that other people think they do, know what I mean?"

"Yeah, I can see that ..."

"Do you see that operating in Woody's life, or do you have any examples?"

"Woody... . Actually, I had other kids in mind, easier, like Eric. You know that thing that 'Eric doesn't like African American females' and how he sits there in front of the TV, and says how he's going to beat them up?"

"Yup."

"Well, that's just not true. Think. Gwen is a black woman; Linda is a black woman; his teacher is a black woman and he never went after them. He loves them! What happened was that people were thinking of reasons that Eric might attack people and they theorized 'African American black women.' And talked about it, figured it *all* out, right in front of him. Then he started saying he was going to hurt the black women on TV."

Woody comes in the kitchen with Greg and me. He pops his tongue against the top of his palate. Then he says, "Oh...ho, ho, ba-dihgeee."

I pop my tongue in response, and say, "What do you want, dihgeee, dihgeee?"

Greg: "I do that too, talk to him in his own language. Actually, I know all the kids' languages. I could talk it right, each one. *I* don't think I'm regressin' them any, talking in their own language. They know I'm just talking their language."

"What is it Woody," I ask, "you have a searching look in your eyes?"

"Gee, ba-ba-ba, dihgeee!"

Field Notes, October 21, 1997

I walk into the Center at about 8:00 AM, and say hello to the receptionist and move the magnetic black dot opposite my name from "in" to "out," pause, and move it back to "in." The receptionist is buried in the newspaper as I walk by and does not look up as I round the corner and mount the stairs to the second floor. My office is in a corner. Team Leader's (I supervise about 8) offices are in larger rooms, and their desks are grouped together in the manner of TV detective shows, except that there are liberal attempts to personalize one's space.

I head toward my office, nodding to my coworkers. There are "Messages for You" according to the liquid crystal display on my telephone.

The first concerns a visit to one of the children's group homes planned by the director of development to tell a story to a group of our town's finest: "This is the way these poor kids live, but through your support, we will be splitting up these 'Eight Bed *Facilities*' (we have two) into three-to-five-kid *homes*." Unfortunately or otherwise, the director had been out to one of the group homes the day before, and she wanted to cancel, "because I just don't think it would be a good idea—I think we'd, uh, disrupt things."

The day before, at our administrative team meeting, I had been arguing against her visiting the kids homes. The director of development wanted to have the parents of one of the children who live there "on site" to tell our town's finest what a service the Center had performed by relieving them of their child.

I was arguing that I didn't want to be in the business of making group homes for children whose parents didn't want them because of their disabilities, that there are other options; we could give the families more support at home (currently, the state allocates 160 hours of respite care per *year* to any family with a child with disabilities). That if the family was abusive, we could set up foster homes and so on. I was outmaneuvered.

I listen to the rest of my messages which pertain to people wanting me to do things that I've already done, thinking of doing, or probably won't do.

On my desk is a stack of neurological reports from Southern State University on a 22-year-old young man who used to live at one of the Center's 8-bed group homes, then a 4-bed, then an apartment with 24-hr. staff. He proceeded to kick the shit out of everyone, molest little kids, and dash unheedingly into heavily trafficked streets.

Our executive director requested an emergency placement, for a month, at Lincoln Developmental Center (LDC), so that we could figure out what to do. After his placement there, he has had two "incidents" where they had to put him in "client management," restrain him that is, for about two minutes a piece. Since then, about three weeks, he has been the model "client." His mother is frantically trying to get him placed there permanently, more or less, and nobody from LDC is returning my phone calls. The executive director emails or voice-mails me daily "re: My plans for Jim."

I visit him once a week in Lincoln; he likes it there, and although he can't say, he shows me why. He likes the trees, the benches, the basketball court, his (shared) room; I get the feeling he feels safe there. Safe? From himself? From others?

The venerable institution's first "staffing" for this young man was attended by LDC's clinical director and one of his Ph.D. line staff, the medical director and one of his line staff (MD), a speech and language pathologist, a physical therapist, three nurses, a pharmacist, an occupational therapist, a qualified mental retardation professional, the living unit director, the facility director, the young man's mother, a registered dietitian, myself,[2] and our executive director.

Our state supports people in institutions like LDC at the yearly rate of $96,000 per year, and the Center's people at $30,000-$36,000 per year. We can hardly get doctors in our town, let alone other professionals to see our people because they are "on" Medicaid, which reimburses poorly. At Lincoln, we luxuriate in an hour-and-a-half long meeting of minds.

Surrounding and overlapping Jim's medical reports on my desk are documents from Human Resources telling me exactly how much overtime my staff have been accruing, my draft intake procedure, a draft PERT chart for converting our two 8-bed children's homes to five 3-4 kid homes, a position paper I'd written two years ago about why we ought to do this, budget summaries for all the programs I direct, piles of junk from our State's Child Protection agency (there are three notebooks that contain the regulations, and at least twice per week, I get a mailing from them that says something like, "Please remove pages 567-587 and insert the attached documents." Stacked one upon the other, these notebooks are 1.5 feet tall. Miscellany, including reminders for me to encourage staff to attend various mandatory and other trainings, copies of letters to schools threatening them with legal action if they don't provide appropriate services for our kids, folders, notebooks, and pieces of paper on which I try to keep track of my subordinates' activities. My daily planner, and so on, are there but not visible. Beneath it all is a desk blotter that has a calendar on it that marks the month as February 1996. My coffee cup reads, "I am a professional: Do not try to do this at home."

I look in one of my mailboxes (I have three, one on each floor of the Center's floors). I find an incident report there. Incident reports are written when something unusual happens, usually involving an injury of some sort. They are classified as "medical" or "behavioral." This is a behavioral incident report. The incident occurred at 3:30 AM at [Group Home A] on 10/11/97, ten days ago. These reports are supposed to be routed within 24 hours. Sometimes we just *can't* make that deadline, it seems. The incident report is divided into sections that should help us uncover the meaning of the event:

---

2 The old adage 'What goes around, comes around' applies. I am now working at LDC as a behavior analyst associate. After a year of training, and if I pass a state-authored test, I will be a behavior analyst I. If you work in a total institution, and leave your keys in the office, have you locked yourself out or in?

Name of Person Involved: Woody.
Location of Incident: Kitchen.
Antecedent Circumstances: He came out of his room to go to the bathroom. Fifteen minutes after, he went back to his bedroom and started vocalizing frustrations.
Description of Incident: As I went to check on him, he came out of his room screaming. He went towards me, grabbed my arms, and attempted to bite me. He did this three different times, each time lasting only a few seconds. Between and after his attempts, he continuously bit his arms, slapped himself on the sides of his head, and jumped up and down. This lasted for about ten minutes.
Staff Intervention: As calmly as I could I asked him if he would like to sit down. After no response, I asked him if he could show me what he wanted or what he would like to do. Client Reaction: Woody went into the bathroom, took off his pajamas, and jumped into the bathtub. He sat up next to the faucet for the next 25 minutes. He was still hyper, but no longer upset when he decided to get out of the tub.
Verbal Contact—Name of Person(s) and Job Title/Relationship: Chauncey Gardener/co-staff, member.
Verbal Contact—Response/Recommendation Given by the Contact Person(s): The situation was already under control.
Action Following Notification: I had Woody put his pajamas back on after he got out of the tub. He voluntarily went back to bed. I checked up on him twice within the past hour. He eventually fell asleep between 4:40 AM & 5:00 AM.

There are some places for people to sign off and date the report. I sign the thing, wondering if Woody had the water running in the bathtub, figuring that he didn't, feeling something of a failure, organizationally, administratively, pedagogically, and personally. He was probably just sitting there naked in an empty tub. Woody spends a large part of his time wandering the perimeter of the fence at [Group Home A]. The path is beaten down where he walks, and I think about the tiger at our zoo, who has rubbed the fur off his hide at his right shoulder and hip, the places where he hits the bars of his cage as he paces his solitary route.

January 12, 1998 (Four days before My Preliminary Oral Examinations at the University of Illinois at Champaign-Urbana)

The executive director of the Center calls me into his office and offers me the choice of demotion or termination within 90 days for not much reason that I could discern. I think it had to do with my not getting our children's group homes downsized quickly enough, even though he had not purchased houses, secured funding, or responded to my insistent demands that during the downsizing, we should adhere to the Illinois

Department of Children and Family Services (DCFS) regulations. I quickly think this offer over and knowing, that I needed to keep my research base, decide to stay.

January 15, 1998

Administrative Team meeting. I notice that the resignation of my assistant executive director position is on the agenda. When it comes time for me to talk about it, I ask that the executive director explain what happened. He slammed his fist on the table and said that he wasn't going to talk about "personnel issues" in that particular forum. After the meeting, he asks me and the director of "Human Resources" to stay, and he says that he thought we had an agreement that I would say that I was stepping down because it was too much trouble for me to be an administrator and work on my dissertation. I told him that was a lie, and I wasn't going to lie. He fired me and gave me thirty days notice. A quick conference with the director of human resources turned him around and it was back to demotion. We left it like that.

The Next Week of January 1998

I contact a lawyer friend of mine, and she tells me that _____ is free to demote me at any time for any reason based on Illinois law but that he is not allowed to make me lie. She says that if he keeps bugging me, I should give him her card and say she'd be talking to him re: my Fourth Amendment rights. He keeps bugging me, so on Wed., I go to his office and say, "_____, I understand your right to demote or fire me, but I am not comfortable lying about it. I've secured a lawyer to protect that right." He called me a "motherfuckin' asshole," and that he wasn't going to talk to any "god damn lawyer," threw the business card in my face, and said that I was effectively terminated within thirty days. I said "OK."

Thursday

The executive director and the director human resources call me on the carpet and tell me that I can basically write my own job description as long as I'd stay. I say "OK," again, based on the need for dissertation data.

Friday

I bring in a job description that suits me nicely, and they agree to it as long as I'd lie and say that I was voluntarily stepping down. I say "OK." I have a paper I want them to sign that says that they would keep the position funded for a year, and they won't sign, because it's "like a contract," but that we could have a "Gentle(person's)men's Agreement" that he would keep the position intact for a year. We shake hands on this. I tell him I want more. He says what do you want? I say, "I want you to promise." He promises.

February 8, 1998

I distribute a letter that I'm stepping down so that I'd be under less pressure and could more rapidly complete my dissertation.

March-April 1998

I work at my job whilst my new boss, the director human resources micromanages my activities. A new "restructuring" of the organization is announced. I do not see a clinical coordinator position in the new "mix."[3] I ask for a meeting with the executive director and my boss, and they say that there is not. I do not whine and say "but you PROMISED!", but say "OK," instead.

April 30, 1998

I turn in my resignation, effective immediately. They ask me to stay on a week so the organization can "Celebrate my time at the Center."

May 5, 1998

Last day at the Center. No celebration. I walk out the door at noon. They are having a big meeting to explain the re-organization to wage-slaves. I'd been working at the Center in one way or another since January of 1981.

May 7, 1998

Director of Special Education at Bloomington Schools calls and asks me to be a one-on-one "teacher's assistant" for Woody. She says that she'll pay me regular teacher's salary to do this. I say "OK."

---

[3] We'd reorganized at least on a quarterly basis from Dec. 1996 to my termination date, May 5, 1998. We had a specialized language to gloss the technicalities reorganization. "New Mix," for instance, couches the various personal and organizational ordeals of managerial and line reconfiguration in an agreeable cast.

May-June 1998

I work with Woody. He stops biting people, learns some stuff (probably not as much as me). I notice that my last paycheck from the Center has been "docked" 4 hours, presumably, because I'd left and not attended the BIG meeting at noon, my last day.

May 15, 1998

On Fridays, we go to the "community." Our students are given a little bit of money to buy *"personal items."* Their IEP's have goals that read, "_____ will purchase *personal items* of their choice in the community."

Most of the kids go to Schnuck's, an upscale grocery store. I ask Woody's teacher if we can go to Angelica's instead.

"What's Angelica's?"

I tell her that it's "...a store, kind of like, uh, an, what's that word for little store that sells expensive stuff?"

"Boutique."

"Yeah!, boutique, and they sell women's stuff, like clothes and jewelry, but they specialize in aroma and massage therapy. That's where I get Woody's hand cream. It's kind of like a Head Shop for the State Farm crowd."

"We'll have to talk to the bus driver."

"It's right around the corner from Schnook's," I say.

I take all my research subjects to Angelica's. I've told the women who work there that I'm interested in alternative therapies for kids with autism. I don't tell them too much more, but they like the kids. A little girl I work with is allowed to spread $50.00 beanie babies all over the floor, but she usually buys something like a 75¢ plastic crawdad.

Woody and I arrive at the store. Woody looks around with what I interpret as wonder. We walk up to the counter.

"Hi," I say, "this is Woody. We came to pick up some more lotion."

"Hi, Woody," says the lady. "Are you here to get some lotion?"

Woody smiles vaguely.

"Let's clear off a spot on the floor, and you can sit down, and I'll bring you some different scents."

"Uh," I say, "let's stay away from like patchouli, and anything like sandalwood. The other teachers come in the class and say it smells like wood and wrinkle their noses."

"OK, Woody, let me go get a couple."

In hushed tones, I hear another worker at the store explaining my activities to a couple of customers. She says: "He's a teacher. He brings his students in here because it's a quiet environment, and we play classical music. It's soothing to them. We let them smell the different fragrances. You can see the change in *them* the more they come in."

"Woody," says the lady, "I brought you a couple of scents."

"Dighee, ba-ba-ba, dighee!"

Woody is getting a little worked up. He reaches around and grabs a silver spoon that has a piece of natural twine tied to it. Woody pulls the twine off the spoon and puts it in his mouth. Properly wetted, he begins to twirl it. The lady goes behind the counter and gets Woody a piece of the same twine and some yin-yang steel balls. These balls have chimes inside of them. Woody is not interested in the balls but accepts the twine, wets it, and twirls it: He holds it between his thumb and index finger with his palm down. By moving his hand in a tight circle; the laws governing that part of the physical world with which I am familiar cause the tail end of the string to remain stationary, while the length curves into an arc, constricting as Woody spins it faster. Woody takes his other hand and holds it about ten inches in front of his eyes, palm toward the twine. He wiggles his fingers, an incantation of sorts.

The woman comes back with several scents she thinks might appeal to Woody. I take away Woody's string, and Woody smells the scents. We think he chooses "Forest Rain." I give Woody his string back, and the woman mixes some of the essential oils into a neutral base. We pay, and since the bus is late, or on time, we go to the frozen yogurt store and get some cones.

August 19, 1998

The walls at [Group Home A] are hung with faux wood paneling. This is so the kids can't punch through the drywall. Nonetheless, where the drywall still persists, in such places as the stairway and in the bathrooms, there are holes. It takes a long time to patch up the holes; there is only one maintenance person. The windows are all Plexiglas. Long ago, when the house opened in 1982, the kids made short work of the original glass panes. The windows now are so scratched that "For now [they] see through...[Plexi]glass, darkly;...And now abideth faith, hope, charity, these three; but the greatest of these is charity" (I Corinthians, 12-13).

At grocery store check-out lanes in town, the Center has distributed jars with "some clip-art from the ARC of Illinois" (formerly the Association of Retarded Children of Illinois, then the Association of

Retarded Citizens of Illinois, and now just, "The ARC of Illinois"). The labels say, "Help them become all they can be" and have silhouettes of little kids dancing about.

The jars should not be in the store: they should all have all been turned into the Center. We are entering the "Blackout Period," which starts in August and ends sometime in November. During the blackout, United Way funded agencies may not actively seek charity because this is the time of the national United Way Fund Drive. Across the nation, workers will be handed red markers and asked to fill in thermometers indicating progress toward the goal.

Woody's been moved downstairs at the group home where he (still) lives. He does not want to be downstairs, but he bites people, so he lives downstairs. His old upstairs room is unoccupied (the Children's Home downsizing was more or less completed in late July, 1998, leaving some vacant rooms at [Group Home A]) and unadorned with any football posters, movie posters, lamps; the closet doors hang open, no clothing. The paneling in this room is white with blue-gray accents in the grain. Electrical outlets have either been covered with metal or are punched out. The bare lightbulb at the ceiling is unlit. The floor is dusty, and the unwaxed linoleum has some holes in it. There is no furniture here, save a white plastic lawn-chair, propped at a precarious angle with the two front legs in the air. Here in the darkest corner sits Woody. His face is broken out badly, and some of the pimples are bleeding.

Individualized Program Planning, May 29, 1998

We are jealous of the better funded Special Education Cooperative in our sister city. Woody's teacher, his mother, and myself, walk into the brand new high school where Woody will be placed next year. None of us are really clear on why Woody is moving to this district, although I suspect that it has to do with the downsizing at the Center, even though no one has moved anywhere nor have houses been purchased.

Woody's mother tells me: "I always wanted him to be in this district, but I gave up fighting with them years ago. I hope the director doesn't remember me."

We walk in and I suddenly realize why Woody's teacher is so on edge: She is destined to look the failure. Her IEP will be deemed inadequate, her behavioral programming lacking, and her related services laughable.

No wonder *these* people will do so much better with Woody! The 'staffing' commences. "Are those marks on your arm from *Woody?*" they ask derisively.

"Yes," I tell them. "I wasn't thinking this morning." Woody bit me while we were playing basketball.

With a very broad brush, the IEP team from the new school veneers the canvas of a community-oriented, vocationally-based (but segregated) special educational program for Woody. His mother wants to know: "Will he *ever* be with the other kids?"

"Our program is *Community-based, and Functional,*" says an alumnus of my master's program at U of I. "I think Woody will *benefit* from our work with him. He'll be having *lunch* here," she says, looking at her nodding, smiling colleagues. In the past, community-based has meant, at least for the Center children, "Take the kid back to [Group Home A] every day with an underpaid teacher's assistant, and pray that they learn some *domestic* skills, and take them to Wal-Mart once or twice a week to shop for *personal items.*"

My inner voice tells me to shut up. "Don't you dare bring up the fact that these people have kicked two kids who lived at [Group Home A] out of their school because of their aberrant behavior! And don't talk about how you had to retain attorneys to get them back in or at least provide them with home-bound instruction for more than an hour a day," it says. I try to fold my arms so the bite marks don't show.

I ask what kind of programming they have in mind to support positive behaviors on Woody's part. While I begin to talk about the interventions I've been using for the last month, how successful they've been, the team begins to fold up their notebooks, zipping and clasping their bookbags and briefcases... . Glancing at my watch, I see that it *is* 3:30. I hand what I've learned from Woody to one of the specialists.

The last staffing I'd been to concerning Woody was in April of 1998. The director of special education for the district was trying to suggest that the school be permitted to use, "a, a, kind of mask? Something Woody could wear on his head that would prevent him from biting?"

"Like a muzzle?" I asked. "Maybe we could get one at Medusa's!" I offered cheerfully. Medusa's is the only dirty book store/adult emporium in our town. But it turned out that the director had a catalog from a special education materials purveyor that had at least two pages of devices.

The director didn't appreciate my humor and looked like she was not doing very well. I volunteered the Center's services (me) to help them work out some sort of intervention so that Woody wouldn't bite anyone.

Usually, the Center does not permit this kind of activity of its employees (schools are mandated and funded to provide a FAPE, a free and appropriate public education, and the Center is not). I thought, "What the hell? They can't really say anything; Woody's mom is on the Center's Board of Directors."

"How can you be sure that he won't bite anyone?" asked the principal.

"I only said he wouldn't while I was here," I said.

"How do you know he won't?"

"I just know," I said.

What I've Learned from Woody: May 28, 1998 (A Memo to Woody's New IEP Team)

General Comments. Since the time that I've worked with Woody in a school setting, I've found that he is generally compliant, in terms of moving from one class to another, one activity to another, and so on. He requires little preparation for these transitions. He sits quietly on the bus.

This is not to say that Woody will do exactly as you want as these transitions take place and afterward. For instance, when Woody moves from class to class, he may ramble about in a seemingly aimless fashion. In class, when he is not sitting, his pattern of motion is circular, clockwise.

A mistake, in my opinion, is to "chase" after Woody, block his way, attempt to maneuver him, and so on. This leads to frustration, both for Woody and the teacher. It also makes one feel ridiculous, as Woody will always succeed in outsmarting you, or you will surely get into a confrontation (please see comments on effective teaching strategies below).

The effect is somewhat like attempting to view a squirrel as he or she scampers to the other side of a tree as you try to keep the creature in view. Or perhaps like rounding up a stray steer.

Woody will try to defend himself if he is "cornered," usually by "blocking" a person, or running, or biting. The "run" is usually a short burst; in our classroom, he will run toward one of the doors, toward the blackboard, the windows—actually toward any of the four walls, avoiding corners. The "run" is more than that; his arms can be raised or lowered to his waist, and there is a prancing quality to the movement. Note that Woody choreographs a similar performance when he is excited or happy, but there seems to be a difference—perhaps it's the expression on his face, the look in his eyes, or one's simply knowing the context in which Woody "takes off."

For instance, today at lunch, I gave Woody some hot sauce on his pizza, and he rose from his chair, galloped up to one of the food service women, hugged her, and kissed her on the neck, bounced back to our table and had another bite. Next he pranced over to the water fountain.

Woody's Unusual Behaviors. Woody has a number of behaviors that most people would consider unusual. Without extensive analysis, I think that I can say with some confidence that these behaviors serve to keep Woody "in." Let me explain. You see, I think that it is at least convenient if not correct to think of Woody being either "in" or "out." When Woody is "in," he seems to be in his own world. When he is "out," he is with us. There's not much point in talking with Woody when he is "in."

When Woody is in, he will use many behaviors characteristic of the autistic spectrum, including finger-flapping, pressing his fingers to his ears, holding the palm of his hand to his mouth with his fingers positioned over his ears (I call this 'communicating with his satellite'—just a note here, it would be helpful to operationally define each of Woody's unusual behaviors and the behaviors that indicate that he is out and write them down, out of respect for Woody, so everyone can 'speak and understand his language'), using a loud voice, twirling string or similar material, and so on.

Disconcertingly, Woody seems to enjoy sticking his fingers into small crevices, holes, and other confining spaces, such as the chain on swings, seat belt clasps, etc. He occasionally gets stuck, and this is distressing for him, panics him. It's almost like a game that he plays to see "just how far can I go!" Woody's fingers usually have some kind of blister or cut on them. The first joint of Woody's fingers seems disproportionately small compared to the second joint. I always carry a tube of chap-stick when I am working with Woody, and I use this as a lubricant to grease his appendage and slowly work it out of whatever clinch or bind he's gotten himself into. He will try to pull his finger directly out, which, most of the time, will not work, because the folded skin will act to increase the diameter of his finger. Using a calm voice and demeanor, I ask him not to panic. I lubricate his finger or thumb, push it further in whatever he's gotten himself into, (to spread the lubrication where it needs to be), and pull out with a slight twisting motion.

Woody will put just about anything in his mouth. Particularly inviting are cigarette butts, old chewing gum, caulk from window glazing, insulation, soft rubber balls in gym class (he will bite these and break them), you name it.

Certain objects hold greater control of "in-ness" for Woody. String and other objects for twirling predominate this category. Woody will tap hard objects, such as pens or combs, on tables which is distracting to students and unnerving to teachers.

Of greater concern have been incidents of biting and other aggressions against students and teachers. These incidents reportedly "come out of the blue," but I dispute this not only because "out of the blueness" is hard to treat educationally or therapeutically, but I have witnessed several potential biting incidents where the precipitating factors did not originate in the blue.

For instance, one time we were walking to the track for gym class. Woody likes to walk on curbs or on the edge of the sidewalks. Suddenly, Woody attacked me and, when he realized he was not going to be able to hurt me, collapsed crying and screaming with both hands over his ears. Tears were streaming down his face. I took Woody back to class, and as we walked, I remembered that just before Woody exploded, he had twisted his ankle. When we arrived back in class, after he was sufficiently relaxed and "out," I checked his feet, and he had some large, festering blisters on his foot. I think that when Woody twisted his foot, he aggravated his blisters and "lashed out" at me.

Early on, Woody tried to bite me "out of the blue," but I think that I had inadvertently cornered him in the classroom, and he saw me as an obstacle to his escape.

Another recent near-attack occurred during a group activity. [His teacher] was leading a group in some kind of educational game that resembled bingo with real objects. Suddenly, Woody was beating the sides of his head. According to our plan, students were removed to another classroom, and Woody was left slouching against the wall, holding his head and crying. [His teacher] thought that maybe Woody was not winning, or perhaps the excited voices of the students somehow undid Woody. In any case, Woody seemed to be in actual pain, like in horror films where evil scientists make your head explode. I took Woody to the nurse to get Tylenol, and he calmed down, and the other kids were invited back into the classroom.

Intervention Strategies–Structured Relaxation with Lotion. At 7:30 or so, I come into the classroom. Woody's bus usually arrives at this time. Usually, Woody stops in the vicinity of his locker and may or may not drop his book bag there. I would like for him to put his own book bag away, which involves walking into the classroom, getting his key, walking out of the classroom, unlocking the locker, putting the book bag away, relocking the locker, and walking back to the classroom. Sometimes he wants to, and sometimes he doesn't; I don't make an issue of it.

I try to "lure" Woody to a semicircle table with the intent that he sit in the chair in the middle and allow me to rub lotion on his hands and arms and Neutrogena anti-acne lotion on his face.

As I stated above, it is not always an easy task to get Woody to sit, and often results in what I described above as an embarrassing game of "chase and cajole Woody." I have tried "waiting him out," but I've not had much luck.

You can tell when Woody is out. He will look at you, smile, laugh, and allow you to touch him.

What has been somewhat successful (about 80 percent) has been putting a dab of hand lotion on my hand, walking over to him, and asking if he would like to use the lotion. Woody usually has something he is "playing" with, such as a string, a ball, a piece of rubber hose, and so on. When we engage in "chase and cajole," Woody shows me that he is "in" by holding his hand to his mouth so that his fingertips encase his ear, saying "eeahhw, wwahhw, eeee," or something like that, along with some combination of the unusual behaviors described above.

Woody often responds to the American Sign Language (ASL) sign, "come," "sit," "more," "stand." Woody will use the sign, "please." I've found that edible rewards or reinforcers are much more effective than chasing him around. Usually, I use Tic-Tacs, a strategy I call Tic-Tactics. My approach is subtle, but Woody is observant. For instance, I can place a Tic-Tac in my hand and sign the word, "come," and when Woody comes, I can slip it to him with no one being the wiser. Tic-Tacs also make a distinctive sound in one's pocket, and I can bang the Tic-Tac container and usually get Woody's attention.

When we are settled at the table, I usually put some lotion on my hands, and Woody will take a dab and rub it on his face, near the lips, often eating a little bit. Then I put some more on my hands. Then, I turn my hands into a crocodile (palms together, fingers apart) and he will place, usually, his left hand in the "jaws." He seems to enjoy it more when I use heavy massaging pressure, using my fingers to rub his palms and my thumbs to rub the top of his hands. When he acclimates to this, I squeeze his fingers (like milking a cow). Usually, I can massage his whole arm like this.

Woody usually offers his hand palm down after transferring his string, ball, or whatever to his right. Of late, however, I trade the "toy" for the massage (in addition, I would like to say that I have discontinued using string and balls in favor of small pieces of rubber objects, such as a piece of a tennis ball. Objects such as these seem to have sufficient allure to hold his attention yet are not so enthralling as to transport him inward). When Woody is very much with you, he will let you massage his feet, and this seems pleasurable to him—but he must be *very much with you.*

There is a delicate balance at play in this interaction, as I try to push the limits of our connection. For instance, if I try to advance too quickly (for example, attempting to rub his hands before I've let him put a little lotion on his face), he will get up and leave, and we are back to ground zero—"chase and cajole." I try to get some lotion on his forearms, but this can only happen toward the end of the session when Woody seems to be relaxed enough to "take it." You can tell when Woody is relaxed because he is not pulling his hands away from you, and he may start murmuring, or speaking in a quiet tone of voice (although the words are not understandable to me at this point) and maintaining eye contact.

When Woody is sufficiently relaxed (a judgment call) I use Neutrogena anti-acne medicine on his face. Once again this is slow process of getting Woody used to my touch. I put a dab on my fingers and tell him I am going to put it on his face and start on his cheek. He'll usually withdraw, and I'll ask if I can try it again. He usually doesn't answer, but if he remains calm, I'll continue to apply it to his cheeks. Once he is into this, Woody will stick his whole face into your palms and rub it back and forth.

Then, I try to rub some on his forehead. I do this by putting some on my forehead while he is watching and then lifting up his hair and stroking it on his forehead. You must be vigilant for any signs of distress, or Woody will lose you (figuratively and literally). Sometimes, Woody will show you that he wants the lotion on his forehead first by leaning his head down from the neck.

After massage is complete and we are both a greasy mess, I try to massage his scalp. The same slow going applies here; first scratch his head a little, then if he leans his head toward you, use both hands to massage the scalp using your finger tips.

Why go through all the trouble? A good question, as it seems that the activities described above at times make Woody feel uncomfortable. However, a massage is pleasurable to most people, and theoretically at least this would apply in Woody's case. In addition, again theoretically, the "therapy" could be seen as one which has the potential to reduce some of

Woody's "tactile defensiveness." Also, it results in prolonged interaction with Woody, and I have had no luck with *any other* activity in terms of duration. Finally, it seems to have the effect of getting Woody "out."

Intervention Strategies—Computer skills. I type with Woody on the computer. I try to use Microsoft Word, and call up a word processing document. When we type, I try to use the font Arianna set at 26-28 points.

I sit to Woody's left and he types with his right hand. When we begin, I mold his fingers such that his typing hand is fisted with his index finger in a pointing position. We try to type different words; I don't, at this point have any evidence that any of these words, such as Woody, [teacher's name], "I want lunch," "What are we going to eat for lunch?" "Woody is cool," etc., have any particular meaning for him. But he will cooperate in typing them. During the session, I try to reduce the assistance I give him by moving the locus of my control from his hand, to his wrist, to his forearm, and then to his elbow. He often succeeds with the prompt at his elbow.

Occasionally, Woody enjoys using my finger to type with. He grabs my finger, and I type words, speaking them as I type.

Often, Woody will stroke the keyboard with his left hand, or if he has a ball or string, will slap at it with that object. I don't try to stop him from doing this, although it results in misspellings.

Interestingly, when Woody is stroking the keyboard, he will use only enough pressure to push the key in to the point at which it will "strike" a letter. This sensitivity is remarkable in that I have extreme difficulty replicating his actions without making letters appear.

After typing, I try to have Woody help me put all of his materials (hand lotion, acne medicine, and so on) into a box. Many times, I can just hold the box and say, "Let's put our things away," and that is enough to move him to action.

I have been teaching the other young adults in the class how to greet Woody. This is simple. I tell them, just walk up to Woody, and offer your hand palm up, and he will stroke it. Students are less afraid of Woody, and he is becoming a popular member of his class; for instance, he is often chosen by team captains first in gym class.

Using Tic-Tactics, I have been able to support Woody in gym class. I have been successful at standing behind him and making shots with the basketball, engaging in team sports such as kickball, and having him at least sit in a circle while the rest of the class does exercises. Here, I do not usually "reinforce correct behavior" with the Tic-Tacs, as much as "get his attention and give him the Tic-Tac"; this seems to put him in the right mind-set for participation.

Just a word about the Tic-Tactics. Please do not confuse these with "reinforcement." Reinforcement can only be defined in terms of its effect on behavior. In other words, reinforcement is a stimulus that, when given in conjunction with a particular behavior, increases the likelihood that the same behavior will occur when the organism is presented once again with the same stimulus. I don't believe that getting Woody in a frame of mind that is conducive to learning falls into this category of stimuli. If you're thinking, "Well, Woody's just getting whatever he wants, and it will 'reinforce' the negative behavior," don't bother. Tic-Tactics are merely a measure to get Woody OUT. Out of whatever trouble he's in or out of his own world.

I have also been teaching Woody to discriminate between coins. The payoff is getting a soda. He seems to like to have you pour a small amount of soda into a glass, and he will sniff the bubbles. I started with nickels (you need 10) and moved to dimes and now quarters. I believe the reason that I am having luck here is that using the vending machine holds a certain distress for Woody. He does not like to put the coins in the machine but wants the pop. So, I can say, "we'll use dimes," and since we only need 5 dimes (fewer coins), he discriminates nicely.

Cautionary Notes. Woody has a history of biting people, and I recommend that anyone that works with him be versed in aggression management techniques. Particularly, if you feel Woody is coming toward you with the intention of hurting you, *do not pay attention to his hands* (they don't hurt as much as his teeth). Hold your hands together, place them at his sternum, and lock your elbows. Use his momentum to guide him to the side of you and step away. Woody's attacks are seldom prolonged. Speak to him gently, and say something like, "Woody, listen to me, listen to me." When he is calm enough, use the lotion to get him "out" again. Then try to figure out what the problem is.

If Woody gets his teeth on you, do not pull away, but bring the affected limb closer to his mouth. This way, there is less chance that your skin will be torn. While you are calmly enduring incredible pain, try to insert an index finger (gently, you could hurt him) in between Woody's jaws through his cheek. When he releases you, move away slowly, and use the calming techniques described above.

Be wary though; sometimes Woody will come at you with the intention of hugging you.

Final Notes. Recently, I believe Woody has begun using sentences, or at least two-word utterances. He pokes me in the chest and then signs "please." Usually I can figure out what he wants from me from the context of the situation but not always. He is also beginning to understand ASL and spoken, "Help me," as in "Help me understand."

Interview with Woody's Mom (Janet), July 1, 1998

I told Janet a "funny" story of how when it was real hot last week at [Group Home A], they'd asked him to go close the door when he came inside. He went outside and shut the door and just stood there in the heat. They finally taught him how to pull the door closed from the inside. A staff member who I'd interviewed thought this was because so many staff want him outside (out of their hair) that when they asked him to shut the door, they were in essence, in Woody's mind, "kicking him out."

Janet told another possible explanation: he doesn't like to pull things, and he would have to pull the door shut if he stood inside. Woody has never liked to pull things. Just push them. Janet used the words "Woody may push things but not pull them." As if there is some sort of permission that Woody must ask of himself.

According to my interview strategy, I asked if she had any similarly engaging stories. She said that she might have some "horror stories."

Janet told me one time some people built a house next door, and Janet and Ken wanted to go meet them. They took Woody along with them. She said, "Woody looks normal enough, but when they got close to the neighbors" and the pond behind their house, "Woody took a flying leap into the pond." It was early April, cold, and they were wearing sweatshirts, because, you know, it was "sweatshirt weather." Soon as Woody leaped into the pond, Woody's dad jumped in after him (before Janet even had a chance to scream), "boots coveralls, and everything, and fished him out" (the water was over his head). They walked home and dried out. Later, Janet talked to the neighbors and said, "You must have thought .... Dan, there was no possible way to explain it..."

The Next to the Last Day of School, 1998

We were going swimming in the school pool. I was swimming around with Woody. He can do somersaults in the water. He taught himself this, as he has, according to his mother, most everything. I figured Woody must be pretty good in the water, so I lured him out toward the deep end. Woody's mom bought a couple of large plastic livestock troughs for the kids at [Group Home A] to swim in. They don't take the kids to the pool very often, if at all.

I was swimming underneath the water, pretending I was a dolphin. From the bottom, I looked up and saw Woody drowning. It looked just like it does on TV. His arms and legs were flailing, and he couldn't get a breath. I put my feet on the bottom and shot up to him, and just like it says in the lifesaving books, Woody tried to climb on top of me to get some air. So just like it says in the lifesaving books, I got behind him and grabbed his chin and swam him to safety. He hugged me, and even though he had a regular Woody face on, I could feel his heart throbbing against my chest.

How do you tell when Woody is scared? I know how to tell when people are scared of Woody.

Interview with Janet, July 1, 1998

"Woody gets scared when he knows he's out of control. He needs to have 'body awareness and presence.' He used to walk on a railing (when he was three) on our deck and was fine doing this. One day my daughter went out and yelled something like 'Woody, hhhuuuhhh, you're going to fall off.' And he fell off. It's the same with trampolines. He can do all kinds of things on the tramp, but he's very careful to stay in the middle. I think it's an instinct he has."

I ask Janet when she started noticing anything different about Woody.

"He had the chicken pox, when he was two and a half, then he started spinning things, started looking at the tires on the cars, the holes in the pegboards, but I didn't think much of it, and I thought it was kind of funny. It didn't mean anything to us at the time. It was when he started screaming all the time, day and night. After about six months of that I was able convince Ken that we had a problem here. They diagnosed it in Champaign, then in Peoria, and it was downhill ever thereafter. We had five kids, and by the time he was three we knew. We talked to other parents. Abe's parents, for instance, knew right away.

"Woody went to Hammit School (a segregated school for kids with disabilities) when he was four. They gave him 'the boot' after about a year and a half. Now they have a program for autistic kids. They did some kind of administrative turn-around, but those kids are a little more 'cognitive' than Woody. Six months after Woody left, they gave Abe the boot."

"What do you mean by 'cognitive,'" I asked.

"Well, it's hard to describe, maybe a little more speech, and a little more manageability. Back then, Hammit billed themselves as—they did not take retarded children, and Woody wasn't testable then. Guess what? He still isn't!" [I laugh loud enough that I peg the VU meter on the tape recorder].

They took basically behavior-disordered kids back then. And Woody definitely had some aberrant behaviors, and so did Abe. I think that that's where Woody learned compliance, because they made him stand up and sit down several hundred times a day. Maybe it stood him in good stead 'cause he's willing to take simple instructions, but lately he's getting a little more belligerent."

"Tired of simple instructions?" I smiled.

"Maybe he's adolescent. Can you be adolescent and autistic at the same time? That's the explanation I have for it. He's adolescent and 15, so what?"

Dan: "I was wondering about that when you told me he treated you like wallpaper."

"Yesterday," Janet said, "I went to see him, and said something about a haircut, and he started twisting his hair around in knots, that's how I know that he knew what I was talking about, and I told him, 'Woody, you don't have to worry, we're not going to cut your hair today.' He shoved me away and laid down on Abe's bed [upstairs], and I just left. Getting a haircut is Woody's and my least favorite activity. I can't stand people touching my hair or my feet.

"But the day before, he acted like he was really happy to see me, and the time before that it was wallpaper. You just never know, it's just something he does, and that's the way it is."

I asked Janet what she meant by the kids at Hammit being more cognitive.

She said that some of them can use augmentative communication devices but doesn't know if the kids are necessarily learning anything, just that the parents seem satisfied.

"I've always thought that Abe was more cognitive than Woody. Abe will go home and take the Crisco and make a big mess with it or fling sugar or flour around just to make a mess, but Woody never makes a mess intentionally, just as a matter of course," and Janet laughs, as do I.

"Woody will make off with the coffee pot," she continued, "if there's coffee in it cause he likes coffee. I say to them, 'Just give him some coffee.' But there's some sort of tradition at the kid's group homes where 'children should not drink coffee.' I guess it's because of some women who ran the group home in the past felt like there should be 'no coffee for children.'

But I told them, it's either give Woody a cup of coffee, or he'll take yours.

"Drinking coffee together was one of the few things we could do together when he was growing up; when he was awake late at night, I would make some coffee, and Woody would sit there and drink it with me. He'd get up every couple of minutes, but he'd come back and get some more. Then he'd take mine, and I'd get up and get myself another cup.

"He's been drinking coffee for ten years, I think it's because of the strong taste. When he wants some, he'll go up to the coffee pot and tap on it."

I ask Janet if Woody thinks about things.

"I don't know if Woody thinks about stuff. I've thought for a number of years that he understands perfectly what's going on as long as it's not too complicated. But it's uneven. When he was a kid, I'd say, 'Woody, lets go outside,' and he'd go to the door, and there were other times when he'd just wander around in confusion. Same with going in the car, going downstairs, putting on shoes."

"Janet," I ask, "do you think he's thinking about something else, not thinking, or what?"

"I think it's like he's just 'out' and not 'in.' It could be anything, inattention, lack of understanding, or just not caring."

Janet thinks at one point in history, autism was the diagnosis of choice— but why someone would choose that diagnosis is beyond her. She thinks because of the historical "fashionability" of the diagnosis, there are a lot of kids out there who are misdiagnosed.

"When I took Woody to Ritvo's clinic in LA, they had a whole ward full of autistic kids, and I spent quite a bit of time watching them. I never watch Woody in situations like that because I already know what Woody does. I think I can tell 'real' autism from something that's not autism."

"What do you think Woody wants out of life," I ask, thinking of the charity cups at Kroger's.

"What Woody really wants is to be left alone," she said without hesitation. "They've been dragging him around all creation this summer. They've used picture symbols, and I think that he's learned that if he taps one, 'they'll leave me alone.' But, they did have activity cards for him at one point, and they'd give him a choice between staying home and going somewhere and he'd almost always pick staying at home, unless it involved food—he loves McDonald's french fries."

I ask Janet if she ever dreams about Woody talking.

"I don't," she said, "but my kids have dreams where he can talk sometimes. I don't remember what the kids say he said. I told them, 'Sometimes dreams come true.'"

Janet doesn't feel like she knows him as well as others right now because she doesn't spend as much time with him anymore. She knows certain things but not everything. She *knows* that he's not a little boy any more.

Janet told me that Woody moved into [Group Home A] August 20th, seven years ago. When they came back from California, it was obvious to her that they wouldn't be able to keep him at home. They were turned down two times, and she was thankful, but the sleeping disturbance was too much—they were desperate.

"The third time was a charm, I guess. But I still didn't want him to go... .

"Woody's got four good staff now, Carlos, Greg, Aaron, Brian. Usually one or two is the most I can hope for."

"What do you think makes a good staff person?" I ask.

"Well, they're not afraid of Woody, for one thing. Woody has to like them, then Woody doesn't resist," she says. "You can just tell. I know that staff are not going to stay too long. I know that they'll get good and bad staff. I just hope the bad leave sooner than the good. It's a college student job."

August 19, 1998

I go to visit Woody at [Group Home A]. In the time since I've left the Center, the electric door alarms (they shrieked when someone exited or entered without turning the key) have been replaced with the kind of security chains you see in regular households. Of course, in the real world, these chains are not meant to keep people in. I'm certain that none of the kids whose roaming is a concern will be taught to operate them. I pause to consider the rhetorical machinations necessary to resolve the cognitive dissonance that must arise in this situation.

In the locked med cabinet, I find the body lotion I'd got Woody at an aroma therapy store, sitting where I left it in May. There is dust on the bottle. I take it, along with the Neutrogena, and knock on Woody's door, and sit down next to him in his white chair.

"Dighee, dighee, dighee," he tells me.

"How yuh doin', Woody?" I ask, squirting some of the lotion into my palm.

Woody reaches out, and takes a dab, lifts it to his lips, and says, "Pa-tee, pa-tee." Then he grabs my head roughly with both hands and pulls me to his face so our foreheads touch. He stares at me directly in the eyes and smiles: "Dighee, dighee, dighee."

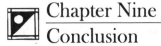# Chapter Nine
Conclusion

*God hath chosen the foolish things of the world to confound the wise;
and God hath chosen the weak things of the world
to confound the things that are mighty.*

—1 Corinthians I, 27.

Making myself understood by others does not usually present *me* with the same kinds of troubles[1] that bedevil the children of whom I've written. But on August 1, 1998, I checked myself in to the Bro-Menn Hospital in Normal, Illinois, for "detox."[2] I'd been drinking heavily for a week. I remember drunkenly asking nurses, doctors, psychologists, psychiatrists, anybody who I could force my self on, what the word "detox" meant. Detoxification? Detoxicated? Detoxified? Nobody knew.

Our small family (my girlfriend and two dogs) decided earlier that day that it was time for me to get some serious alcohol addiction treatment. We called the treatment center, and the woman told us that the best way to "get in" (read: jump ahead on the 'waiting list' and facilitate the necessary insurance transactions) was to go to the hospital, and, as they say, "present."

My girlfriend tried not to giggle as I laboriously explained to the nurse who had asked, "Why did you get so drunk?"

---

[1] Buckholdt and Gubrium (1979, 225) explain that human service professionals are trained to treat a wide variety of troubles.

[2] My girlfriend and I, being seasoned social workers, knowing that there was probably some kind of "system," found out that this is the quickest way to get into 'treatment' (i.e., get completely drunk and go to the hospital), otherwise, you are placed on the inevitable waiting list.

"Weltschmerz," I replied.

"What?"

"It's a *German* word," I said, "literally, it means world-hurt, a kind of psychic pain, a romantic sadness that haunts German sociologists when their Weltanschauung collides with a world in which they seem to have no place."

"Weltanschauung?"

"World-view," I explained, "I think Freudians get anomie. And the French get *mal du siècle*, I just got drunk."

Turning to the doctor who'd walked in on this, the nurse said, "He's incoherent." My French (and English) pronunciation *could* use a little work, I'd admitted to myself.

The 'detox center' at the hospital was closed or being moved, I don't know. I wound up in the Psychiatric Intensive Care Unit.

I feel different from everyone. I am in an institution. The doors are locked. I am not trusted, and I don't trust myself. I don't want to see anyone. The nurses talk about me outside the door. There is a camera trained on me at the corner of the room. My possessions are locked up. The windows have heavy plastic-coated steel screens over them. I must remove my necklace so I don't kill myself. Staff take away the chairs my few visitors use immediately after they leave so I can't stand on them and hang myself or perhaps take a flying leap and with arms outstretched impale my throbbing heart on one of the chromium-plated, spindly legs. People who try to call me at the hospital are told that I am not a patient here.

A social worker friend of mine gets in because she knows how to do things like that (e.g., visit people who are [not?] on locked wards in hospitals). I am not thrilled to see her.

A couple of days later, I was released and started intensive outpatient treatment for "alcohol addiction" as I call it. Many call it "alcoholism," a widely used term (of abuse) which more or less describes alcohol addiction: but *doing* alcoholism was something I had to learn, a performance, a dance.[3]

---

[3] Norman Denzin has compiled an extensive body of research on the alcoholic 'self' including: Denzin, Norman K. (1993). *The alcoholic society: Addiction and recovery of the self.* New Brunswick, NJ: Transaction Publishers; Denzin, Norman K. (1991) *Hollywood shot by shot: Alcoholism in American cinema.* New York: A. de Gruyter; Denzin, Norman K. (1987). *Treating alcoholism: An Alcoholics Anonymous approach.*

Many of my fellow (we were, in the main, separated by sex) "clients" at the treatment center had been adjudicated there in lieu of or in hopes of reduced jail sentences. Some had been there longer (and in most instances, more often) than myself, and were better alcoholics than I. One guy was such a good alcoholic that they weren't going to let him in because he was so "treatment savvy."

A new staff member started the same day I did, and a more seasoned employee was helping her learn the ropes. They walked through the day room talking.

"Working on detox," said the veteran, "can be a pain in the ass, but you'll get used to it, don't worry." I was working on the MMPI (Minnesota Multi-Phasic Personality Inventory) at a table with some others. Just for the record, despite the distractions, the test revealed that my tendency toward delusion and psychosis were within normal limits.

I go up to the staff area (there's a chest-high Formica bar) to give a blood alcohol count—breathalyzer—and go home for the day. Another seasoned staff member is talking to the newbie five feet away from me.

"Excuse me," I intone, "I'd like to take my breathalyzer and go home."

They do not look up, they keep talking about the Avon catalog they're looking at. The newbie finds out when orders are to be placed and other rites and rituals of the local Avon practices.[4]

One of my fellow clients has been standing there longer than me; he wants a highlighter. "Excuse me," I repeat, louder now. Still no response. I don't know these people's names yet. I wait. I knock my knuckles on the bar, and the staffers look up. "I'd like to take my breathalyzer." Concluding their communion, the seasoned staffer moves toward us after casting a knowing glance over her shoulder at the newbie. I saw her eyebrows start to rise and her lips curl as she turned her head.

"What do you want?" she asks me. I will find out later that in treatment, day-patients are a rung or two higher than the inpatients. "He was first," I say.

"I'd like a highlighter," he says.

"What for?" asks she.

He explains, in the language of a street-smart crackhead, that he'd like

Newbury Park, CA: Sage Publications, 1987.
4 This ethnography has yet to be written although I believe it would be compelling.

to emphasize certain parts of our treatment texts he found particularly relevant to his situation, and having done so, would be more able to quickly reference those sections.

"How long do you want it for?" she asked.

"Just forget it, I'll use my pen." He walks away. She nods her head sadly at me, and I say "he only wanted a highlighter."

She looks at me and asks "What do you want?"

"I'd like to take my breathalyzer."

"BAC?" she asks.

"Yeah, I guess that's it."

She walks over to the swinging door, lifts the hinged part of the bar and folds it over, so I can get back to the machine. I blow in the machine. She hands me the paper that is proof-positive(ist) of several days of sobriety. I tell her:

"It seems like you are angry about the interruption."

"No I'm not. It's my job."

"Your body language and tone of voice..."

"I'm not angry!"

"OK," I say, feeling downtrodden, and I think to myself that I'll file a grievance, and I do the next day. "People," I thought nobly, "who are at risk for feeling like dirt, shouldn't be treated like it."

My counselor wanted me to try to work this out with the functionary, who has a master's degree in social work. I told her that I wasn't going to talk about it with her, that her behavior was an organizational issue, not a personal one with me. She said that it would be good for me to be assertive about this matter.

"I was," I said, "I filed a grievance. Do you have a policy and procedure concerning the time required to resolve the grievance?" It had been a few days, and I hadn't heard from anyone.

Therapist: "Well, I told [name] that you'd be coming to talk to her about your interaction with her."

"Why'd you do that?"

"Because I think it would be helpful for you to work this through with her."

"I'm not going to solve your personnel issues," I tell her, "I'm not an administrator anymore."

For an ungodly amount of time, we go back and forth about whether this is an personal or personnel 'issue.' My counselor says that she will look into it. I say that it's an administrative issue, not a counselor-client matter. She says that it's interfering with my therapy, and that makes it a counselor-client issue. I said that it's not interfering; I dealt with it through the grievance process outlined in my admission documents, and I would follow the process as far as it led.

I never did hear from the administration. I didn't follow up on my grievance either because, you see, by the time I was ready to file a second grievance, I was an alcoholic. I'd come to understand that my anger directed against the functionary was a result of a "disease"—that because I'd always drowned my anger in Budweiser, I'd never learned appropriate ways to deal with it. I *saw* how I'd turned my bottled-up (if you'll forgive me *un bon mot*) anger against this person who *may have* behaved inappropriately, overlooking the *responsibility* of dealing with my own feelings toward her.

I learned not to think so much about things because it interfered with my therapy. "There you go again," my therapist would frequently point out. Usually, at least in the beginning, the 'point of departure' (i.e., where I was 'going') had to do with my reluctance to say, "I am powerless over alcohol." She would write in my progress notes and treatment plan, "Dan still has trouble admitting his powerlessness over alcohol."

"Your HMO is concerned with your lack of progress," she told me one time. At about $1000 per day of treatment, my HMO's "concerns" held some control over my cognition.

I said, "I don't see how a bottle of beer has any power over me."

"There," I was told, "You go again."

"OK," I said, "I admit that once it's in my body, I'm sunk.'

Oh, how I'd cherished my ability to intellectualize matters of importance to me!

As I said, I don't know what it's like to experience the kind of difficulty making myself understood that the children I wrote about did. But I hope this somewhat prolonged foray into self-disclosure has served several purposes.

First, mindedness is something abiding not entirely within one's self. Each of my behaviors in "treatment" were assigned to two mutually exclusive categories: those verbalized cognitions that were indicative of recovery and those that were not.

Second, social roles carry powerful expectations. The sanctions and rewards of correct performance are relentless.

Third, mindedness has a political-economic dimension. In order to receive treatment, I had to "present" my abnormal self for correct categorization by professionals, subsequent indemnity, analysis, and correction.

Fourth, having been normalized, I have obtained, in the words of Goffman, "...not the acquisition of fully normal status, but a transformation of the self from someone with a particular blemish into someone with a record of having corrected a particular blemish" (1963/1986, 9). I am a recovering alcoholic, with all that implies socially, psychologically, politically, and economically. I've left a trail a mile wide.

From this perspective I will now examine the stories I've told.

Foremost, I tried to paint word pictures: Renoir's soft pastels, Hopper's stark realism, Munch's scream, or Magritte's assault on the gap between looking and seeing. I indulged myself in this luxury, casting my gaze from a certain standpoint informed by the notion that mindedness to a large extent depends on others granting that accession. Mental retardation, autism, developmental disability, I assumed, exist to the degree that *this* social assertion becomes possible: "Access Denied."[5]

I situated and emphasized Cassie and Sean as children in the middle of our part of the world, its little towns, flat farmland, straight roads, meandering rivers, and mud. Our historical and geographical (and even if not until recently, social) connections personally helped me keep the dogs of nomothetic thinking at bay.

Emily and I lived in our own little cyberworld that was a friendly place for us. It didn't strike me as odd or unusual until much reflection, that all of *that* could go on in a tiny little office room in a suburban house.

Woody and I coexisted in "the system," both of us casualties. The consequences were exasperating to me but life-threatening for him.

Ferguson's question posed in Chapter One of this book presented itself repeatedly in my work: "What do we do with those examples [people?, social situations?] where culture seems beside the point; where physiology [and observed behavior] has gone so far awry that it threatens to overwhelm the social context?" (Ferguson, 1987 54).

Shamelessly I sidestepped the question, holding to Blatt's assertion:

---

[5] Another study is suggested by this use of cybertalk. I remember as a young boy watching a particular episode of the Walter Cronkite Show. He stood in front of a 15-foot-tall monstrosity, with his hand held high, palm outward: "This, is the computer," he said, "it is like a human mind." A proper question to ask of our age is, "What happened in the transformation of the perception of computers being "mind-like" to minds becoming "computer-like?"

"*[t]he best way to cure an invented disease is to forget it ...*" (1981, 131). It's an easy detail to overlook from where I sit, but not from where I found Janet, Mary, Harry, and Melanie. The social cost (ecology) of their children's behavior *and that of others* will have significance long after I wrote this, you read it, and we all went on about our business.

At the outset, I intended to demonstrate that people construct mental retardation (and as Trent [1994] terms the converse, 'mental acceleration') based on scientifically or normatively imposed expectations. Through Woody, Cassie, Sean, and Emily I tried to convey some evidence to illustrate my belief that expectations of mindedness are only as limiting or as engaging as their interpretation.

Gubrium (1986) puts it another way: "Where mind is a poignantly problematic category, [it becomes] the common responsibility of those concerned" (49). This stands in opposition to functional definitions of mental retardation that position it as a quantifiable trait people possess.

When personal traits become quantifiable, unexplored avenues of minded research stretch before us. For example Budd (1992), in a recent article entitled "Rorschach Assessment of the Non-Living: Hardly a Dead Subject,"[6] found evidence linking the dead (perhaps more correctly, at least to some, according to Budd, "persons with problems in non-living", [12]) with the Rorschach's traditional indicators of cognitive rigidity. Budd conjectured that this finding suggested a "...rigorous adherence to standard modes of thinking. This rigid perfectionism, or inability to "loosen up," is striking in view of the uncanny frequency of the adjective "stiff" in formal characterizations of dead persons" (15).

Informal characterizations of people with severe disabilities, mental retardation *with extensive support needs (wants?) across all adaptive dimensions* often include the descriptor 'vegetable' (Ferguson 1987) . Although I attempted to dismiss "mindedness" as a solely human domain early on by including minded(-like) portraits of animals created by their caretakers, some writers have gone further in their attempts to broaden the construct. The Mothers of Invention,produced a song in the late sixties—"*Call Any Vegetable*"—(Zappa 1995/1967) that flaunted the abundant pleasure inherent in reciprocal communication with vegetables

---

6 This is humor, or a stab at it. The article is from the *Journal of Polymorphous Perversity*. A reader of a very early draft of this chapter likened its meandering nature to the title of my Uncle Bill's 1951 poem, "Six Pallbearers in Search of a Corpse*". This got me thinking about people with problems in nonliving.

(despite what the neighbors might say). Vegetables, the songsters counseled, and our selves deserve nothing less.

Less radical and perhaps less invasive was the subjective hopefulness I admittedly possessed as I attempted to take on the "common responsibility" of constructing the children I've written of as minded, very human creatures.

"When will '*it*' happen," I wondered? "It" being the *moment* when I would *see* Woody, Sean, Cassie, and Emily as little people; little people who had a name, a mother and a father, sisters, brothers, uncles and aunts, a face, a voice, a dream, and a story. As it turned out, I didn't have to wait long for the *moment* with any of these kids: When I dragged Cassie by her red boots on her tummy, screaming her protests, she turned her head and I saw not tears but a smile of conspiratorial delight (I didn't know who her co-conspirator was but suspected that, in some manner, it was I).

Woody, cherub-like at 10 or 11 jumped in my lap, and said "Dighee-dighee?" I responded in kind, and he offered his arm for me to, presumably (according to staff, at least), bite. "He don't usually do that with men," they told me. He was sitting in my lap. "Probably he's doin' it 'cause you're talking to him, talking *like him*, and we don't encourage that."

When Emily blew up her Kid Pix creation, backed into my arms, and dropped her jaw (with sincere apologies to the Beatles), I knew that I'd just met a girl, or shall I say, she'd just met me?

Sean and I took a little longer. I watched him for many visits (separated by weeks), wandering, seemingly aimlessly about the house clutching two or three videotapes to his chest. I *found* him dancing with me to the do-dah of King Louis.

I "kidnapped" *Emily* from some of my own unpublished work. In that context, she served me well as a mirror from which I could reflect on notions of teaching (Is it Art? Or Science?) and Foucauldian normalization (who cares if it's art or science, it's still an ecology of power with sinister overtones). These days, for what it's worth, I think the *real* question is, "To what degree, if at all, is teaching anything other than magic?"

This is why I am able to state with authority things like, "I just know," when I actually do not. But I just knew Woody was not going to bite anyone at that high school, ever (except the one time with me). Peter Abelard studied the Greeks (and I don't think the Greeks often refers to sophists) and declared in the thirteenth century that *knowledge must* precede belief (which led to trumped up charges of heresy for which he was duly castrated). Like the great teachers of the past, Protagoras, Gorgias, Hippias of Elis, and Prodicus of Ceos, I could argue either side of the question, but in your average teaching situation, I think that magical thinking suffices.

Greg and I tried to work out just what it was that made some people more effective as staff with Woody. Greg said that he thought that he could communicate with Woody more effectively because Woody knew that he was not afraid of him. Without delving into the pathos of this state of affairs (can *you* imagine what it would be like to be in Woody's shoes? To have people so afraid of you? Only finding security in your self around others who were not afraid of you? To scare people that much?), consider what Greg and I were doing with Woody's mind. First off, we took his mind for granted. Constructing Woody's behavior for us was only possible by labeling Woody thoughtful and emotive. The task at hand was to recreate Woody not as an object of fear, in need of analysis and corrective programs, but as a fairly rational sort of fellow who only needed a little understanding.

Second, how could Woody *know* that Greg, or myself for that matter, were not afraid of him? Woody's long-standing diagnosis of autism in many ways precludes this kind of social sensitivity.

Third, how could Greg or myself know that Woody felt safe around others who he knew were not afraid of him? Greg and I came up with this notion independently, apparently naturally, and seemingly without thinking about it too much ourselves.

Humanity, as I argued at the beginning, is linked with mindedness. Sanders and Arluke (1993) asked the question concerning relationships among people and nonhumans, "how does the central activity of 'taking the role of the other' proceed apart from conventional linguistic exchanges? What methods do actors use to define situations so as to contextualize interactions and thereby imbue them with meaning and order? What is the role of emotional experience in the structuring of intersubjective encounters?" (384).

In part, I addressed these questions with the work of Bogdan and Taylor (1989), who found among the accepting relationships between people (with and without differences that put them at risk of being "somewhat less than human") that attributions of thought, presuming individuality, and creating social space for *the other* constituted the social construction of humanity.

If you ever work with people at risk for dehumanization, you will notice immediately that others will talk over their heads. Personal pronouns are replaced by he, she, and so on. "He's got a sore in the middle of his head, always had it, cause he keeps banging it," for instance. It doesn't seem to matter that the guy's sitting two feet away.

What puts the children I wrote about at risk for dehumanization is their perceived lack of formal language and ostensibly odd behavior. Certainly it was not their looks.

One time, while I still worked at the Center, I had to go get Woody from school because he'd bit some other child. We stopped at a convenience market (one without gas pumps) so we could get some soda (I was later questioned as to whether I was reinforcing Woody's less than desirable behavior by doing this—you see, I was getting him 'out' of school, *in addition to* providing him with an apparently scarce commodity—Diet-Pepsi). Two young women swirled up on roller-blades and crashed into one another giggling, so distracted were they by what they saw through my windshield. My heart went pitter-patter as I thought that something like this, distracting (attracting) the attentions of pretty young women hadn't happened to me in decades. It was only as this thought was crossing my mind (feminist analysis had yet to kick in) that I noticed that their gaze was directed at Woody, not me.

Tan, muscular, with his shaggy blonde hair; he looked like he rode the curl out here from Malibu Beach. The only thing lacking was a rack with surfboards atop my late model, four-wheel drive fire-engine-red pickup truck with extra-wide tires. Woody waited patiently while I unbuckled his seat-belt and then opened up his door, hoping that his youthful admirers would think him the quiet, brooding type with strong, capable hands.

Woody though, bites people, makes funny sounds, and prances, and this is going to get him into trouble. I don't think he stands a chance. The common responsibility of Woody's mind will create, what we in special education caustically refer to as a "person with a severe reputation."

When I first met Emily, she did not talk, and when I finished writing about her in 1994, she was not talking much. Still, we had a relationship, a very human one. It was filled with the little mysteries, nuances, embarrassments, guilt, triumphs, joy, sadness, regrets, agony, insight, frustration, and boredom to which any relationship is subject.

I think it was easy to accept Emily on these terms, especially for me personally because of her fascination with my Macintosh computer (which has stood accused in all of my romantic relationships of competing for my loving attention). That nexus could have been replaced by some other artifice, but that's what we had together.

Nicki, early on, granted me what Gubrium (1986) calls "discernment credentials," that is, a guarantor-interpreter of the "mind" of the apparently mindless "because of experience, education, or insight, among a host of interpretive warrants" (43). This (with *notable exceptions* which include interpersonal and/or organizational one-upspersonship, power-brokering, and, among other enticements, personal vendettas) can be an uncomfortable position in which to find one's self.

"I like to play with Emily!" Despite common sense notions that play connotes reciprocity, social place, thinking and individuality, I don't think that this statement would hold the same weight as say, a speech and language therapist relegating Emily's 'manding' competence to that of a 14-month infant.

Nonetheless, I found myself credentialed in discerning Emily's mind. I was able, in some respects, to take advantage of this position. How did I know when Emily was behaving in a minded manner? The question came up enough: Was she pointing and clicking at random, selecting the right responses occasionally? Was she acting in a "rote" manner?

All I had to go by was feeling: I could sense her movements, I'd say to myself, "What would I do in a situation like this?" To the extent that I could relate to what she was doing in, say, a problem-solving situation, I could say to Nicki, "Emily is figuring out how to solve *this* problem." The only way I could tell was to sense how her hands were moving, where she was looking, how she backtracked through multiple commands whose outcome was undesirable, and so on.

Emily and I, years later, conversed regarding computer operation, and along with our conversation of gestures, surreptitious glances, subversion, teasing, and glee, we did some serious talking. I never knew for sure why Emily held my head when we worked, but I was glad to find that it was to prevent its imminent explosion. Interestingly, I'd always felt this to be the case. Something about the little four-year old's grip on my head made me think she thought that she was somehow helping me keep my thoughts together.

I tried not to direct Emily's education in any formal way, instead following Dewey, I hoped that "[w]hen external authority is rejected, it does not follow that all authority should be rejected, but rather that there is need to search for a more effective source of authority. Because...older education imposed the knowledge, methods, and the rules of conduct of the mature person upon the young, it does not follow...that the knowledge and skill of the mature person has no directive value for the experience of the immature. On the contrary, basing education upon personal experience [of young people] may mean more multiplied and more intimate contacts between the mature and immature than ever existed" (Dewey 1938, 21).[7] In this way, I hoped to find Emily's mind and to aid her in self-discovery.

The assumption of mindedness and humanity, I've mentioned, should not be taken lightly. I related my own experience and that of other researchers who have traveled beyond the apparently natural[8] aversion to people who possess noticeable and negatively socially valued characteristics. In addition, I opened that delightful can of worms labeled, "Are nonhumans minded?"

Of course, a larger question might be, "What constitutes mindedness?"

In his biography of Herman Melville, Lewis Mumford (Miller 1986, 299) observed, "To produce a mighty volume, you must choose a mighty theme." Mumford thought that the creation of a volume describing the origin and development of the modern world and the modern mind would serve a function of sufficient gravity.

In his anthology of Lewis Mumford's work, Donald L. Miller (1986) stated that Mumford, "[d]rawing on the latest German scholarship, ...analyzed the process of ideological transformation for full mechanization, arguing that the Industrial Revolution began as far back as the Middle Ages, when a number of cultural transformations occurred that prepared the ground for the larger technical revolution that altered all of Western culture" (299).

Mumford actually traced these transformations back to the building of the great pyramids in Egypt. "Men became mechanical," according to Mumford, "before they perfected complicated machines to express their new bent and interest" (Mumford 1963, 12-22).

The building of the great pyramids required a new form of social

---

[7] The tragedy is that an exercise of power is an exercise of power.

[8] The degree to which this "apparently natural" aversion is a cultural artifact is questionable. For instance, Lou Brown, et al. (1989) point out that having children with obvious disabilities as classmates would in all probability reduce the stigma that these children might otherwise experience. Their classmates, after all, will go on to be doctors, lawyers, social workers, television producers, supervisors, and so on.

organization, one Mumford calls the Megamachine. The Megamachine, in its original configuration, was composed almost entirely of human parts. Arms for grasping, hauling, and chipping stone, legs for pushing; bodies acting in uniform precision, under the direction of the incarnation of the Sun God.

Mediating between the two, and essential for the machine's operation were organized knowledge—natural and supernatural—represented by the priesthood, and a nascent bureaucracy, capable of passing orders, unerringly and unquestioningly to the disciplined laborers.

Mumford writes in *The Myth of the Megamachine* that: "This condition remains true today, even though the existence of automated factories and computer-regulated units conceals the human components essential even to automation" (cited in Miller 1986, 319).

Over the stunningly compact time span of 300 years, the Megamachine became perfected. From Mumford, I quote at length: "The kind of mind that designed the pyramid was a new human type, capable of abstraction of high order using astronomical observations for the siting of the structure...But the workers who carried out the design also had minds of a new order: trained in obedience to the letter, limited in response to the word of command descending from the king through a bureaucratic hierarchy, forfeiting during the period of service any trace of autonomy or initiative; slavishly undeviating in performance...the men employed left their names in red ocher...on the blocks of the Meidum pyramid: 'Boat Gang,' 'Vigorous Gang.' They themselves would have felt at home today on an assembly line..."

"Only the naked pin-up girl," Mumford tells us, "was lacking" (cited in Miller 1986, 318-319). These minds of the new order, I argue, are minds of this [dis?]order: ones of Mindlessness.

Along with double cheeseburger value meals, Social Security cards, video tape rental stores located invariably adjacent rent-to-own stores, and the World Wide Web (a recent manifestation of individualizing/totalizing panoptic projects) we get mindless mindedness. People who don't fit get spun out with tedious regularity, but like a black hole, they are sucked back into the vortex, revolving mercilessly and mercurially at the edges of la société. To quote Itard once again: *"Unhappy creature,' I cried as if he could hear me, and with real anguish of heart, 'since my labors are wasted and your efforts fruitless, take again the road to your forests and the taste for your primitive life. Or if your new needs make you dependent on a society in which you have no place, go, expiate your misfortune, die of misery and boredom at Bicêtre'"* (Itard, 73-74).

Hahn (1987) equates this observation with the social, economic, and political correlates of the rise of industrialization and capitalism in the eighteenth and nineteenth centuries. "As factories replaced private dwellings as the primary sites of production," he writes,

> [r]outines and architectural configurations were standardized to suit nondisabled workers. Both the design of worksites and of the products that were manufactured gave virtually no attention to the needs of people with disabilities. As a result, patterns of aversion and avoidance toward people with disabilities were embedded in the construction of commodities, landscapes and buildings that would remain for centuries.... Perhaps even more significantly, the growth of mass production eventually spawned an increased emphasis on mass consumption. In a variety of ways, capitalists sought to persuade workers that they should spend the wages they were earning in factories on items they formerly produced themselves.... Industrialists were not merely attempting to sell their products; they were also promoting a vision of satisfaction that could become available to those prepared to reshape themselves. What seems to be missing in most analyses of the growth of consumerism is a realization that the images depicted in these appeals may have been even more important than their content, or the specific product they were attempting to sell. When other kinds of messages failed, pleas addressed to personal vanity or the narcissistic feelings of the dominant majority were remarkably successful (557-558).

The theme of normalization has presented itself in various guises throughout these stories. I am aware of at least three writers who have used the term for sociopolitical ends: In the work of Goffman, Foucault, and Wolfensberger the term shoulders different burdens but taken together form an interesting perspective from which to take on Emily, Sean, Cassie, and Woody.

Each child was and is at risk for evaluation, categorization, and treatment (education?). Yet I found many examples of people, knowingly and otherwise, attributing mindfulness and humanity to these children, and doing so in such a way that did not cast judgment on them. Cassie noticed the stars, Margaret told me, before her cousin Arianna.

"And the kids love him," says Karrie speaking of her son, "he just attracts them somehow. I don't know what it is, it's almost like he has some sort of glow about him. They just come around."

The principle of normalization, first articulated for United States audiences in 1972 by Wolf Wolfensberger, posits "The use of means which are culturally normative to offer a person life conditions at least as good as the average citizen's, and to as much as possible, enhance or support personal behaviors, appearances, experience, status, and reputation to the greatest degree possible, at any given time, for each individual according to his or her developmental needs" (28).

For one to say that "normalization" has been a rallying cry for special education and for those who work with people with disabilities would be to understate its importance. The principle lays a foundation for determining how people should appear, where and how they should live, how others who care for them should act, the rhythms of their daily life and, importantly, a vision of society that offers each of its members a valued place (unfortunately, no matter how he tried, Wolfensberger was never able to make clear his philosophy's endgame: Normalize environments, not people).

There is, therefore, what Laird Heal (1988) calls a "conservative corollary" to Wolfensberger's theory of normalization. That is, in developing environments for people with disabilities, the task becomes one of "conform[ing] to the positive end of the culturally normative continuum to compensate for the negative imagery that cultural norms associate with handicap. There seems to be a measure of self-contradiction in this application of imagery. Why should the disinherited emulate the disinheritor? Why shouldn't the disinherited instead resist the association of minorities with any particular image, good or bad? Why shouldn't the quality of 'human-ness' supersede all other qualities as the basis for human valuation?" (67).

Why indeed? I believe, and have attempted to demonstrate, the answer lies in this contested territory: "the quality of 'human-ness.'"

Human-ness or humanness (Bogdan and Taylor 1987) has taken on various disguises in this book. The above-mentioned authors found it when people in relationships with others whose characteristics put them at risk for being labeled "mentally retarded" attributed thinking, reciprocity, individuality, and (valued) social place for the other person. For all practical purposes, I have equated these notions with mindedness.

Occasionally, I found instances in my experience with the children I wrote about where humanness didn't seem to matter. For me, reading Sean's neurological report that characterized him as a "3 and a half year little boy, with the above noted problems, [who] has not yet started smoking cigarettes or using tobacco products," smacks not only of careless use of computer templates but of dehumanization. Similarly, Sean's dad complained, "[t]hese doctors all say the same damn thing, I think they all read the same fuckin' books on autism, 'cause I keep hearing the same shit."

More subtle was Cassie's speech and language therapist. She literally had a bag of tricks, and presented tasks according to her assessment of Cassie's level of functioning. One interpretation of how to teach Cassie would follow these lines: Although she is at risk for a medical diagnosis of some kind of autismlike disability, Cassie deserves opportunities similar to everyone else in society. There should be no assumption that Cassie cannot learn the things she needs to know in order to participate fully with other people in domestic, vocational, recreational, and community environments. Analyze these environments. Compare how Cassie is functioning in these environments to that of others. Find the discrepancies. Consider instruction for those skills that Cassie can learn to help her participate fully. Develop adaptations in environments to ensure her engagement where instruction is not an alternative (Baumgart et al. 1982). One can see how normalization and instruction work together in the above illustration. The mechanistic face of special instruction is hard to miss.

Translating the above process into the language of operant conditioning makes the alliance, according to one line of thought, unholy. A criticism of this approach is that the mechanistic orientation of special education instructions recreates students as objects whose difference from others makes them somehow deviant (Guess and Thompson 1993). The student-deviant-object is subjected to technology whose aim is shaping their behavior until it approximates a terminal state largely determined by others (Iano 1986).

Consider what Cassie's speech and language therapist had to tell me concerning her therapeutic methods: "But even just like the progress of sweeping, the first day I did that, it was the most horrible thing I'd ever done to Cassie. Today, she asked for the broom and swept up the rice because it was bothering her where she was sitting. Without me asking. So it seems that the structure, when it's given to her, helps her to be able to move toward more appropriate behavior."

Wolfensberger seems to have arrived at his notion of normalization independently of Michel Foucault (1977/1979). For Foucault, normalization is bringing the tactics of discipline to bear on individuals; calculating discrepancies and shaping behavior until it approaches that of a norm. Although they go by different names, disciplinary tactics are familiar to most people who work with and care for people with obvious and stigmatizing differences. Interestingly, Foucault marks Itard's time (the

Enlightenment) as the epoch during which the codification of discipline as a technology began.

Discipline proceeds along several trajectories. Separate individuals from the crowd. Create a space for each; distribute them so that minute observation becomes possible. Regulate their behavior by a timetable. Analyze activity so that a detailed description of the correlation of body and task becomes possible. Do not place before the individual tasks which are beyond mastery. Exercise, repeated practice, becomes the means to ensure success and the punishment for failure. In a way, people are penalized for being abnormal, and "[t]he ideal point of penalty today would be an indefinite discipline: an interrogation without end, an investigation that would be extended without limit to a meticulous and ever more analytical observation, a judgment that would at the same time be in the constitution of a file that was never closed, the calculated leniency of a penalty that would be interlaced with the ruthless curiosity of an examination, a procedure that would be at the same time the permanent measure of a gap in relation to an inaccessible norm and the asymptotic movement that strives to meet in infinity" (Foucault 1977/1979, 227).

The penalty for the children presented in my stories follows the diagnosis of mental retardation, autism, or some other as yet untestable but obvious disability.

The beauty of disciplinary tactics is that the more you use them, the more you find out about what is and what is not normal, and further, what you can do about it. In this way, teaching itself is a dividing practice that separates, defines, and distributes along a curve that discipline renders precise.

Accepting Foucauldian notions of normalization means implicating the other "normalization" as complicit (as Heal [1988] above deftly brought to light) in creating at least some of the initial conditions of disability. In other words, using culturally valued means to produce culturally valued outcomes reinforces socially constructed notions of difference. But in his assertion of the normalizing tendencies of western culture since the Enlightenment, Foucault also partially answers an implicit question in the section above, that is: "Why is it that certain perceptions of (or preoccupation with) mindedness seem so appropriate for some people whose characteristics are so exceptional?" The technical, mechanistic face of Mumford's Megamachine takes on prescriptive meaning.

Erving Goffman? His book, *Stigma: Notes on the Management of Spoiled Identity* defines normalization as the social process of "showing just how far normals [can] go in treating the stigmatized person as if he didn't have a stigma" (1963/1986, 30-31). A deconstructive act would be to see just how far normals go in unknowingly treating the mindless-by-definition as if he or she had a mind.

I called them *Hidden Treasures!*—speech acts performed by others who in their descriptions of children showing mindedness and humanity, according to canonry of disability theory, had no business doing so. I wrote about normalization to frame the discussion.

Speaking of Cassie, Jake (her grandfather) told me, "She's smart, smart as a whip.... She just don't talk." Jake was making a supposition about Cassie's mindedness; I believe that he simply assumed it was there. The assumption of mindedness was common among some observers of the children I wrote about. Especially myself, because I was looking for it. I modified my own behavior on many occasions based on what I thought Cassie was thinking. For instance, I learned to run through commercial establishments, "We run," I wrote, "into the gas station, because I've had enough experience with Cassie wanting to go where I didn't in stores, and go there quick, that I figured if I ran with her, she'd at least think we were going somewhere interesting."

One time Woody became very upset: During a bingolike game, Woody started beating the sides of his head. Once we had the kids safely out of the room, Woody sufficiently safe from himself, slouched against a wall crying, I asked [his teacher] what *she* thought drove him to act as he did. She thought that maybe Woody wasn't winning the game...

It's remarkable that Woody's teacher took for granted his ability to not only understand the game, but to keep score (at least in a general sense—winning or losing), to recognize he was losing, to see this matter as one of some importance to him (or perhaps others), and to react strongly to his pending defeat. All this from a young man whose résumé includes only aborted attempts at intelligence testing, whose use of language is (on the face of it) nonsymbolic, and to many, nonfunctional, who relies on others for virtually all of his physical and social well being: a person whose mother says that he has never been taught anything by anyone. His only knowledge being that gained by way of his own means.

These stories, for me, are stories of hope, hope that operates on a couple of different levels.

I made some attempt at deconstructing common sense and scientifically derived significations of mental retardation by attempting to show that in day-to-day life, mental retardation as a construct is at least frayed at the edges. As such, in this paradigmatic warfare,[9] I declared myself a border skirmisher. I hit and I ran.

Despite its absence in the majority of scientific discourse policing the boundaries of disability, people do, consciously or otherwise, use mindedness as a tool to describe the actions, behaviors, and thinking of people who by definition, should have a measurable lack of mentality. Sometimes mindedness manifests itself as empowering, dignifying attributions; sometimes not. (When I began writing this book, my guiding principle was this: Question—"What can the dumbest person in the world do to the most intelligent?" Answer—"Outsmart them").[10]

If this point is not clear in the children's stories, the fault is my own. The stories are short, both in the sense of "short story," and that of duration. Perhaps more prolonged "being with" the children and subsequent additions to the anecdotal "evidence" would have clarified this. Particularly helpful would have been the opportunity to talk with, listen to—generally thicken—the descriptions of the children's interpretive communities. My excuse, couched in an ethical dilemma, was that I wanted to teach the kids something, to help out in some way, because, you see, they were helping me out in a *big* way.

This kind of research is no walk in the park. To get close enough to people so that you know what they're thinking, or get a feeling of what they might be thinking, you run the risk of developing relationships with them, always a gamble in our day-to-day lives. You wind up caring about them, wondering what they might think of you, wanting them to like you, feeling inadequate, conflating clinical empathy with genuine sympathy, and the other foibles that plague human bonds. In my case, I came to be friends with all of the kids I wrote about, and to varying degrees, their parents.

Situated as such, researchers become part of a particular person's interpretive community. Thoughts of scholarly objectivity drift like the falling leaves outside my window. My hopes and dreams for the kids by design became entwined with those of their significant others.

Hope, according to Scot Danforth (1997), "[d]espite [its] powerful and assumed role in special education,...is an unexamined aspect of work in this professional field" (93). In his article entitled, "On What Basis Hope? Modern Progress and Postmodern Possibilities," he takes a good, hard

---

[9] Forgive me the militaristic metaphorical language. Nothing else comes to mind.

[10] Bob Stake (personal communication, 1994), helped me turn this tirade into something more constructive(ist).

look at hope. Hope in its "unexamined" guise derives from faith in progress, "a rejection of an attitude that has characterized most human communities throughout history." (Frankel 1967, 483). For most of our western past, change, when people "have been aware of it at all" (483), has been seen as moral decay. It was only the machinations of modernist philosophers (Sir Francis Bacon [1561-1626])[11] is one of my personal favorites) that elevated progressive change—directed by the cold light of an enlightened science—to its current status.

I've gone to some length to demonstrate some of the more heinous outcomes of this mentality. But a person must (at least *I* must, given what I've done to myself rhetorically) apply one's self to Danforth's (1997, 93) question, "On What *Basis* Hope?" (my emphasis).

His answer is simple: Seek democracy over science, community over objective truth. Hope and truth become fruitful and multiply (Genesis 1:22) as conversations are vested among interpretive communities whose object is not to objectify, but to create a space (Bérubé 1996, 249) where "3, 5, 10, or 12 persons devoted to the well-being of the individual labeled as having mental retardation have the opportunity to set aside scientific talk and disability constructs in favor of language and relationships that value the labeled individual" (Danforth 1997, 105).[12]

Bérubé makes *his* strategic maneuver clear: trying "to represent [his son] to the best of my ability. I have done so in the belief that my textual representations of him might make his claims on the world as broadly and as strongly as possible" (263).

---

11 Sir Francis was well aware that the scientific improvement of humankind would cost a lot of money and went to great lengths to make this clear to his King and the power elite of his time. He died after contracting bronchitis while stuffing a chicken with snow to see just how long the treatment would preserve its flesh. Instead of retiring to the modest, but warm and dry accommodations of the commoners, he chose to recuperate in a damp and drafty nobleman's estate. He made a mistake.

12 There is a growing body of literature concerning planning processes that put the person first. MAPS (Vandercook et al. 1989), Lifestyle Planning (O'Brien 1987) and Personal Futures Planning (Mount, 1987) are early and hopeful examples of procedures which people can use to reduce the risk of "what we have is what you get" style planning for people with disabilities. Lately, Mount (1994) in the manner of Dr. Frankenstein, has beheld the movement she created becoming hide-bound through the same sociopolitical metamorphoses as its predecessors. The important question here is posed by Fine and Asch (1988): "We wonder what keeps researchers from imagining a context in which disability would not be handicapping?" (17).

I hope that the stories I've told harmonize with that challenge.

My writing has examined the development of the science of mental retardation, its consequences for the humanity and mindedness of its subjects, both the defined and the definers, and four stories in which I attempted to dispute and reconstruct children at risk for rejection as "full-fledged" (Bogdan and Taylor 1989, 280), minded members of their interpretive, human communities.

References

American Psychiatric Association. (1994). *Diagnostic and statistical manual of mental disorders, 4th edition.* Washington, DC: American Psychiatric Association.

Barnes, C. (1992). Qualitative research: Valuable or irrelevant? *Disability, Handicap and Society,* 7: 115-124.

Barton, L. (Ed). (1996). *Disability and society: Emerging issues and insights.* New York: Longman.

Baumgart, D., L. Brown, I. Pumpian, M. Nisbet, A. Ford, M. Sweet, R. Messina, and Schroeder, J. (1982). The principle of partial participation and individual adaptations in educational programs for severely handicapped students. *Journal of the Association for the Severely Handicapped,* 7: 17-27.

Becker, H. S. (1963). *Outsiders: Studies in the sociology of deviance.* New York: Free Press.

Begab, M. J., and S. A. Richardson (Eds.). (1975). *The mentally retarded in society: A social science perspective.* Baltimore: University Park Press.

Bérubé, M. (1996). *Life as we know it: A father, a family, and an exceptional child.* New York: Pantheon.

Bettelheim, B. (1967). *The empty fortress: Infantile autism and the birth of the self.* New York: Free Press.

Biklen, D. (1988). The myth of clinical judgement. *Journal of Social Issues,* 44, 127-140.

—— (1995). The social construction of mental retardation: Facilitated communication. *The Journal of the Association for Persons with Severe Handicaps,* 17: 23-37

Blatt, B. (1977/1994). The definition of mental retardation. *Mental*

Retardation, 14: 69-72.

——— (1981). *In and out of mental retardation: Essays on educability, disability, and human policy.* Baltimore, MD: University Park Press.

Blatt, B., and F. Kaplan (1974). *Christmas in purgatory: a photographic essay on mental retardation.* Syracuse, NY: Human Policy Press.

Bogdan, R. (1987). The exhibition of humans for amusement and profit. *Policy Studies Journal*, 15: 537-550.

Bogdan R., and S. J. Taylor (1989). The social construction of humanness: Relationships with severely disabled people. In P. M. Ferguson, and S. J. Taylor (Eds.), *Interpreting disability: A qualitative reader.* New York: Teachers College Press.

Bogdan, R. and S. J. Taylor (1987). Toward a sociology of acceptance: The other side of the study of deviance. *Social Policy*, 27: 35-39.

Bogdan, R., Taylor, S. J., deGrandpre, D., and Haynes, S. (1974). Let them eat programs: Attendants' perspectives and programming on wards in state schools. *Journal of Health and Social Behavior*, 15: 142-151.

Borg, W. R., and M. D. Gall (1989). *Educational research: An introduction, 5th edition.* White Plains, NY: Longmans.

Brown, F. and D. H. Lehr (1989). *Persons with profound disabilities: Issues and practices.* Baltimore MD: Brookes.

Brown, L., E. Long, L. D. Udvari-Solner, P. VanDeventer, C. Ahlgren, F. Johnson, L. Gruenewald, and J. Jorgensen (1989). The home school: Why students with severe intellectual disabilities must attend the schools of their brothers, sisters, friends, and neighbors. *The Journal of the Association for Persons with Severe Handicaps*, 14: 1-7.

Brown, N. H. (1952/1994). Singing in the Rain. On *Singing in the rain: The original soundtrack* [CD]. Hollywood, CA: Reprize. [Song originally written 1929.]

Buckholdt, D. R., and J. F. Gubrium (1979). Doing staffings. *Human Organization*, 38: 255-264.

Budd, R. (1992). Rorschach assessment of the non-living: Hardly a dead subject. *Journal of Polymorphous Perversity*, 9 (1): 12-16.

Bullock, A., O. Stallybrass, and S. Trombley (1988). *The Harper dictionary of modern thought, revised ed.* New York: Harper and Row.

Chaplin, J. P. (1985). *Dictionary of psychology.* New York: Dell.

Danforth, S. (1997). On what basis hope? Modern progress and postmodern possibilities. *Mental Retardation*, 35: 93-106.

Davis, L. J. (Ed.). (1997). *The disability studies reader.* New York: Routledge.

Denzin, N. K. (1994) The art and politics of interpretation. In N. K. Denzin and Y. S. Lincoln (Eds.), *Handbook of qualitative research*. Beverly Hills, CA: Sage.

Dewey, J. (1938/1963). *Experience and education*. New York: Collier Books.

Ferguson, D. L. (1994). Is communication really the point? Some thoughts on interventions and membership. *Mental Retardation*, 32: 7-18.

Ferguson, P. M. (1987). The social construction of mental retardation. *Social Policy*, 27: 51-56.

Fine, M., and A. Asch (1988). Disability beyond stigma: Social interactions, discrimination, and activism. *Journal of Social Issues*, 44: 3-21.

Foucault, M. (1965/1988). *Madness and civilization: A history of insanity in the age of reason*. New York: Vintage.

—— (1977/1979). *Discipline and punish: The birth of the prison*. New York: Vintage.

Frankel, C. (1967). The idea of progress. In *Encyclopedia of Philosophy*, 483-487.

Freud, S. (1930/1962). *Civilization and Its Discontents*. New York: W. W. Norton.

Goffman, E. (1974) *Frame analysis: An essay on the organization of experience*. Cambridge, MA: Harvard University Press.

—— (1959). *The presentation of self in everyday life*. Garden City, NY: Doubleday Anchor Books.

—— (1963/1986). *Stigma: Notes on the management of spoiled identity*. Englewood Cliffs, NJ: Doubleday.

Golander, H. and A. E. Raz (1986). The mask of dementia: Images of 'demented residents' in a nursing ward. *Aging and Society*, 16: 269-285.

Goode, D. A. (1994) *A world without words: the social construction of children born deaf and blind*. Philadelphia: Temple University Press.

—— (1984). Socially produced identities, intimacy, and the problem of competence among the retarded. In L. Barton and S. Tomlinson (Eds.), *Special education and social interests*. New York: Nichols.

—— (1980). The world of the congenitally deaf-blind: Toward the grounds for achieving human understanding. In J. Jacobs (Ed.), *Mental retardation: A phenomenological approach*. Springfield, IL: Charles Thomas.

Gubrium, J. F. (1986). The social preservation of mind: The Alzheimer's experience. *Symbolic Interaction*, 9: 37-51.

Gubrium J. F., and J. A. Holstein (1995). Individual agency, the ordinary, and postmodern life. *The Sociological Quarterly*, 36: 555-570.

Guess, D., and Thompson, B. (1993). Preparation of personnel to educate students with multiple disabilities: Time for a change? In L. Meyer, C. Peck, and L. Brown, (Eds.), *Issues in the lives of persons with disabilities*. Baltimore MD: Brooks.

Hahn, H. (1988). The politics of physical differences: Disability and discrimination. *Journal of Social Issues*, 44: 39-47.

—— (1987). Advertising the acceptably employable image: Disability and capitalism. *Policy Studies Journal*, 15: 551-570.

Heal, L. W. (1988). The ideological responses of society to its handicapped members. In L. W. Heal, J. J. Haney, and A. R. Novak Amado (Eds.), *Integration of Developmentally Disabled Individuals into the Community*. Baltimore, MD: Brookes.

Heshusius, L. (1989). The Newtonian mechanistic paradigm, special education, and contours or alternatives: An overview. *Journal of Learning Disabilities*, 22: 403-421.

Heward, W. L., and Orlansky, M. D. (1992). *Exceptional children: An introductory survey of special education*. New York: Macmillan.

Hickson, L., L. S. Blackman, and E. M. Reis (1995). *Mental retardation: Foundations of educational programming*. Boston: Allyn and Bacon.

Iano, R. P. (1986). The study and development of teaching: With implications for the advancement of special education. *Remedial and Special Education*, 7: 50-61,

Itard, J. G. (1962). *The wild boy of Aveyron*. (Humphrey, G., and Humphrey, M., Trans.). Englewood Cliffs, NJ: Prentice Hall. (Original work written in 1801 [*First Developments of the Young Savage of Aveyron*] and 1806 [*A Report made to His Excellency the Minister of the Interior*], published in 1894 as *Rapports et Mémoirs sur le Sauvage de L'Aveyron*, Paris).

Kuhn, T. S. (1962/1970). *The structure of scientific revolutions*. Chicago: University of Chicago Press.

Lane, H. (1977). *The wild boy of Aveyron*. London: George Allen and Unwin.

Linneman, D. (1992). *The web of experience: Attitudes and perspectives in an inclusive classroom*. Poster presented at the 119th Annual Convention of the Society for Persons with Severe Handicaps, San Francisco.

Linneman, W. R. (Undated). *Poems: A collection.* Author.

Luckasson, R., D. L. Coulter, E. A. Polloway, S. Reiss, R. L. Schalock, M. E. Snell, D. M. Spitalnick, and J. A. Stark (1992). *Mental retardation: Definition, classification, and systems of supports,* 9*th* edition. Washington, DC: American Association on Mental Retardation.

Luckasson, R., and D. Spitalnik (1994). Political and programmatic shifts of the 1992 definition of mental retardation. In V. J. Bradley, J. W. Ashbaugh, and B. C. Blaney (Eds.), *Creating individual supports for people with developmental disabilities: A mandate for change at many levels.* Baltimore MD: Brookes.

Lynch, M., and S. Woolgar (1988). Introduction: Sociological orientations to representational practice in science. In Lynch, M. and S. Woolgar (Eds.), *Representation in scientific practice.* Cambridge, MA: MIT Press.

Mannoni, O. (1972). Itard and his savage. *New Left Review,* 74: 38-50.

McKnight, J. (1977). Valuable deficiencies. *The Co-evolution Quarterly,* 14: 36-38.

Miller D. L. (1986). *The Lewis Mumford reader.* New York: Pantheon Books.

Mitchell, S. (1997). Flying blind on purpose? Thoughts on the banishment of developmental theories from clinical settings. *Mental Retardation,* 38: 1997.

Montessori, M. (1912). *The Montessori method.* New York: Stokes.

Mount, B. (1987). *Personal futures planning: Finding directions for change.* University of Michigan Dissertation Service.

Mount, B. (1994). Benefits and limitations of personal futures planning. In V. Bradley, J. Ashbaugh, B. Blaney (Eds.), *Creating individual supports for people with developmental disabilities* (pp. 97-108). Baltimore, MD: Brookes.

Mumford, L. (1963) *Technics and civilization.* New York: Harcourt, Brace and World.

O'Brien, J. (1987). A guide to life-style planning: Using the activities catalog to integrate services and natural support systems. In G. T. Bellamy and B. Wilcox (Eds.), *A comprehensive guide to the activities catalog: An alternative curriculum for adults and with severe disabilities* (pp. 175-189). Baltimore, MD: Brookes.

Oliver, M. (1992). Changing the social relations of research production? *Disability, Handicap and Society,* 7: 101-114.

Passmore, J. (1967). Logical positivism. *Encyclopedia of Philosophy.* N.Y.

Collier-Macmillan.

Pollner, M., and L. McDonald-Wikler (1985). The social construction of unreality: A case study of a family's attribution of competence to a severely retarded child. *Family Process*, 24: 241-254.

Reichle, J., and D. P. Wacker (1993). *Communicative alternatives to challenging behavior: Integrating functional assessment and intervention strategies*. Baltimore, MD: Brookes.

Richardson, L. (1994). Writing: A method of inquiry. In N. K. Denzin and Y. S. Lincoln (Eds.), *Handbook of qualitative research*. Beverly Hills, CA: Sage.

Romski, M. A., and R. A. Sevick (1996). *Breaking the speech barrier: Language development through augmented means*. Baltimore, MD: Brookes.

Rose, D. (1993). Ethnography as a form of life: The written word and the work of the world. In P. Benson (Ed.), *Anthropology and literature*. Urbana, IL: University of Illinois Press.

Sanders C. R., and A. Arluke (1993). If lions could speak: Investigating the animal-human relationship and the perspectives of nonhuman others. *Sociological Quarterly*, 34: 377-390.

Sands, D. J., M. L. Wehmeyer (Eds.). (1996). *Self determination across the life span: Independence and choice for people with disabilities*. Baltimore, MD: Brookes.

Schalock, R., J. A. Stark, M. A, Snell, D. L., Coulter, E. A. Polloway, R. Luckasson, S. Reiss, and D. M. Spitalnik (1994). The changing conception of mental retardation: Implications for the field. *Mental Retardation*, 32: 181-193.

Scheerenberger, R. C. (1983). *A history of mental retardation*. Baltimore, MD: Brookes.

Schwartz, J., and M. McGuinness (1979). *Einstein for beginners*. New York: Pantheon.

Shattuck, R. (1980). *The forbidden experiment: The story of the wild boy of Aveyron*. New York: Ferrar, Strauss & Giroux.

Sheridan, A. (1980/1990). *Michel Foucault: The will to truth*. London: Routledge.

Sherman, R. M., and Sherman R. B. (1966). *I wan'na be like you: The monkey song*. Wonderland Music Company.

Skrtic, T. M. (1986). The crisis in special education knowledge: A perspective on perspective. *Focus on Exceptional Children*, 18, 1-16.

—— (1991). The special education paradox: Equity as the way to excellence. *Harvard Educational Review,* 61: 148-206.

Stake, R. (1994). Case studies. In N. K. Denzin and Y. S. Lincoln (Eds.), *Handbook of qualitative research.* Beverly Hills: Sage.

—— (1982). Naturalistic generalizations. *Review Journal of Philosophy and Social Science,* 7: 1-11.

Taylor, S. J., and R. Bogdan, (1989). On accepting relationships between people with mental retardation and non-disabled people: Towards an understanding of acceptance. *Disability, Handicap and Society,* 4: 21-36.

Trent, J. W. (1995). Suffering fools. *The Sciences,* 37: 18-22.

—— (1994). *Inventing the feeble mind: A history of mental retardation in the United States.* Berkeley, CA: University of California Press.

Turnbull A., R. Turnbull, M. Shank, D. Leal (1999). *Exceptional lives: Special education in today's schools, 2nd edition.* Upper Saddle River, NJ: Merrill.

Vandercook, T., J. York, and M. Forest (1989). The McGill Action Planning System (MAPS): A strategy for building the vision. *Journal of the Association of Severe Handicaps,* 14: 205-215.

Winzer, M. A. (1993). *The history of special education: From isolation to integration.* Washington, DC: Gallaudet University Press.

Wolfensberger, W. (1972). *The principle of normalization in human services.* Toronto: National Institute on Mental Retardation.

—— (1989). Bill F.: Signs of the times read from the life of one mentally retarded man. *Mental Retardation,* 27: 396-373.

—— (1991). Reflections on a lifetime in human services and mental retardation. *Mental Retardation, 29,* 1-13.

Wright, D., and A. Digby (1996). *From idiocy to mental deficiency: Historical perspectives on people with learning disabilities.* London: Routledge.

Zappa, F. (1967/1995). Call any vegetable. On *The Mothers of Invention, Absolutely Free* [CD]. Rykodisc.

Zarb, G. (1992). On the road to Damascus: First steps towards changing the relations of disability research production. *Disability, Handicap and Society,* 7:125-138

Index